SOPHIA SPEAKS FROM THE HEART

About her tragic girlhood, her famous battles, international stardom, and the men in her life. . .

CARY GRANT: "I never doubted for a second that Cary loved me as much as I could hope to be loved by any man."

CARLO PONTI: "In my heart, I wanted him to discard everything for me. I did not want to be an undeclared mistress, or any kind of mistress."

RICHARD BURTON: "During the sad period when I knew him, he was a tragic figure, the way kings in Shakespeare, once grand, are broken upon the wheel of preordained tragedy."

SOPHIA

"My philosophy is that it's better to explore life and make mistakes than to play it safe and not to explore it all."

Intensely personal, candid and inspiring . . . The triumphant and totally captivating story of a living, loving legend.

SHE IS ALL SHE SEEMS TO BE
AND MORE!

Sophia
Living and Loving
Her Own Story

A.E. Hotchner

SOPHIA: LIVING AND LOVING

*A Bantam Book / published in association with
William Morrow and Company, Inc.*

PRINTING HISTORY

*William Morrow edition published February 1979
Eight printings through April 1979
Book-of-the-Month Club edition April 1979
Movie/Entertainment Book Club edition May 1979
Newsweek Condensed Books edition July/August 1979
Serialized by United Features Syndicate March 1979
and East/West Network June 1979.
An excerpt appeared in Book Digest June 1979.
Bantam edition / November 1979
2nd printing*

*Picture Editor, Ursula Hotchner.
Cover photo by Albert Watson.*

ISBN 0–553–13030–7

Published simultaneously in the United States and Canada

PRINTED IN THE UNITED STATES OF AMERICA

There was once a little girl with very thin legs, huge eyes, and a worried mouth. She disliked herself so much that she feared that fairies did not like her. But she loved every blade of grass and flower on the land, and she believed that those who seek a treasure must never mention it. She had been born in a knot of bitter roots, in the flower of which she eventually discovered the world: mountains to climb, streets to run.

She embraced the whole universe; everything was to be seen and experienced. But she feared the role that life gave to her, feared having to walk straight, with great effort, toward a faraway destination; feared weakness and love. But she persevered. And she overcame her fears.

This book is dedicated to her, and to all little girls with big eyes and spindly legs who are born in a knot of bitter roots.

I was born wise. Street-wise, people-wise, self-wise. This wisdom was my birthright.

I was also born old.

And illegitimate.

But the two big advantages I had at birth were to have been born wise and to have been born in poverty.

Out of chaos comes the birth of a star.
—CHARLIE CHAPLIN

PROLOGUE

I am in a small room in a hospital in Rome where my father lies dying. I sit on the bed beside him, holding his cold hand. In this room are four other people whose eyes are fixed upon the agony of his slow death: my mother, whom he seduced and abandoned; my sister, who suffered terribly because of his refusal to give her his name; a young man, Giuseppe, one of my father's legitimate sons from his marriage to a woman who is not present; Carol, a small blond German woman with whom my father lived for the last ten years of his life.

As he lies dying, I think: Despite his negativism, his rejection of the good we wanted to bring to him, my father has managed to bring together in this room a family of people. He has emotionally joined me to strangers.

And I think: For so much of my life he has been a source of pain and rejection and humiliation, yet now, here at the conclusion of his life, whatever negative feelings I have had about him have been erased by a wash of pity; and a glow of love has somehow managed to penetrate the grim events of our past relationship.

Pity and love.

How seldom I saw him, how many times during my agonies of surviving he refused to help—yet, incomprehensibly, he was a forceful factor in my existence. As I look back now, I realize that the story of my life must begin and end with my father. I sought him everywhere. I married him. I made my best films

with him. I curried his favor. I sat on his lap and
snuggled him.

Yet I saw him only a few times in my life. Once
when he came to Pozzuoli and brought me a little blue
car. Once in a courtroom. Once toward the end of his
life when I visited him in his home. A few isolated
meetings, that's all, yet he dominated my life.

And now, as he breathes his last, despite the painful incidents which occurred between us, I feel that
he has been a father to me. Perhaps it is only a delu-
sion, one of death's little distortions. It may be that
in thinking about my life, in recalling old events and
emotions for this book, I can come upon the truth
about him.

And about myself.

One

We were only ten minutes out of Paris when the plane hit a stone wall, rocked violently, and fell interminably before righting itself. It creaked and strained and groaned in every joint. Again it hit a wall head on, shuddered and dropped in its tracks, straight down, a runaway elevator, and I screamed as fear filled my mouth. The movie screen, wrenched from its invisible moorings, shot out of the ceiling and down to the floor; then, as the Caravelle nosed up to break the fall, the screen snapped back up into the ceiling with a screechy whine, as if manipulated by the same giant hand that was assaulting the aircraft.

I screamed again as the plane was rammed from the left side, the force hurling it up and rocking it, a chip on violent waves. The closet doors in front of me popped open and an avalanche of blankets spewed out. A woman across the aisle was now also screaming, and behind me I could hear the commotion of panic. With each violent movement of the plane, I screamed and dug my nails deeper into the armrests. The crew was strapped in, holding on for dear life as we were.

I had left my Paris apartment early that morning for the hour flight to Nice. Carlo was already there. My two little sons delayed me on leaving and I had been a trifle testy with them. The car was waiting in the garage basement and I would leave from there because the lobby was under siege by photographers who had been keeping a vigil for two days because they

1

knew that I was going to Cannes for the film festival. But they are often in the lobby, film festival or not. How often I long for a few days' respite, somewhere beyond the reach of the long lens.

How could I have anticipated that on May 19, a lovely spring morning in Paris, an hour's flight to Nice, how could I have known that my life would end like this, in this turbulently doomed airplane? My body can barely be restrained by the seat belt as we plunge and spin and stagger. The movie screen appears and disappears erratically. Each time the closet doors pop open a few more blankets catapult out. There is an eternity of time and distance between here and Nice. My mind is both clear and in panic. I cry out, God! God! but I do not pray. I am no longer religious in that way. But I try to pull the spiritual, cosmic force of God around me for protection. The woman across the aisle is now sobbing hysterically. I am in the first row so I see nothing but the frenzied screen and closet doors; in back of me, though, I hear the tumult.

I think of my two little sons and what will happen to them if I die this miserable death; all the trouble, the pain, the agony I went through to bear them and then to throw away my life with them, never to see them again, just for vanity, because I was summoned to Cannes for my film—and what will their life be without me? And what about Carlo? Glimpses of my life roll across my eyes, like film being edited: my mother, who vicariously lives my life; my sister, our lifetime of intimacy and interdependence; flashes of moments from forgotten memory, glorious, painful, wistful, interrupted by the violently lurching plane; I am certain now that death is imminent, since the airplane (which I fear even in normal flight) is unable to evade the vise of this frightening, destructive barrage. Only once before in my life have I been so near to death, when I was almost asphyxiated during the filming of *Legend of the Lost*, but I was semiconscious then, which diluted my fear. Now my fear has no dilution. It is real and sharp and unbearable.

When I was a child, fear was common to my life

—fear of having nothing to eat, fear of the other children taunting me at school because I was illegitimate, and particularly fear of the big bombers appearing overhead and dropping their lethal bursts from the sky. We were forever running for the protection of the train tunnel, trying to reach it before the barrage began. But that was a child's fear and a child's fear is not the same as that of an adult.

Carlo holds my arm securely and steers me across the tarmac of the airport. Someone has handed me a bouquet of red roses. I am still violently airborne but I smile fixedly for the phalanx of photographers backpedaling in front of us in a clicking, flashing arc. I have not been able to tell Carlo about the flight but he knows how upset I am. Carlo. His instincts. His strength. The haven of his arm wrapped around mine. His strong smile. Never have I needed him more than at this moment when I must reenter the earth, having died a hundred deaths in that boiling sky.

Yesterday a "friend" called (of course, these "friends" are always *so* reluctant to have to bring these items to my attention) to read to me an account that ran in a magazine, with a picture of Carlo and me on the cover, about how our marriage was on the jagged rocks, how we had separated and were living apart, and how it was just a question of working out details with the lawyers. Scarcely a week passes that an obituary doesn't run in some publication for our marriage, a requiem written by someone with "real inside knowledge." It disturbs the journalists who observe the so-called celebrity world that Carlo and I, who are in a profession where alliances are fragile and transitory, are still together after twenty-five years. I met him at fifteen, got seriously involved with him at nineteen, and now at forty-four he means as much to me as he ever did. We endured terrible years together, when the church pilloried us and the Italian government prosecuted us for bigamy, but it was a fire of calumny that tempered the steel of our relationship and made it all the stronger.

Carlo tightens his grip on my arm and whispers, "We are almost there. See, there's our car." Carlo—lover, protector, friend, sensitive and creative; a father image for me? Yes, I suppose he's the father I never had, the father I needed in my life. Even now. I'm forty-four, but the little, shy, illegitimate, fatherless girl of Pozzuoli is still very much inside me, and I need the fathering of Carlo as much today as I ever did.

In ten minutes I will be leaving my hotel room for the premiere of my film *A Special Day*. The effects of the terrifying experience in the airplane have receded, and now I am glad to be here because this film represents a new and important and risky involvement for me. Performing without makeup, I play a drab, forlorn fortyish housewife during the days of Mussolini's Rome. But now, for the premiere, I am wearing a new gown, gay, colorful, gypsy-inspired, all the more to heighten the contrast between what I play on the screen and the glamour role I am playing tonight. The gown suits me, it fits the occasion, and it makes me feel especially good—my criteria for being well dressed.

There is enormous tension in the hotel room, much more than the usual tension that precedes every premiere, which is the first taste of public judgment.

Two plainclothes detectives are here with walkie-talkies, keeping in touch with special police in the lobby and outside the hotel. They tell me that in all the years of the Cannes Film Festival, they have never had a situation like the one they face tonight. The lobby is packed solid with hundreds of spectators, photographers, and press. Outside the hotel, a mob has jammed itself around the entrance, and all along the five-minute route to the theater, dense crowds have gathered.

"We have a big problem trying to get you through the lobby and into your car without your getting crushed," one of the detectives says.

"Then we have the problem of trying to move you

along the street," says the other detective. "But the biggest problem of all is how to get you out of that car and up all those steps into the theater."

Mastroianni is now in the room, black tie, handsome, and smiling. The detectives explain. He shrugs, an Italian shrug, comes over, kisses my neck, and smiles upon me. This is our eighth film together; there's no doubt by now that our marriage will last. We respect each other and love each other and on the set we have wonderful rapport. Many laughs. Marcello can be mercilessly funny.

But we rarely see each other away from the movie set. Marcello is a man beset with problems, continually buffeted by problems he cannot solve but which torment him, and for twenty years they have always been the same. The people in his life have changed but the problems remain the same, and Marcello has steadfastly refused to change his life in order to ease those problems. I figure that he must like the problems, and the torment. But on those rare occasions when we have gone out to dinner and he has permitted his spirits to soar above his problems, he has been the funniest, gayest man I ever encountered. He has an offbeat sense of humor, dry and sophisticated, that particularly appeals to me.

But it is a very rare occasion when Marcello indulges his spirited, funny side; when he is immersed in his thoughts, which is more often than not, he becomes sober and noncommunicative.

He adores the little daughter he had during his love relationship with Catherine Deneuve, but he lives in Italy and she is in Paris and he rarely sees her. Things like that depress him, and he can see no way out of the morass of these problems which fill the well of his private life.

The walkie-talkie detectives are consulting their watches and talking a kind of code language to their confederates below. Marcello and I step from the elevator into the lobby as an enormous burst of light from hundreds of flashbulbs goes off in our faces. The lobby is compacted with people jammed between us and the lobby doors. Arrayed in back of them and literally hanging from the ceiling are the photographers working feverishly with their cameras.

There is a roar of welcome from the mass of spectators. A wedge of sweating special police, their arms locked, with Marcello and me in the pocket of the wedge, starts to move toward the doors, the crowd not giving way until forced to, pressing in on us, striving to touch us, pushing in the sides of the moving wedge.

Somehow, despite little flares of violence, despite moments when the police wedge was in danger of collapsing and crushing us, we reach the car, where other special police are trying to maintain a path to the open door of the car. Miraculously we land inside the car, but now the crowds in the street impede the car, rocking it, banging on the windows, chanting, Sophia! Sophia! Marcello! Marcello!, only giving ground as police around the car physically move them out of the way.

This is the fifth time I have been to Cannes for a film of mine in competition, but I have never before experienced anything even approaching this. You would think I was some electrifying newcomer, some pop idol from the Elysian fields of Woodstock moving among the grassed cultists, but these are the rather proper people of Cannes and movie professionals, and their reception baffles me.

It is even worse when we get to the Palace, where the picture is to be shown. The crowd is bigger, denser, and noisier. This time there is a double wedge of police to move us up the long, steep steps into the crowd which is pressing down on us from above. Again the chant, Sophia! Sophia! fills the air. Now we are pushed and shoved from side to side, people reaching over the police to grasp at us. I stumble but hands grab me and keep me from falling down the steps. I hear the sounds of my dress as it rips and tears. At times like this I honestly don't know whether to be frightened or to be elated, because these people are communicating something to me that makes this moment unique, a moment perhaps never to be repeated in my lifetime.

When this kind of thing happens to me, I feel that I am in a dream, and I seem to step outside of myself and look at Sophia struggling inside a police wedge, trying to reach the doors at the top of the steps. I see myself as if I were watching myself on television. This phenomenon of viewing myself from outside myself is something I've been doing all my life. It helps me keep my balance.

What is particularly gratifying is that I feel that these people like me as a person and appreciate me as an actress and are telling me this in the most demonstrative way they can. They are showing me how they feel about my past films. And about me. You cannot fool movie audiences about your true self. The close-up is as honest as truth serum or a lie detector. No matter how much makeup or histrionics, who you truly are shines through. Blemishes and all. You are what you are and the audience sees it under the totally revealing microscope of the close-up.

Now in the hushed presence of obligatory black ties and the glitter of Van Cleef & Arpels, I wait for the verdict of the audience. A film is shot in isolation, as a book is written, and there is no way to predetermine how the mass audience for whom the film is intended will react. The terrifying moment comes when the end titles start to appear and the audience responds. Will they applaud? Will it be perfunctory applause or will it be a wholehearted outpouring of approval? It is quite easy to tell. I am not one who with my imagination magnifies audience reaction, or who quickly stands up to provoke a heartier applause.

But on this night, I do not have any doubt. The audience has been involved and enthralled and their applause is deafening. They shout approval and finally, at their insistence, Marcello and I rise and acknowledge their acclaim.

For me it is a moment of sweet fulfillment, as gratifying as any moment in my career. This was an extremely difficult movie to make and the most difficult role I ever performed. Thus, this day that started so terribly has ended wonderfully well.

Which, it seems to me, is as good a starting point as any for what I have to tell you about my life, which also started terribly.

Two

In the Clinica Regina Margherita in Rome, there was a charity ward for unmarried women, and it was there that I was born in 1934, the year before Mussolini bombed Ethiopia. My name was entered in the hospital records as "Sofia Scicolone" by virtue of the fact that my father, whose name was Riccardo Scicolone, made an affidavit that affirmed that I was his issue. He had refused to marry my mother, or even to see her during the months she was pregnant, but strangely he did come to the hospital and give me his name.

My mother, though, had to keep her maiden name, Romilda Villani. She had brought terrible disgrace and humiliation to her family in the little seaport town of Pozzuoli, which is about twenty-five kilometers from Naples, but painful as it must have been for my grandmother, she nevertheless came to Rome to be with her daughter when I was born. Considering my father's brutish behavior prior to my birth, my grandmother was surprised to meet (for the first time) Riccardo Scicolone at the hospital, and more surprised when he announced that he intended to give me his name and to live with my mother after her discharge from the hospital. But he was careful to point out that he had absolutely no intention of marrying her.

I was a skinny, pale, ugly little thing but my mother tells me that despite my unattractiveness and her humiliating and precarious condition, it never crossed

9

her mind to put me in the orphanage which was run by a nearby convent for the accommodation of babies from my mother's ward. She was and is a fiercely determined woman and she had determined that I was going to be a part of her life.

In the Italy of 1934, the prospects facing my mother were certainly not good. The strict Catholic tenets which governed life in Italy gave no comfort to those who sinned against the church's precepts, and having an illegitimate baby was one of the severest sins. In the small town of Pozzuoli, where everybody knew everybody else, illegitimate childbearing was virtually unheard of and certainly would be subject to ostracism and contempt.

But, temporarily at least, my mother was able to avoid facing the moral hostility of Pozzuoli. My father, who had little money and no job, asked his mother whether he and his new family could stay at her house while he looked for work, but his mother turned him down. "I have no desire to have the ugly thing squalling in the house all the time, and the best thing you can do is to get rid of both the woman and her baby."

My father found a tiny room in a boardinghouse and that was where my mother and I went to live with him on leaving the hospital. Although he had studied to be an engineer, my father had never followed it up and remained without any trade or profession, so finding work was not easy. He was probably too pretentious to take menial work and not qualified for the kind of jobs that he fancied were commensurate with the impression he had of himself.

As soon as my mother could, she too went out every day to look for work, leaving me in the care of the woman who ran the boardinghouse. But Italy in the thirties had virtually no job opportunities for women. Mussolini had ordered them to stay at home and bear children, which, of course, reinforced the traditional attitude of Italian men as far back as the Romans. The little money my father had quickly dwindled to nothing. The landlady was aware of my parents' plight and tried to convince my mother to get rid of me. "Why don't you let this ugly thing die?" she asked. "Just look what you're going through—and for what? You're not married, neither of you can find a job, your husband has no money—why are you clinging to this baby? It's ridiculous. I can't keep you on here if you can't pay rent. His mother won't have anything to do with you. Where will you go? What will you do? Your breasts are dry and the baby sucks on you without getting anything to eat—look at her . . . she's all skin and bones. Just let her die. No one will blame you. I'll take care of everything."

My mother's answer was to redouble her job-seeking efforts, but with no better results. Finally, one day when I was alone with the landlady she took matters into her own hands. The reason my mother's breasts were dry was attributable to my father's mother. A few weeks after we had moved into the boardinghouse, my paternal grandmother came to visit us. She discovered that my mother was suffering from severe constipation and brought her a powerful laxative, which she insisted that my mother take. These pills relieved my mother's condition, but a few days after she took them, most of the milk in her breasts disappeared. As a consequence, I had grown even thinner and had become progressively weaker. I was badly in need of nutriment.

On the particular day I mentioned when I was alone with the landlady, she decided to put some food in me; the food which she forced down my throat was a mixture of lentils and stewed tomatoes. I was about six weeks old. Of course I became violently ill and developed severe colitis. When my mother found out what the landlady had done she furiously railed at her, but the landlady replied that my demise would be the best thing that could happen for my mother's well-being. There was no money for a doctor nor for medicine. I cried constantly, and my intestines could retain nothing.

My mother tried to contact my father but he had disappeared. In desperation, my mother took me to the clinic but they said there was nothing they could do for a condition as severe as mine. There was no medi-

cine to prescribe for it. They did say that a baby af-
flicted as I was must not have cow's milk, which
would only make the colitis worse, but had to subsist
entirely on natural milk from the mother. Survival,
they said, was simply a matter of luck.

The grim facts that my mother had to face were
that her breasts were now completely dry, Riccardo
Scicolone had departed for good without leaving her
so much as a lira, the landlady was demanding her
rent, now considerably in arrears, and I was dying.
On top of all this, my mother was aware that her
family in Pozzuoli did not want her malevolent presence in their house.

It was a situation made to order for her natural
defiance of life's darker forces. Actually, my mother
had been born much too soon. At a time when women
were docile and obedient to the strictures of a male-
dominated society, she was a vehement iconoclast—
fiery, eccentric, beautiful, uninhibited, stubborn. She
still is. At nineteen she belonged behind the Paris
barricades of the sixties, or on the streets of Chicago
during the Democratic National Convention. That
my mother's personality and attitudes developed as
they did in the small, poverty-stricken narrow-minded
town of Pozzuoli is nothing short of miraculous. My
mother had no interest in school but a great affinity
for the piano; despite the fact that it was a struggle
to buy food and pay the rent, somehow my grandmother, that remarkable woman, contrived to get a
piano, which she crammed into the small living room.
It was a big piano which filled most of the room, big
because the local philosophy was that if you got
something unusual in a little town like Pozzuoli, it
was better if it was big.

My mother quickly established her talent for playing the piano, and was given a scholarship for lessons
at the conservatory in Naples. By the time she was
sixteen, she was already so accomplished that the
conservatory awarded her a professorship and authorized her to give lessons.

But more remarkable than my mother's ability at

the keyboard was her resemblance to Greta Garbo, who at that time was one of Hollywood's great stars. People would stop my mother on the streets of Naples and ask for her autograph. Not only did my mother bear a striking resemblance to Garbo, but she also had a resolute dream that she would achieve a fame that would equal Garbo's. As luck would have it, when my mother was seventeen, MGM announced a Greta Garbo look-alike contest that would be held throughout Italy, the winner to go on an all-expenses-paid trip to Hollywood, a first-class steamship ticket included, and be given a screen test in MGM's Culver City studios.

From the moment she read about the contest, my mother never had a moment's doubt that she would win. She took a bus to Naples, paraded before the judges, and was ultimately crowned the winner over three hundred and fifty other entrants. My mother's temperament and eccentricity had already figuratively liberated her from the bonds of Pozzuoli, but now this prize was a true liberation. Her ecstasy was boundless. A girl born into the poverty of Pozzuoli has only her dreams, as I was to have a generation later, but the dreams almost always die aborning, and the dreamer eventually has to accept the dismal reality of the hard, confined existence of Pozzuoli.

So you can imagine my mother's elation when she rushed back from Naples to tell the good news to my grandmother and grandfather. My grandmother, however, didn't regard it as good news at all. I adored my grandmother, who was destined to be one of the most important persons in my young life, but she was a totally provincial person, devout, hard-working, and suspicious. Very Neapolitan. "No," she said to my mother, "you cannot go. Look what just happened to Rudolph Valentino."

My mother was stunned. "He died," my mother said. "What's that got to do with my going to America?"

"He didn't just die," my grandmother said. "He was killed. Murdered."

"What? What do you mean? Who murdered him?"

"The Black Hand. And if you go to America, they will be after you."

"Why? Why in heaven's name would the Black Hand want to kill me? I'm just an unknown girl from Italy."

"The fans of Greta Garbo would hire the Black Hand—they would be jealous of you. Ask anyone what they did to poor Valentino. The Black Hand. Just ask anyone."

Valentino was a great hero in Italy, and after his recent untimely death, a rumor had swept the country that he had been murdered by the New York Mafia, which at that time was called the Black Hand.

MGM officials came to Pozzuoli to see my grandmother but she stood her ground. She did not cite the menace of the Black Hand as her reason for refusing permission for her daughter to go to Hollywood; to their astonishment she told them that her daughter could not go because she didn't have a fur coat. No amount of assurance or persuasion would budge my grandmother, and since her permission was necessary, because my mother was only seventeen, the movie people eventually left and switched the award to the runner-up. To this day my mother doesn't really know if her mother believed the Black Hand stories or if she had simply invented them as a way to keep my mother from going to Hollywood.

It was a bitter and infuriating frustration for my mother. To have gotten so close to her dream and then been thwarted; it was not something that her volatile disposition could easily deal with. Thus, it was in the wake of these events that she had, without my grandmother's permission, gone to Rome to try to get into the movies, which were then being made in quantity at Cinecittà, the vast cinema complex that Mussolini intended as his answer to Hollywood.

I don't know how much ambition my mother really had. I think she was more piqued at being denied the Hollywood trip than she was ambitious for a career. At any rate, it was while she was in Rome in this frame of mind that she met Riccardo Scicolone, and as her pregnant belly grew, her dreams of ever becoming a concert pianist, which perhaps she could have done, or a movie star, receded.

Now on that day in Rome when she was alone with me, faced with the reality that the father of her child had abandoned her, that the child itself was near death, that she had no money, no food, no job, and was about to be evicted, she did the only sensible thing she could do to survive: she somehow managed to acquire a bus ticket to Pozzuoli. Her family would not be glad to see her, but she hoped they would not shut the door in her face. If her baby died, she needed her mother to comfort her in her grief.

Sophia's mother

The past destroys me because all my memories are ugly. Riccardo Scicolone picked me up on a Rome street. I had gone there to further my piano career— I was a marvel at the piano—when he came up to me on the street and told me he was a film producer and that I was so beautiful he couldn't resist talking to me. I thought he was sincere. I was just a country girl, fresh out of Pozzuoli, knowing nothing. I met him a few times and then he came to my rented room and got me into bed; two months later I was pregnant. He refused to marry me. It was a terrible disgrace, but my family did not throw me out. I gave birth to Sophia as easily as a cow in the field.

It was not easy for me to go back to live in Pozzuoli. No other girl in Pozzuoli was unmarried with a baby. Pozzuoli girls were virgins until they married. It was a strict rule of life. I knew the townspeople would think of me as indecent, unfit, a whore. But I stood up to all of them. I am a fighter and I fought for myself and my baby. And my family stood by me. That is what saved us, the way the Villanis embraced us.

Three

The town of Pozzuoli is built on volcanic ash and it rises and falls with the tides. At the end of Via Solfatara, the street on which we lived, is a semiactive volcano which occasionally spits boiling stones and lava. Naples has Vesuvius, Pozzuoli has Solfatara. There was a fear, during the war, that if aerial bombs scored a direct hit on Solfatara it would cause a major eruption that would bury the town; I don't know if that was actually true or just another of the many war rumors.

Pozzuoli is an ancient town with some well-preserved Roman remains, especially an amphitheater, which was located directly behind our flat. From the kitchen window we could look out on the beautifully formed and preserved arena, with the blue of the Tyrrhenian Sea behind it. Although the people of Pozzuoli were very poor and life was no better than in other slums, we did have the advantage of having the beauty of the sea and the Roman ruins around us.

Also, it helped that *all* of Pozzuoli was equally poverty-stricken, unlike big-city slums, like those of Naples, which are adjacent to luxurious sections of the cities. We children of Pozzuoli were not very aware of being underprivileged since everyone was poor and struggling to get enough to eat, and there were no rich kids to envy.

The ancient occupations of the town had been shipbuilding and fishing, but both had fallen on hard times. There was no longer much demand for Pozzuoli's hand-wrought ships, and the fishing fleet, such as it was, was outmoded and barely earned an existence for the fishermen. The only other activity in the town was a munitions factory which paid poorly but employed a large number of Pozzuoli's menfolk.

The Villani family lived over a vinegar factory in a compact flat that consisted of a small living room, a narrow dining room, two modest bedrooms, and a small kitchen. There was a toilet but no bath. We were seven in all (grandfather, grandmother, two uncles, an aunt, my mother, and I), eight after my sister was born; we slept four to a bed. Until I left Pozzuoli I never slept in a bed with fewer than three people in it. In true Neapolitan fashion, the living room existed only to receive company; since we never had any company, we rarely set foot in it from one week to the next. Except for Sunday, we ate most of our meals on a wooden table in the little kitchen.

My grandfather was a tiny man, short and small-boned, who cared about little else than his work. He was a foreman at the munitions factory, and we considered him quite an important man, but his title was more impressive than his pay. He worked hard, long hours, and when he came home he wanted to be left in peace to read his paper, but my grandmother insisted on discussing her problems, which mostly concerned family finances, prodding him and provoking him until he angrily put down his paper and responded; these nightly quarrels were a regular part of life in the Villani household.

My grandmother carried the burden of the family on her shoulders. She was the wellspring, the spirit, the evaluator, the prodder, the comforter, the voice of doom and of hope—but above all she was a positive, rather optimistic force. At fifty, hardship had already turned her old, grayed her hair, bent her, saddened her. I patterned some of the middle-aged housewife I depict in *A Special Day* after my grandmother.

My grandfather brought home his paycheck on the twenty-seventh of the month, but by the thirtieth my grandmother had used it up for the family's expenses, and every month she had to face the remaining month of maneuvering our existence with IOU's and other devices. My two uncles had sporadic menial jobs at the munitions factory, but the total earning power of the family did not put food on the table seven days a week. Actually, the aggregate effort of the Villanis was directed toward the Sunday lunch. For six days we barely subsisted; you might say we practiced a variant on the old biblical exhortation that you will work six days and rest on the seventh—with us, we starved for six days and on the seventh we ate. It was Grandma Luisa who week in and week out managed the miracle of the Sunday lunch.

And it was Grandma Luisa who opened the door that evening when my fearful mother, fatigued from the long bus ride from Rome, stood there with her sick baby, desperately wondering if she would be received or turned away. The Villanis had no telephone, of course, and there had been no way to inform my grandmother that she was arriving.

Without a moment's hesitation my grandmother opened her arms and pulled her daughter and granddaughter against her breast. A bottle of liquor, preserved for important occasions, was taken from the cupboard in the dining room, and all the family drank a toast to me, the new addition. Then my grandmother turned her attention to the grave condition of her granddaughter. "The clean sea air will help her," she said, "but she must have milk immediately. It's the only hope."

My mother had explained what had happened to her milk. "There's only one thing to do," my grandmother announced. "We will immediately put her to feed with the wet nurse Zaranella, who is the most prolific fountain of milk in all Campania."

Not only did my grandmother pay the prodigious Zaranella fifty lire a month to enable me to join the dozen or so babies who suckled her bountiful breasts, but my grandmother also decreed that for however long it took me to recover, all meat that she normally bought for the family table would go to Zaranella to nourish and improve the quality of her milk.

None of the Villanis protested the meatless months that followed. Later on, when Grandma Luisa told me all these details, she said that giving that meat to Zaranella, knowing how it would benefit me, made dinner more enjoyable for her than if the missing meat had been on the table.

That is the kind of love which, to this day, I especially prize. Giving like that without expectation of anything in return. Giving out of love, and love alone.

Four

I was either the first one in the schoolyard, at eight o'clock, or the last, arriving just as the last girl was filing into class at eight fifty-five. I had learned, through painful experience, that that was the way to be inconspicuous, and only by being inconspicuous could I avoid the whispers, derisive glances, snickers, and taunts that my schoolmates directed at me because I was the illegitimate offspring of an unmarried mother. I was painfully shy and introverted and totally unable to cope with this cruelty. The nuns at the parochial school which I attended were indifferent to my ostracism. They were formal and remote and it was unthinkable that I could go to any of them and discuss my plight. Actually, I was scared to death of them and I felt that they were no more kindly disposed toward me than my classmates. Every morning of my childhood I dreaded having to go to school. I felt that the stigma of my illegitimacy was tattooed on my forehead.

I suffered doubly from the fact that my mother was tall and beautiful and didn't look like any of the other mothers. She sometimes picked me up after school and my classmates reacted with the same derisiveness that greeted me in the morning. I tried to avoid being picked up by leaving school as quickly as I could. I would always go home very fast, running.

My mother earned what money she could by playing piano in the little cafés and trattorias. Sometimes she went to Naples and to Rome. One evening, pale and fearful, she got up her courage and con-

fessed to my grandmother that she had seen my father
a few times in Rome, hoping to persuade him to
marry her. But in the process, she had become pregnant again.

My grandmother bowed her head and put her
hand over her eyes. But she had a forgiving heart
and she accepted my sister, Maria, into the family,
as she had accepted me. I was four years old when
Maria was born.

I do not know if I am withdrawn by nature or as a
consequence of how I was treated by my classmates.
Even now, I am terribly shy and almost always find
an excuse not to attend parties to which I'm invited.
It is ironic that my elder son, Carlo, Jr., who is nine,
is quite the same as I am. He is embarrassed and
self-conscious whenever I pick him up after school.
You're not like other mothers, he complains. You're
special-looking and all the kids look at us and point
you out.

I wear jeans and try to be as inconspicuous as I
can but inevitably Carlo sees a reaction to my appearance. When we get in the car, though, Carlo often tells me how happy he is that I came to get him.
God knows I understand the duality of his feelings;
perhaps when he's older, he'll understand mine.

I was five years old when I met my father for the
first time. As a ruse to get him to Pozzuoli, my mother
had sent him a telegram that I was very sick and he
should come as quickly as possible. I recall how nervous and excited my mother was on the day he arrived. She had not told me he was coming, but I
sensed that something special was happening from
the way she fussed over my hair and dress, trying to
make her skinny, sallow, homely daughter look as
attractive as she could.

She brought me into the rarely used living room,
where a tall, handsome man was standing with his
back to the window. He was considerably taller than
any of the men in the Villani family, and he was
much more elegantly dressed. He had a rather pro-

nounced nose but it suited the size of him. On the floor in front of him was a blue pedal car, fashioned after one of the Italian roadsters. No child in Pozzuoli had a car like that, and certainly I had never seen anything like it. Painted on the car was my nickname, Lella. My mother put her hand on my back and pushed me toward him. "Here is your father," she said. My father bent down and extended his hand to me. He had a charming smile. "I brought you this little present," he said.

This much I remember, but curiously I'm fuzzy about what followed. My mother says I recoiled from him and refused to believe he was my father; that I told him to go away, told him that I had a father and that he was not at all my father and that I didn't want to see him. Whereupon, in tears, I ran from the room.

My mother should have prepared me for this confrontation. It was simply too big an event for an outcast five-year-old to handle. I suppose my father was hurt by my rejection of him, but the fact was that I had never considered him my father, or even a member of my family. I called my grandfather "Papa," and my grandmother "Mamma," and my mother "Mammina." The word *father* means nothing to a child if she doesn't live with that man and share her life with him, and if he's not there to pick her up and console her when she falls down. Also, when my father's name was mentioned in the house it was always in a derogatory way. No one had a nice word to say about him. So if you talk to a child about a man who is always put down, the child has no desire to see that man or be nice to him even if she is told it's her father. *Father* is only a word. A label without a meaning. How can a child have affection and feeling for someone who should be with her but isn't? This man called father never came to see us, didn't care about us. My grandfather and grandmother did. They were warm and loving and gentle, and until my grandfather's death a few years ago, I continued to call him "Papa" and thought of him as such.

As for Grandmother, when I came home from

school in the afternoon and we were alone in the kitchen, her whole personality changed. She used to cast off her cares for an hour or two and be gay and funny with me. While a big pot of *pasta e fagiole* was bubbling on the stove, she sang songs to me that she had made up, about how life would be for me when I grew up—a wonderful life filled with Pozzuoli dream objects such as automobiles and fur coats and diamond rings. She would be sitting there sewing me a garment she was making out of an old blanket and singing to me of this sumptuous life in the fairyland of tomorrow. At the same time I was making shoes for myself from two flats of leather to which I'd affix strings to bind around my ankles. Grandmother had a lovely imagination and often invented wonderfully whimsical stories about princesses and enchanted forests. Her father, who had been a *granatiere* (a special army detachment distinguished by the height of its members), and her brother had both been accomplished guitarists and musicians, and it is this strain in the family that I think had asserted itself in my mother.

How I loved Grandma Luisa! The first success I had in the movies, *The Gold of Naples,* I took what little money I earned and bought a ring with a tiny diamond in it. By then, my grandmother was sick and bedridden. I went all the way to Pozzuoli on the bus from Rome to surprise her with my diamond ring. "Look, Mamma," I told her, holding up my hand in front of her face, "your dreams for me have come true." She was so happy to see the little diamond on my finger you would have thought it was twenty carats of the finest stone. Grandma Luisa died six months later but her voice lives on inside me. It is a voice that I shall hear all the rest of my life.

After that first time in Pozzuoli, my mother often sent telegrams to my father urging him to come immediately because of my grave illness, but he never again fell for that hoax. A few years after my sister was born, he got in touch with my mother and told her that he had met a girl whom he had made pregnant, and he threatened to marry this girl unless my mother came to Rome and asserted her prior rights. "She's a good deal younger than you and quite pretty," my father had said, "and I'm going to marry her unless you show up and stop me." My mother was angry and disgusted with him by then and told him to do whatever he wanted, that she was through with him. So he married this girl and had two sons with her. But some years later, he left her and went back to live for a while with my mother.

While my father was alive, my mother often denounced him in violent terms and said she hated him. I don't know how she feels about him now that he is dead, but as I said at the start, I think I was born quite wise and it always seemed to me that what my mother had for my father was not hate but enormous love. She conceived two children with him, she never married nor had any other true love, and until the day he died Riccardo Scicolone aroused her deepest emotions. I have kept a notebook for many years in which I record things I read which I want to remember. One of those quotes is, "As a person, he didn't exist any more and she didn't desire him, didn't desire to have him, desired only to get rid of him. He was a man once, but now he had transformed himself into a situation. Hate is only an unfinished love."

I know I never really hated my father—oh, a momentary flash of hatred when he did something outrageous, but I always try to understand why people act as they do, and as I got older I think I developed a pretty good understanding of my father and his failures. Even though absent, he was a very important element in my life, a long shadow of influence. In thinking about him like this, for this book, about his visit to Pozzuoli that summer of my fifth year, I was drawn back to Pozzuoli to visit our old flat. My aunt and uncle still live there and things are pretty much the same in the house as they were when I was a girl. I asked my uncle about the little blue car I used to ride up and down Via Solfatara, what had happened to it. He went into the kitchen and climbed up on the old wooden table and reached into a storage area close to the ceiling.

There was the little blue car, cobwebby and faded, an old wasp's nest under the steering wheel. My uncle put it on the floor and it rolled easily to the kitchen door. It was a poignant moment for me; I felt it in my breast, a sliver of pain, a little difficulty breathing. "It's silly to keep the little car," I said, but I did not tell my uncle to throw it away.

Five

In 1940, when I was six, war came to Pozzuoli. It
seemed that overnight German soldiers were everywhere. They were our allies then, and friendly, and
my earliest memories are of delightedly watching the
young, handsome soldiers in their beautiful uniforms,
playing war games in the back yards of the houses
on our street. I don't think I had ever seen a blond,
blue-eyed man before the German soldiers arrived.
It was exciting to stand in front of our house and
watch the troops march by, and it was especially exciting when long columns of tanks rumbled down the
street. After the war began, everything in Pozzuoli
gradually shut down and finally there was nothing at
all for a child to do—no school or movies or library or
radio or anything at all, so that all we had as a diver-
sion was the war itself. The war became our play-
thing. Our flat was not far from the railroad station
and since the tracks through Pozzuoli joined the important Naples–Rome line, German soldiers were always in our area, patrolling the railroad station on one
side of us and the harbor on the other.

It wasn't long, however, before the twin magnets of
the munitions factory and the harbor began to draw
the attention of the Allied planes. Bombing raids
became more and more frequent, shattering Pozzuoli's
tranquillity and putting all of our lives in jeopardy.
As the bombing intensified, food and water began to
disappear; the food, because transportation was cut off,
the water, because the bombs destroyed the water
mains. For safety, the people of the town had to

crowd into the railroad tunnel every night after the last train left for Naples. In the morning, everyone had to get out of the tunnel by four-thirty, when the first train from Naples came roaring into the tunnel.

The tunnel became the focal point of our lives. Every night we dragged our mattresses and, in the winter, our blankets, into its pitch-black interior—no light, not even a candle, was permitted. No one was allowed near the entrance, where there was some air, because of the possibility that fragments of a bomb, falling in that vicinity, could penetrate a certain distance into the interior of the tunnel. The central part of the tunnel, where we were all squeezed together, was very dark and humid, a hot, stinking atmosphere, putrid with the smell of unwashed bodies, overripe, half-rotten food, urine, feces, and garbage. Cockroaches were everywhere and enormous tunnel rats scurried around and over us to get to the food. Night after night after night, for unending months. But there was no revulsion, no reluctance to go there. We knew it was the only way to survive, and one's tolerance stretches far to accommodate survival.

Running for the shelter when the alarm sounded became an exciting event for me. I remember one night when I wandered out of the shelter to watch the awesome spectacle of a sky full of flares that the Allied planes were dropping to illuminate the area before they dropped their bombs. The landscape appeared painted by a silvery magic sheen, and the sea reflected the trembling, intense glare of the floating flares. I thought that the sky had somehow lowered the glory of its stars very close to the earth. It was far more exciting and magical than the meager fireworks I had sometimes seen in the village of Pozzuoli for the Festa of the Madonna di Pompei. My poor mother, searching everywhere, dying with anxiety, shouting my name, finally found me standing in a very exposed area, my silvery face upturned to the blazing sky, clapping my hands with excitement.

A sound slap in the face brought me back to reality. My mother was crying tears of relief as she dragged me back to the shelter. There, in the darkness of the fetid tunnel, I too began to cry. Not because of my mother's slap, but because the magic spell of the night sky had been broken.

But even more stark in my memory is one devastating raid that caught us by surprise. The air raid alarm had failed to sound, and we were asleep in our beds when tons of bombs began exploding all around us, shaking the walls, shattering windows. My mother shouted to me to dress as fast as I could, but instead of putting on my clothes, I was so scared and befuddled that I got completely undressed, and when my mother came into the room to get me she found me standing stark naked, shivering with fear.

We ran for cover but a shard of shrapnel caught me in the chin, and by the time we got to the air raid shelter my face was all bloody. The following morning, when we returned to our rooms, the streets were covered with blood and with badly injured people and with devastation. My sister had lost her shoes and her feet got badly cut by broken glass. Many of the injured people called out to us for help but there was nothing we could do. When we got back to our house, it was half ruined. That was a night of fear for child and adult alike. It seared my memory, and now when I think of it I feel the fright of my awakening that night as keenly as when it happened.

In the winter the tunnel became freezing cold and we never had enough warm clothes and blankets. Crying babies, husbands and wives screaming at each other, couples making love, snorers, teeth-grinders, lost children, people bitten by the rats, sickness, laughter, drunkenness, death, and childbirth were all part of the interminable nights in the tunnel. To this day, as a result of those terrible black nights, I have a phobia about the dark. When Carlo is away and I am alone, I cannot go to sleep if the lights are not on. And sometimes if I awake alone in the dark, I am panic-stricken.

Under the pressure of the shortages of food and water, and of the bomb hits on the munitions factory, which drastically reduced work days, the marginal existence of the Villanis collapsed. The specter of starvation was omnipresent. My mother devoted herself to foraging for enough food to feed me and my sister but she often didn't succeed. In the evening, when it was time to eat, I could always tell by the expression on my mother's face when she had nothing for us, and on those occasions I would always pretend to be busy to ease her discomfort.

More days than not, we didn't have a crust of bread nor a swallow of milk. Our hunger was constant and numbing. My grandparents continually worried and argued about food, and living on top of each other, as we did, it was impossible for them to conceal their worries and fears from me. When they were not worrying about food, they worried about the jobs at the munitions plant, whether the bomb damage of the previous night's raid could be repaired or whether the factory would have to shut down and even the meager paychecks would cease.

The only source of water for all of Pozzuoli was a spring-fed little fountain that was a ten-minute walk from our house. All the townspeople queued up there and it was a long, long wait to fill a couple of bottles. My sister was continually sick in bed, with one illness after another, but despite my emaciated look I was quite healthy. The other children made fun of me, though, calling me *steccheta* (stick) and scrawling "Sofia Stuzzicadente" (toothpick) on the wall of our building.

Of course, we no longer had meals together or ever sat down at the dinner table. We would immediately devour any food that found its way to us. When you are starving, knives, forks, napkins, and table manners disappear. When our weekly loaf of bread was brought in, my grandmother immediately cut it into equal pieces and handed them around, and they were ravenously consumed right there and then. But there is a confession I have to make about the bread, something I did which troubles my conscience to this day. Bread was very scarce and it was distributed by the town on the basis of coupons which were allotted to each family. It was my duty to take our coupons to the bakery each week and get our allotment. We were given the number of grams allotted for eight people, and this always came out to a large loaf plus an extra little piece. On the way home, I always ate that little extra piece and I never told my family about it, although my grandmother used to weigh the bread and I think she suspected my pilferage.

Of course, when you are seven years old, and you have painful contractions in your stomach from not eating, the sight and smell of fresh bread is beyond your willpower. I simply could not restrain myself. I have always had strong control of myself but starvation incites you to do things contrary to your nature. This bread pilferage is the only time in my memory when I lost that control. As I said, I still feel a kind of shame for what I did way back then.

That is not to say, however, that I didn't commit other childhood transgressions, all related to food. I can recall sneaking into the concierge's garden and stealing fruit from her trees. She finally caught me and raised her voice for the neighborhood to hear. "Look at her! Look at this Sofia Stuzzicadente who steals my apples! Look at her eyes! They are the eyes of a thief!"

The only other food thievery fortunately escaped detection. Before the war, I used to filch religious postcards and sell them to get money for an ice cream or a piece of candy. It was wrong, of course, but at least I was helping to spread the faith. When the war caused ice cream and candy to disappear, my career as a thief of religious postcards also came to an end.

I had one other secret source of food, but this was my mother's secret, not mine. Some mornings at dawn, when the wake-up cries resounded through the tunnel, urging us to leave quickly because the first train was approaching, my mother would take me by the hand and, making sure she wasn't followed, hurry me along into the open country. We followed a path that led to a series of small caves, from one of which emanated smoke from a wood fire. In this cave there was a goatherd who was a friend of one of my uncles. He had an empathy for me as he would have had for one of his little goats that was undernourished. The goatherd would milk one of his goats, filling a big mug with frothy, warm milk which he would hand to me. I cannot possibly describe the exquisite taste of that fresh milk as I felt its warm little river run down my insides and settle in my empty stomach. That cup of milk lifted me physically and spiritually; on those mornings when my mother took me to the goatherd, it really didn't matter if there was no food for the rest of that day. I was uplifted. I was sustained. Food has always played an important part in my life, and as an adult I have eaten remarkable dishes prepared by some of the world's great chefs, but I prize two memories above all else: the memory of that warm goat's milk, and the *pasta e fagiole* that used to burble in my grandmother's kitchen.

My mother's sacrifices were boundless. Her most cherished possession, and she didn't have many, was a camel's-hair coat that seemed to heighten her Greta Garbo resemblance. She adored that coat. But that first freezing winter in the tunnel, when I had nothing to wear to keep warm, she unhesitatingly took a scissors to her coat, recut it and sewed it into a dress for me. She did the same thing to one of her two dresses for my sister.

As the war worsened for the Germans, they began a wholesale conscription of able-bodied Italian men, both for the army and for their work forces in Germany. My uncles, Guido and Mario, who were in their late twenties, had to go into hiding to escape the regular conscription sweeps of the Germans. They no longer stayed in our house, nor could they sleep in the tunnel, but they had to hide out in various secret places they knew in and around Pozzuoli. Of course, they could not work in the munitions factory any longer, for the Germans had grabbed all the young men who worked there and replaced them with old men and women. So we suffered the loss of

their paychecks, and to our many anxieties we had
to add the fear that they would be captured and
sent to Germany.

As a result of this confusion and suffering and fear,
with the fabric of our family torn apart, I felt a
keen isolation, a kind of loneliness that caused me to
be more withdrawn than ever. In my loneliness, I
would climb a small fig tree in our front yard and
hide myself in its thick foliage. I felt secure there, in
the green world of its broad leaves. I often sat there
for hours at a time.

A proclamation, signed by the mayor, appeared on
all the bulletin boards of Pozzuoli and on the radio. All
citizens of Pozzuoli were to evacuate the town within
forty-eight hours. The bombing raids had become intolerable. The Germans were moving out. There were
rumors that big American warships were on their way
to shell the port as a prelude to an invasion attack.
There were other rumors that the attack would be
coming from the north, off the beaches at Anzio.

There was no organized evacuation. Everyone had
to leave but where we went and how we got there
had to be our own concern. My grandparents' only
relatives, outside of Pozzuoli, were a family named
Mattia that lived in Naples. Signora Mattia was the
cousin of my grandmother. Unfortunately, they had
not seen each other for years, nor kept in touch; my
grandmother warned us that her cousin had a rather
selfish personality and that we were not to expect a
warm welcome, or, in fact, any welcome at all.

Even though our house had been somewhat damaged, a few windows broken, some plaster cracked,
it was still an important haven to me, the only home
I had ever known. Now my grandmother was saying
that we would take a few clothes and blankets and
go to the big city of Naples, where I had never been,
and ask to be taken in by people who didn't really
want us.

On the way to the railroad station, I clung to my
mother, who carried my sister. We struggled with
our pitiful belongings. Our uncles came out of hiding

and met us at the train. All eight of us crowded into a compartment that was already occupied by several nuns. Halfway to Naples, the train was stopped and boarded by German soldiers who began searching the cars, seizing those men who looked fit enough to work in German labor camps. Germany was experiencing a severe manpower shortage and they needed all the able-bodied men they could find.

It looked like my two uncles were finally trapped. There was no way to avoid the search parties who were working from both ends of the car toward the middle compartment, where we were. Aware of our agitation over the impending fate of my uncles, two of the nuns motioned to my uncles and each nun stuffed one of them under her big black skirt, just as the Nazis entered our compartment. My uncles stayed hidden under the nuns' skirts until we reached Naples and thereby escaped detection, but afterward Guido said that he had passed out, probably out of fear.

As my grandmother had predicted, the Mattias were certainly not hospitable, but they didn't turn us away. My mother, my sister, and I shared a tiny room which fortunately had a balcony. For the five months we stayed in Naples, that balcony was my only contact with the outside world; my mother and grandmother feared that if we left the room the Mattias might not let us back in, so my sister and I acted as room insurance. The Mattias had tins of biscuits and a cache of other food which they had put aside for themselves, but which they never shared with us. We never got so much as a crumb of bread or a glass of water from them; as a matter of fact, they went to great pains to hide their food and water. I understood this. It was a desperate time when people were dying of starvation and dehydration and my grandmother's cousin had to insure the survival of her own family.

The survival of ours was something else again. My uncles went back into hiding, this time joining some other men who were hidden in a storeroom that had been ingeniously covered over with a large cupboard

full of china. So they were relatively safe, but we
found that conditions in Naples were even worse
than they had been in Pozzuoli. There was no water
at all, not even spring water. All that people had to
drink was whatever rainwater they could accumulate.
Apart from a virtually inedible black bread that was
severely rationed, there was absolutely no food, except on the black market. In the house, we could feel
the hatred of the Mattias. The nightly bombing raids
were much more intensive and destructive than we
had known in Pozzuoli. Naples was the most bombed
city in Italy, and when the air raid sirens started wail-
ing it really sounded as if the world were ending.

My mother, who is by nature a very nervous woman, had a terrible time those months in Naples. Her
nerves were always on or over the edge. When the
mass of sirens sent up their wail, my mother would
scream at the top of her lungs, scream right along with
the screaming sirens. She used to scare me to death.
My mother reacts more strongly to nerve-racking
events than other people. She does to this day. My
mother still screams at life.

I bear no grudge against the Mattias for hating our
presence. As a child, I discovered that more terrible
than the physical effects of war—the death, devastation, and ruin—more terrible was the ruin of the
human spirit, the transformation of a human being into an animal. People paid a terrible price to survive,
and the mutilation of the soul was the worst part of
the war.

My sister was ill all during our stay in Naples, and
this added immeasurably to my mother's nervousness.
Maria had measles and then, barely over them, she
developed typhoid. She had a high fever which gave
her a terrible thirst. All that my mother had for her
to drink was dirty rainwater which she had collected
in a pot on the balcony and which she kept hidden
under the bed. Another time, when there wasn't even
dirty rainwater to drink, my mother went down into
the street and drained some water from the radiator
of a German army truck. The soldier-driver came

upon her as she was leaving but he was more amused than angry.

Luckily, I didn't catch any of Maria's diseases, but I was a skeleton. Sometimes my mother or my grandmother would bring home a sack of rice or potatoes, which would be our entire diet for a week or ten days, but more often than not, all that Maria and I had to eat was a hunk of that gooey black bread. This bread was rock-hard on the outside and gummy within. The inside was like modeling clay and it would stick to the knife when you cut the bread. My sister and I would eat the thin hard crust and then mold little animals out of the inside dough and put them in the window to dry. But usually we were so hungry the following morning that somehow we managed to eat those indigestible objects, which dropped into our stomachs like paper weights.

I remember one desperate occasion when my mother hung over our little balcony, inspecting the people passing below. She spotted a mother pushing a baby carriage, with a bag of food in one of her arms. My mother rushed down, and I watched her go up to the woman, point to me, and ask the mother if she had any food she could share with us. The woman took out a loaf of bread, broke it in two, and gave her half. My mother had to beg food like that on many occasions, and people, more often than not, were kind and sharing. Much more so than our own relatives. As our situation became more and more desperate, my grandmother had angry food discussions with her cousin which we could hear from our part of the flat. When there is poverty, there are always angry voices. I spent my entire childhood among screams and protests, and a living atmosphere that was always very tense. I instinctively knew, however, that it was not the ordinary way to live. I could sense that inside of me; I hid from these confrontations because I couldn't bear to hear people scream.

As the war worsened for the Nazis, they became uglier toward the Italians, whose sentiments were now staunchly with the Americans. Reprisal executions in public, vicious anti-Jewish propaganda, torture by pulling out fingernails, burying people alive, burning them in ovens, human soap factories, concentration camps—these were some of the things I heard my family talking about, and the victims were non-Jewish as well as Jewish Italians. But the things I heard were really too terrible for my young mind to accept.

Toward the end of their occupation of Naples, however, when the Nazis knew they would soon have to give ground to the Americans, they began to kill the Neapolitans indiscriminately, and then, seeing it for myself, I really understood the appalling viciousness of war. Inanimate bombs dropping from the sky, wounded people lying in the streets, the absence of food and water, were awful, but not the same as a human being, dressed in a soldier's costume, committing an atrocity against another, defenseless human being. Now that I actually observed these mounting atrocities from my balcony, I finally understood the full terribleness of war. I saw men grabbed on the streets below me, beaten, thrown into German army trucks and hauled away. People were shot in the streets without warning. My young eyes saw one appalling, gruesome spectacle after another.

And then came the worst bloodbath of all—what became known as the Four Days of Naples, when ragged little boys from the slums finally rebelled against the German oppression and took matters into their own hands. What these little boys did I witnessed with my own eyes, but even so, I find it difficult to believe that what I remember actually happened. Armed with bottles filled with gasoline they had stolen from the Germans, these boys ignited rags they had stuffed into the bottles to serve as wicks, and then darted from side streets and swarmed over the huge German tanks, stuffing the bottles into the gun slits in the tanks just as the gasoline exploded. These were ragamuffin little boys, mind you, ranging from five to ten years of age, whose courage was unbelievable. They attacked tanks and trucks and installations, and no German soldier on the street was immune from their swarming attacks. Their fire bombs were exploding everywhere, and some of them had grenades and ammunition, which they had stolen from the Germans. I couldn't believe my eyes. Many of these boys were shot and killed by the Germans, their bloody little bodies dotting the streets, but nothing daunted their attacks.

I also saw them run at tanks with flaming straw held over their heads, and then somehow twist the straw into the tanks, often being killed in the process. Groups of these boys scurried around the rooftops dropping paving stones, sacks of rocks, and every manner of heavy object on troop carriers, trucks, and marchers passing below. It was a fanatical attack, waged with scissors, knives, nail-spiked boards, and virtually any potentially lethal object they could get their hands on.

For four days these incredible boys were a continual, deadly harassment. Day and night I watched them running, dodging, scurrying in and out of alleys and over walls and rooftops, ever attacking, achieving with their courage and brazen tactics what the Italian men, who were now in work camps or in hiding, had failed even to attempt.

Those boys from the slums of Naples were very much like the boys of Pozzuoli. The hard life of the slums had taken away their boyhood and required manhood of them at an early age. They ran with their flaming bottles in the face of guns firing at them, and even when wounded, persisted to their goal, if they possibly could. To my horror, I saw some of them blown up by exploding tanks when they couldn't get away in time. The most gruesome sight I saw was two German soldiers scrambling from their burning tank, themselves on fire, running after the escaping boy who had attacked their tank, firing at him with their pistols. Flames were trailing from their hair and their burning uniforms but they were intent on pursuing the little boy and trying to kill him. The three of them disappeared into an alleyway but for some time I continued to hear their pistols firing.

After four days, incredible as it may seem, the boys of Naples had brought the German army to its knees;

to our amazement, the entire German military estab-
lishment withdrew from Naples. By the end of the
fifth day, there wasn't a Nazi soldier left on the
streets. But the fury of the Nazis was still to be
reckoned with. They had taken all the food and water with them, and as they left they had blown up
sewer mains and what remained of the water system. They then stationed snipers in the hills and
mountains which surround Naples to the north. Directly above our house was Monte Santo. And directly
below us was a food store which constantly had a
long queue of people in front of it, patiently waiting
to buy some black bread and what little other food
was available. Almost all the people on line were
women, children, and old persons. The Nazi snipers
on Monte Santo would fire on these bread queues,
wounding and killing people indiscriminately. That
seemed to me the worst of their atrocities, the most
mindless. When the snipers scored a hit, the wounded or dead would be taken away, but the people did
not give up their places in the line.

Two days after the German retreat, the Allies came
marching in. We knew they were on their way and
there was great anticipatory excitement. On the
morning when everyone poured out of the houses,
and all the men came out of hiding to welcome the
new soldiers, my mother allowed me to leave our
room for the first time. What a surprise I had when
the first troops I saw were a regiment of men in skirts.
I had never heard of kilts or Scotsmen, and neither
had the Naples ragamuffins, who darted among them,
trying to look up their skirts.

It was a day of jubilation. The Americans came in
jeeps and trucks and right away started to hand out
candies and biscuits and other forgotten delicacies. A
soldier threw me a piece of chocolate but I didn't
know what it was. I had never tasted any. I tried to
catch some of the marvelous boxes and cans and
packages that were flying through the air but all I
snared was a little can of concentrated coffee. I gave
it to my grandmother but we couldn't figure out what

to do with it. My grandmother knew from the smell that it was coffee but it obviously wouldn't work in her espresso machine. Eventually she discovered the miracle of adding hot water.

As soon as the Americans started to bring food into Naples, a black market began to flourish. Our family had no money, nor anything of value to sell, but those who could afford the black market began to eat quite well. The Neapolitans were very adroit at stocking the black market. As trains and trucks and ships began to arrive, laden with American foodstuffs, clothing, and nonmilitary supplies, it was not uncommon for entire railroad cars to disappear and for trucks not to reach their destination. In fact, on a couple of occasions, unloaded ships simply disappeared from the harbor, never to be found again. Not a trace.

We had to leave Naples as precipitously as we had arrived. The Allied military requisitioned our building and we were forced to depart on a few hours' notice. The train tracks to Pozzuoli had been destroyed, and no other transportation existed (penniless, we couldn't have bought tickets anyway), so we were obliged to travel the twenty-five kilometers on foot, with our possessions on our backs. We left Naples very early in the morning, before dawn. I don't recall saying good-bye to Cousin Mattia. Maria was too ill to walk, so my uncle Mario carried her on his shoulders all the way to Pozzuoli.

The road to Pozzuoli was choked with refugees, lugging their possessions on their backs, and in carts and wagons and all manner of wheeled contrivances. The road itself was in terrible condition, covered with bomb craters. People got in each other's way, carts broke down and blocked the road, some people tumbled into the craters, there was yelling and screaming and joyful reunions and fistfights and exhausted people sitting on the roadside, but withal, I felt elated because we were going home.

Of course, we all shared a common fearfulness about our house and what may have happened to it —in fact, if we had a house at all. The assault on

Pozzuoli had been devastating, and we were prepared for the worst. But, never mind, at the end of that long trek we would be in our hometown, house or no house, and to my ten-year-old mind that would be a lovely awakening from a nightmare.

As we neared Pozzuoli in the late afternoon, the throngs of refugees became even denser and we began to run into friends and neighbors. That day on the road stays in my memory like flashes of a well-cut film. (In fact, the refugee road that de Sica created in *Two Women* was very much like what happened that day going back to Pozzuoli. Much of *Two Women* corresponded to this childhood period of my life.) Friends we ran into told us rumors about what had happened to this person and that person, who had been killed, what houses had been wiped out, and so forth. As we trudged through the outskirts of the town, my apprehension grew because the desolation was terrible. We were climbing up and down huge mounds of rubble and twisted girders—the unrecognizable remains of stores and paved streets and houses.

Then, suddenly, there was our house, badly damaged but still standing. All the windows had been blown out, the roof sagged, the walls were cracked, but it was standing. That was the important thing. It was still on its feet. We would eventually patch up the broken furniture, tape newspapers over the windows, repair the broken plaster, and fix the roof and walls.

But first we had more urgent matters to attend to: our two old nemeses of no water and no food were as much of a problem as ever, and there was a new tribulation—lice. We were covered with them—in our hair, all over our bodies and thick in our clothing. The itching and scratching that they caused were far worse for us than our hunger and thirst. These were not the little black lice that we schoolchildren sometimes got, but a peculiar species—fat and white and tenacious, and no one could recall ever having seen anything like them before the war. They had swept through Naples like a virus, and everyone had them. Unlike ordinary lice, these horrible creatures were very active and crawled constantly around my scalp and body. Just thinking about them now makes my skin crawl, and I start to itch and scratch in vivid remembrance. We used to pick them off us and disgustedly throw them in the fire, getting a little feeling of vengeance from watching them sizzle in the flames. But there was no way to get rid of them. We carried heavy pails of water from the nearby fountain from which a trickle of spring water still flowed. We boiled the water over a wood fire and then threw all our clothes in the boiling water and let them cook for an hour or two. We washed our hair and bodies with a caustic laundry soap and rinsed ourselves with steaming water. But no sooner did we dress than the lice were back, just as pestiferous as before. The problem was that there was no way to kill the eggs, which hatched as soon as we took the clothes out of the water.

We were desperate. My scalp and skin were bleeding from all the scratching. I couldn't sleep. And besides, I had a second affliction that none of the others had: scabies, which is a disease caused by a certain kind of mite that burrows under the skin and deposits its eggs there. As the eggs hatch in ever increasing numbers, the itching they cause becomes more and more unbearable. So I had the double plague of the mites and the strange white lice. I would sometimes weep from the intensity of the itching. I kept moving around as much as I could, because I scratched more when I was quiet.

The shape of those lice, the way they felt when I plucked one from my hair, the satisfaction I got from squeezing one between my fingers and feeling it pop—a horrible memory that I'll never forget. Those dreadful bugs seemed to sum up all the suffering and horror and injustice of the war. As a matter of fact, my family had heard a rumor that these lice had been dropped from airplanes in order to infect the population. After all, they were a breed no one had ever seen before, and they never reappeared after the war. My grandfather was convinced of this, but perhaps they were spawned by all the dirt and improper

sewage and all that. Almost everyone had those lice
but some people pretended not to because they were
ashamed.

I don't know what would have happened to me if
the United States Army had not come to our rescue
with its miracle powder, DDT. The army set up aid
stations in the town, and after one application of DDT
we were miraculously free of this pestilence. But I
still had the mites to contend with. DDT helped, but
not until an American doctor gave me a sulfa com-
pound was I entirely rid of them. The disappearance
of the lice was a sign, for me, that the war was really
over. We had no food on the shelves and we still had
much struggle and hard times ahead, but we had always had a hard life and it all felt familiar and good.

We began to get some food from the army, even
white bread, which was considered a great delicacy,
but our biggest problem, that first winter back in
Pozzuoli, was the cold. It gets very cold in the
winter and we had no fuel and woefully inadequate
clothes. The kitchen was the only room we tried to
heat by burning scraps of wood in the old iron range.
All nine of us (my aunt and uncle now had a child)
would huddle in that little kitchen. If we had to get
something from one of the other rooms, we would
dash out, get it as quick as we could, and dash back.
My sister was ill again, still suffering from the ravages
of the typhoid. When it was time for bed, my grandmother would fill a long-handled receptacle with some
of the hot coals from the stove and warm the sheets
of the bed with them.

But as I said, this part of my life was not much different from what it had been. We had never been able
to afford enough fuel to be adequately warm. The
important thing was that despite all the problems and
privations, I had the love and protection of my mamma and my mammina, and I was surrounded by a big
family, which gave me a sense of security; and for a
kid it was fun to race from the kitchen through the
ice-cold rooms and jump into a bed with a nice warm
sheet on the bottom and an ice-cold one on the top.

∿∿∿∿∿∿∿

Sophia's aunt Dora, who still lives in the
family's original quarters in Pozzuoli

Sophia was a very serious child. She preferred
doing her homework to going outside to play. She
had only two friends, Rosa and Rita. She was very
quiet; it was her sister, Maria, who was the talker.
Sophia did not smile very much, or laugh. Sometimes,
though, she would sing songs with her grandmother
when they were alone in the kitchen. But only when
they were alone. She did not seem to have fun, to
play games and enjoy herself the way other children
did.

∿∿∿∿∿∿∿

Day by day, a little at a time, the mystery of
self-restoration began to be solved. In addition to food
brought in by the American troops, produce began to
appear from farms that farmers had started to rework.
Many people whose houses had been destroyed lived
communally in the city hall and in the schools while
they rebuilt their abodes.

But for us a source of some concern was the contingent of Moroccan soldiers that had been billeted in
the ground-floor quarters of our building. They were
commanded by a French officer, but he didn't exercise much control over them. They were always drinking and playing cards and dancing to the rhythms of
cymbals. To get to our flat on the top floor, we had to
pass by the Moroccans and it was always frightening.
They would talk to us in a language we didn't understand, and with their gestures tease us and pretend
that they were going to go after us. Actually they
never molested us. A couple of times in the dead of
night, though, when they had had much too much to

drink, they had come pounding on our door, to frighten us. But finally my grandmother marched down to the Moroccans' quarters and had a good, tough talk with the French lieutenant. After that, we were never again bothered in the night.

Occasionally, German bombers made a run on Pozzuoli and we had to hurry back to the dread confines of the tunnel, but it was not often, nor were the attacks very concentrated; after all we had been through, those raids seemed pretty tame.

My mother began to earn a little money by playing piano in the little café and restaurant across the road from us which had just reopened with mostly American GIs as clientele. After my sister recovered her health, she often joined my mother in the cafés. For a six-year-old, she had a remarkable voice and she loved having an audience to hear her sing. I yearned to join in the singing, although my voice wasn't as good as Maria's, but I was much too shy even to go to listen to them.

These entertainments by my mother and sister gave my grandmother an idea of how to bring in some badly needed revenue. Aside from a few bare cafés and a couple of shabby restaurants which did not have much to eat or drink, there was virtually nothing to do for the large numbers of GIs who were bivouacked around Pozzuoli. They would come to town on a pass for a few hours but there was no place to go to enjoy themselves—to have a drink, hear some music, get their minds off the war. So my grandmother hit on the notion of turning our unused living room into a kind of home café, where soldiers could have a few drinks, listen to music, sing, have some laughs, and, above all, feel that they were spending a few hours with a family group inside an Italian house. The big problem for my grandmother was how to provide drinks. She solved that by using the little money my mother had earned to buy pure alcohol (on the black market), to which she added essence of cherry Strega, a liqueur. It was a sweet-tasting drink but my mother had discovered, from observing the GIs in the cafés, that they liked sweet drinks. Some of them even put sugar in their wine.

My grandmother's home café caught on immediately. The GIs loved to pass a few hours there, drinking Grandmother's alcoholic concoction (and the rough red wine that began to come in from the country) and listening to my mother play the piano and my little sister sing. They would join in the singing, and our living room began to be a place where they would rendezvous with their friends. We were like a foster family to them. They often brought records to put on our old hand-wound Victrola, and some of the regulars brought PX food such as biscuits, pasta, flour, coffee, and cans of fruit. I helped serve and wash dishes but my shyness prevented me from singing or taking part in the festivities. At ten, I was still stunted in growth, terribly thin, and quite ugly.

Sometimes when they got a little drunk, the GIs would start to think of home and get very sad. My grandmother would keep an eye on them, and when she saw them getting into this condition she began to water their drinks. These boys were very young, not more than twenty, twenty-two, and sometimes, under the release of a few drinks, they would break down and weep. My grandmother and my mother would console them; it was probably cathartic for those boys to be able to talk about their families and girl friends and the life back home which they yearned for. Of course, my mother and grandmother neither spoke nor understood English but it didn't seem to matter.

Most of the GIs simply had a good time; some of them played the piano, often beautifully rendered jazz or swing, and when the piano set the mood, others would dance marvelous boogie-woogie, which was a dance I had never seen before. At six o'clock Grandmother would announce closing. We never entertained at night. Hearing about my grandmother's success, many other families on the block opened their houses to the soldiers in the same way, serving drinks and providing entertainment. After a while there was a spirited competition for GI customers.

One of those American GIs arranged for my mother and me to visit the American army base, where, even though it was against the rules, a doctor performed a minor operation on the shrapnel scar on my chin and succeeded in making it virtually disappear.

Charles Dial was a GI stationed at a training area seven miles outside of Pozzuoli. He kept a diary.

March 5, 1944—Sunday. I went into Pozzuoli with Mike Codega, Jim Lauro, and Yakubisin to take a shower at the Bath Station. We have no water where we are. Afterwards, Jim took us to visit a truly beautiful blonde named Romilda who he said he had completely bowled over (B.S.). She lives with her family in a place on the waterfront near the Rangers' Club. She's a nice gal about my age—plays the piano and sings a bit and sells us vino for 100 lire a bottle.

March 8—Wednesday. Today went to Pozzuoli to take a bath around 3 P.M. It's right next door to the place where we spent Sunday afternoon with the blonde with the piano and the voice. She remembered me and came out with a big hello. Jackson and I went in, and soon the whole shower truck followed along. We had a bit of cherry brandy, sang a few songs and left. She does a mean rendition of *My Blue Heaven*. I don't think she was too happy with me for bringing in the entire company at once.

March 25—Saturday. Went into Pozzuoli with a few of the boys and wandered around town. Went to see my blonde friend, Romilda, about 4 P.M. Sat around alone with her in the early evening batting the breeze, she in Italian and me in English. It's amazing how we can understand each other. She told me she had been trying for the movies. She went back to her bedroom and brought out a group of pic-

tures taken by MGM. She was posed as another Garbo
—Camille, Anna Karenina, etc. She is truly a magnificent beauty and has kept up her spirit during the
war. She has 2 small children and a real struggle. When
I left her about 6–7 P.M., told her that if at all possible to get a ride out to our outfit I would con some
food for her from the cooks. Also said I would see
what I could do about getting the medics to fix the
scar on the face of one of her kids. Left and thumbed
my way back to the outfit.

March 26—Sunday. Went to Mass at 10:00. Yesterday they put up a wire barricade in an area near
Headquarters Co. Any local civilians found wander-
ing in the area are going to be put in there. They say
there's too damn much stealing. I guess it's true but
these people are hard pressed. When I think of all
that Caruso and other Italians have given to us, that
damn barricade is just too much.

I also got word that I had to be on guard duty.
And to make the day complete, about 2 P.M. a guy
on guard from C Co. comes up to the tent and tells
me they've got a blonde and her kid locked up.
She told them she'd been asked out to visit me—and
so she had. I went down and got them out of jail and
brought them back to our area. Romilda had walked
all the way from Pozzuoli with the little girl. She's a
cute little kid. Mom has her all dressed up in a
navy blue coat and little brown kid gloves—a real
effort these days. She's about nine years old—very
quiet and serious with very dark eyes. Unfortunately
she'll never have her mother's looks. She's probably
scared to death of all us dirty smelly GIs.

I took them over to the medics to see what they
could do about the little girl's chin scar. Since I had to
go on guard duty about 4:00, I arranged for them to
be taken to the kitchen after the medics to get fed. I
know George Borkhuis will look after them. Later
George told me that he loaded a jeep with food and
had Bell drive them back to Pozzuoli—Amen.

~~~~~~~~~~

Sophia's sister, Maria

I am not instinctively projected forward. Actually I am full of fantasy about the past, so I have nostalgia even for our life in Pozzuoli, and for that big family we had. We were very poor and we lived on top of each other, but we were closely knit. My childhood was full of trouble, and full of war, but I like problems and my memory of that time is not a bad memory at all. Of course, I was very little—Sophia was much more aware of what was happening and its significance.

Also, by nature she is more sensitive than I am. Very introvert, silent, *meditativa*, shy. She would always be off by herself. Sophia seemed lonely, even in the midst of our crowded kitchen.

I was just the opposite. Extrovert, loving music, singing all the time, especially American songs I learned from the GIs who came to our house, even though I didn't understand the words I was singing. I made costumes, presented plays, had many friends; Sophia would always look at me with her big, shy eyes as if I were a character from a storybook.

~~~~~~~~~~

Six

I did not start to develop physically until I was fourteen, which is quite late for a Neapolitan girl. My friends were all bigger than I was in every way. They had breasts and were menstruating and discussed sexual intercourse and conception. I pretended that I too had become a woman, lying about everything, but in the process I got a pretty good education. In those days it was unheard of to discuss anything that related to the body or to sex with one's family, so that my grandmother and mother never mentioned such things to me. My skinny, breastless body, plus the fact that I had not yet begun to menstruate, made my inferiority complex even worse.

When I was eleven I started to play the piano, which I adored. I think I could have been a very good pianist, that I had the talent for it, but we couldn't afford to pay for lessons and my mother was my teacher. Parents rarely make good teachers for their children, and my mother was certainly no exception. She was terribly impatient with me, and every time I made a mistake she banged me on the head. I finally gave up. I loved everything about the piano, even practicing, but my headaches from being knocked on the head by my mother became so severe that I had to stop.

When Pozzuoli's only movie theater reopened, it offered Hollywood movies for the first time. Before the war only drab Italian films had been shown. The Hollywood films took me into a world far removed from the desolate years of my childhood. But it was not the opulence I saw on the screen that overwhelmed me; it was the stars themselves and the roles they played. Fred Astaire dancing with Ginger Rogers was a fairy-tale dream. Gable, Cary Grant, Linda Darnell, Rita Hayworth, Sinatra, Betty Grable, Gene Kelly, June Allyson, and, above all, Tyrone Power. He was the god of my adolescence. When he appeared in the melodramatic epic *Blood and Sand,* I went to see him twelve times. And each time I sat through as many shows as I could. I had to convince someone in my family, usually my aunt Dora, to sit with me because my grandmother would not allow me to be in the movie house by myself.

Poor Aunt Dora, sometimes sitting through four consecutive showings of *Blood and Sand* just to please me. Some days she would split her chaperoning of me with some other member of our family. I felt a real physical pain each time I had to leave the theater, no matter how many times I saw the film. After I saw Rita Hayworth in *Gilda*, I started to comb my hair the way she wore hers; later I switched to Veronica Lake's hairstyle when one of her pictures captivated me. But I never stood in front of a mirror and tried to imitate their acting. I had no desire to be a star, to be glamorous, to have cars and furs and a castle in Beverly Hills, and not because of the impossibility of attaining them. It was something else. What these movies set off in me was something quite different. It was the intangible of emoting, of *acting* itself. I was not interested in what I could bring *to* myself by being an actress, but in what I could bring *out* of myself.

I have no way of accounting for this reaction. There had been no plays or entertainments at the strict Catholic school I attended. The nuns only cared about the three Rs. But even if there had been plays, I would have been much too shy to appear in them. I used to help my sister cut costumes out of paper for shows which she sometimes put on for the neighbors, but I would never actually take part in the shows themselves. I would just sit in the corner and marvel at her ability to stand up in front of all those people and perform.

There was no library in Pozzuoli, nor did we have any books in the house, so that part of my development, the world of imagination, I guess you'd say, was totally neglected. I had never heard of Shakespeare or Shaw. My family simply had too many problems just keeping all of us alive to pay any attention to books and reading. They were church people who went along with the church's notion that strict adherence to basic studies was all that a girl should concern herself with. My grandmother and my aunt were devout Catholics but my mother was not. As a matter of fact, at one time my mother even considered turning Protestant. Being a musician, she favored Protestant songs because they didn't sound so much like traditional church music. It was a tribute to her cunning, because she had also discovered that if you were Protestant you were eligible to receive packages that were being sent to Italy by Protestant organizations in America. She once took me to a Protestant service with her but my grandmother found out about it and put her foot down. I never went again.

My aunt and my sister are still devoutly religious and go to mass regularly, but I am not. I never go to mass. Not necessarily because I am against the church but because I think you can pray anywhere, and I don't need a church to commune with God. I must confess, however, that the attitude of the church toward Carlo and me has contributed to this feeling.

~~~~~~~~~

Sophia's sister, Maria

My father was the most important man in my life, but not as fathers usually are. There were no secrets in our cramped quarters, and I constantly heard denunciations of my father because of his denials that I was his child, and his refusal to give me his name. I had never seen him, but my mother had a little photo of him which she let me see. If my mother was in a calm, quiet mood about him, probably because she was hearing from him, she would tell us, yes, you have a father, his name is Riccardo Scicolone, he lives in Rome; she would even attribute to him a few virtues. But if she was angry with him, which was more often the case, she would deny that he was alive and tell us how he had died in the war. The story varied in the telling. So, one week he was alive, and another week he was dead, and for me it was a terribly upsetting state of affairs. I tried to condition myself not to think about my father, but Sophia thought about him a lot and suffered.

The first time I actually saw him in the flesh and knew for sure that he existed, was in the *tribunale*, the courtroom. My mother, who is a dangerous fighter, was determined to get me his name so she sued him for paternity. I was brought to the courtroom to stand beside my father before the judge, who, by looking at us, was to decide if I was or was not my father's daughter. Many Pozzuoli townspeople crowded into the courtroom to see for themselves if there was any resemblance. The family was rather disgraced by this confrontation. I recall how I trembled as my mother led me into the courtroom. Sophia suffered even more than I, perhaps because she saw my trembling and because she understood the cruelty of subjecting me, and our family, to this public embarrassment.

I looked up at my father, who did not look at me. His face was our face, and I could see in his features some of Sophia and more of me. But he denied to the judge that I was his child, and he angrily denounced my mother with language that I could not understand except to know that what he said was bad. They did not have such things as blood tests in Pozzuoli (perhaps the technique had not yet been invented), so it was simply a matter of whom the judge believed. To my sorrow, he ruled in favor of my father, officially denying me his name, which left me feeling worse about him than I had felt before, when I was not sure if he was dead or alive.

Every time I entered the hallowed darkness of the Teatro Sacchino I could feel a change in my whole person. The Teatro had been a legitimate theater before it turned to films, and it had a proscenium arch, velour seats, and elaborate friezes in its baroque interior. When the lights went down and I was alone with Rita or Linda or Tyrone, I was suffused with the feeling that that's what I was put on earth to do, to act, to express myself, to let out whatever feelings I had inside; and perhaps a need to escape anonymity. I was not intrigued with the accouterments of success and fame, the furs, jewels, expensive automobiles, and mansions that are success's handmaidens. Of course, later on I had all of these so-called rewards when I became successful, and people tend to think, coming from the life I had, that that was my goal, but I can assure you that these things were not on my mind when I sat spellbound in that Pozzuoli movie house. It was what these performers on the screen were doing, not what they received for doing it. Although there was a far, far distance between the desire of a ten-year-old poor kid and the realization of that desire, curiously I felt a confidence in myself. Naturally, I never confided any of this to anyone, but deep down inside me I felt a conviction that I had been put on earth to be a movie actress.

At fourteen my body miraculously came to life, virtually overnight, and by fourteen and a half the ugly duckling had bloomed into a long-legged, full-breasted swan. It was as if I had burst from an egg and was born. For the first time in my life, when I walked down the street, I heard the mellifluous sound of male whistles. And I definitely knew I had finally and fully matured the day our physical education teacher, a handsome young man who used to supervise calisthenics in the amphitheater, came to see my mother to request permission to marry me. She told him to go home and soak in a cold tub.

A friend of my mother's, who lived across the street, brought us a Naples newspaper that gave details about an impending beauty contest that promised lavish prizes to the girl crowned Queen of the Sea, and to the twelve girls chosen as her princesses. The rules stipulated a minimum age of fifteen, but my mother said that now that I had filled out I looked at least fifteen and she was going to enter me. My shyness being what it was, I tried to protest, but my mother shut me off. "Lella, you are going to enter this contest," she said forcefully, "and you are going to win." I don't know the origin of "Lella" but it's the only name my family ever called me. My grandmother wasn't fond of "Sofia" (which is how it was spelled on my birth certificate) because that was the name of my father's mother and I have already explained how my family felt about him.

The contest was sponsored by the newspaper *Il Mattino* as a device to increase circulation; contestants were required to appear in Naples with an afternoon dress and a gown for the evening. My mother saw in this contest possible vicarious revenge for the Greta Garbo prize she had been denied, and the fact that I didn't have the requisite evening gown was not going to stop her. She enlisted the help of my grandmother, who was a genius with needle and thread. She had just made a brown-and-beige dress for me out of scraps of material she had in her sewing bag, so that would do for the afternoon, but the evening gown was a problem since, as usual, there wasn't a lira in the house.

"I'll tell you what we'll do, Lella," she said, after long reflection, "we will just take down one of the drapes in the living room and I will make you an evening gown out of that. It is very nice pink material that will look good on you." And so she did. And it did look nice, at least to my fourteen-year-old eyes. But I didn't have white shoes to go with the dress. In fact, the only shoes I had were black, and worn, but my mother solved that problem by getting some white paint, and by applying two thick coats, created my white shoes. We prayed it wouldn't rain.

The contest was held at night; my mother and I went to Naples by train, traveling in a crowded third-class compartment. I wore my new pink drapery dress, with my old school coat over it, and I was very careful not to scuff my shoes and let the black show through. I had my hair up, to look older, and my mother let me use some makeup.

We had to walk quite a far distance from the train station to where the contest was being held in a villa called Circolo della Stampa near the sea. It was a rather exclusive press club, and I felt, as my mother led me to it, as if I were the proverbial lamb being led to its execution. I would have given anything, *anything*, not to have to go through the doors.

Above the main drawing room, there was a wide corridor that gave into a huge reception chamber, and there were upwards of two hundred girls and their mothers crowded in that corridor, primping, combing, powdering, perfuming, studying themselves in mirrors, nervously waiting their turn. They wore beautiful gowns which quite obviously had not previously hung in their living room windows, and many of them were wearing jewels and flowers. I sat down quietly in a corner, trying to pull myself into the wall, and patiently waited my turn. My mother was very nervous.

When my time came to appear before the jury, I found, to my astonishment, that when I entered the room where the fourteen jury members were sitting at a long table, my nervousness seemed to fly off me. I walked back and forth before the jurors and answered their questions with composure. Before entering, I had been scared to death. I am always frightened before I do anything that requires me to perform. To this day, before the camera turns, I am still frightened of scenes I must play. I have a negative persuasiveness. I have no arrogance, not even confidence. I never expect anything. Then when it happens, I am doubly happy, but if it doesn't, I am not so badly disappointed. But there is this: once I put myself into a thing, I do my utmost, my very, very best. I never take for granted any demand I put on myself. My attitude is that nothing is going to come of my exertions, and I prepare myself mentally for rejection. But this attitude does not affect my performance: I still perform at the top of my talent—a positive performance, but a negative attitude.

That night in Naples, I was scared to death. It was very late when the last girl had paraded and the judges announced their verdict. I was prepared to console my mother. As it turned out, I was not selected queen, but my name was called as one of the twelve princesses, and I felt a bubble of joy rise inside me such as I had never felt before. Photographers took our pictures, reporters asked me for the spelling of my name, and we were each given a bouquet of flowers. It was my first bouquet.

Then I received my prize: a railroad ticket to Rome, several rolls of wallpaper, a tablecloth with twelve matching napkins, and twenty-three thousand lire (about thirty-five dollars), which to us was a very impressive sum of money. The following day, I appeared in the group photo in the newspaper with my name, incorrectly spelled, in the caption. In the afternoon, the Queen and Her Twelve Princesses were paraded through the streets of Naples in a carriage. People threw flowers at us and there was a marching band. I had the strange illusion, which I have previously mentioned, that I was standing on the sidewalk watching myself go by in the carriage, and that this joyful event was not happening to me but to my alter ego in the carriage.

The wallpaper was immediately pasted over our cracked, peeling walls of the living room, the tablecloth and napkins became fixtures of our Sunday lunch, and I hid the Rome ticket and the lire in a secret place behind a bureau drawer. In seeing her daughter crowned a Princess of the Sea, my mother had received all the encouragement she needed to concentrate on my future as an actress. Her next step was to enroll me in a drama school in Naples, which she paid for out of money she had started to earn giving piano lessons.

The faculty of the drama school consisted of a single professor, a former actor, who had his own approach to acting—a method of what he called "shaping an actor out of stone." What he taught us, pure and simple, was how to make faces. We never read a line of anything or acted anything, we just made faces. He gave us a printed list and we were expected to make faces precisely as they were described on the list. Horror, joy, despair, ecstasy, love, anger, whatever—the professor had a specific face for each and every emotion. Joy—both eyebrows up; surprise—both eyebrows up with the mouth formed in an *O;* skepticism—one eyebrow up; horror—big eyes; pain —little eyes. And so on. The Naples version of the Actors Studio. The professor obviously had never accepted the passing of silent movies.

My lessons at the acting school were only incidental to my main schooling, which I now pursued in the Pozzuoli public school; my goal was to be a teacher. But one day at the acting school, the professor made an announcement which, as it turned out, changed the course of my life. He told us that a colossal American production moving into Cinecittà, called *Quo Vadis*, had put out a call for hundreds of extras. "Those of you who can get to Rome will probably get your chance in the movies," the professor said.

I carried this news to my mother, who made an immediate decision that I should quit school; she decided that we would set out for Rome and really devote ourselves to trying to make me a movie actress. My grandfather and grandmother were as dead set against our going as they had been when my mother won the Greta Garbo contest, but times had changed and on this occasion my mother prevailed. I think that for some time she had been desperately hoping to find a way to escape the monotony and provincialism of Pozzuoli. My mother's personality simply wasn't suited to the subdued life of a small town. I also think that, even though he was now married, my mother hoped that by living in Rome she could somehow establish contact with my father.

As for me, I had no ambition as such to become a

movie actress in Rome. I would have been happy being a teacher in Pozzuoli, marrying a good local fellow, and raising a family, although I did feel in my heart that I had a force in me, a talent, for acting. But without my mother's ambition, her drive, I doubt that on my own I would have pushed myself out of Pozzuoli and into the frightening world that was faraway Rome.

Seven

We had gone to Rome with no preparation, but I didn't realize, until we got off the train, that my mother knew no more about big-city life than I did. She didn't even know how to use the telephone. She made a few futile attempts but finally we had to go into a bar at the railroad station and ask someone to make the call for us. It was my father she was calling.

He was astonished to hear from her. "What are you doing in Rome?" he asked.

"We want to see you. Sophia is here with me and she would like to see you very much because she is quite sick." Countless times my mother had failed to lure my father with my imaginary illnesses; this time it worked.

"All right," my father said. "I'll meet you at my mother's house."

His mother was anything but happy to see us. Rather grudgingly she offered me a glass of milk, and then left us to sit alone and await my father's arrival.

The first thing he said when he came in was, "You can't sleep here." Then he said, "I haven't any money, you know." Finally, he looked at me and said, "She doesn't look sick to me."

My mother told him why we had really come. My father jumped to his feet. "The movies!" he shouted. "Why, you're crazy! You're absolutely insane—you have no idea how tough things are in Rome! The movies? Why, is she such a beauty? Well, do what you like but leave me out of it."

"I just thought, since it's your own daughter," my

mother said, "that you might want to see her get
ahead, make a name for herself."

"How, by making a ridiculous ass out of herself?"
my father said.

"I just thought," my mother continued, "that you
might want to help her out a bit. You've never given
us so much as a lira—"

"I have no money to give you, *especially* for this
wild-goose chase to become a movie star. You do
what you want but *leave me out of it.*" He walked us
firmly to the door and ushered us out.

My mother's only other Rome contact was a cousin
I had never met. The cousin was not at all hospitable,
even before she heard my mother's purpose in bringing me to Rome. She used the same word as my
father, "crazy," and tried to induce my mother to
take the next train back to Pozzuoli. After much
wrangling, my mother wrung out of her a concession
that we could sleep on the couches in the living room
for one week without paying, but that if we stayed
after that we would have to pay a weekly rate.

While we were at my cousin's, every night we went
to bed only after they were through using the living
room, and we got up very early so as to be out of the
living room when my cousins awoke. They did everything they could to make us feel unwelcome. Since
we had very few belongings, our presence was scarcely noticeable. The only thing I wore, night and day,
was a black skirt and a black shirt because my mother
said that if I was dressed in black I would always
look elegant.

Quo Vadis was indeed hiring a horde of extras,
and Cinecittà was packed with thousands of people
seeking to be hired. The director, Mervyn Le Roy,
had all of them parade by him, choosing for interviews those who looked promising. My mother and I
were called forward. My mother had primed me to
answer any question I was asked in English with the
one word yes. No matter what they ask you, she had
said, smile and say yes. So that's what I did, answered all of Mr. Le Roy's questions with a pleasant
yes. But he finally got wise to me when, in response to

his question, "What is your name and address?" I answered yes. He was good-natured about my fakery, however, and although I didn't get the little speaking part he had in mind, he did hire both my mother and me as extras.

We reported to the vast sound stage where all the extras were being processed. An assistant director was summoning each extra by name. He called out, "Villani," and my mother stepped forward. "Scicolone" was next, but when I walked up to the production table, so did another woman. "Which one of you is Scicolone?" the man asked. "I am!" this woman said. "What do you think you're doing?" she said to me. "The man said Scicolone—that's me!"

I was stunned. We were standing in front of several hundred extras, and they were all listening to this confrontation. The woman just stood glowering at me and the sound stage was suddenly as quiet as if cameras were rolling. Then it dawned on me who she was. My stepmother. I had never seen her before but obviously this was the woman my father had married when my mother had refused to come to Rome and bail him out of his predicament. My mother always referred to her by her maiden name, Nella Rivolta, and always with great reticence. Now here she was screaming at me in front of all these people. She was like a fury. What a conflict must have been inside of her, and inside my mother. These two women belonged to the same man, competing for the same job with their daughter. As for the name Scicolone, it meant nothing to me. I had no pride in bearing it. I would have been just as happy with the name Villani. It was a big thing for my sister, important for her psyche to have the name, but I was totally indifferent. I had been born illegitimate, that was the stigma, and the fact that I was called Scicolone did nothing to eradicate the stain of illegitimacy.

I was rescued by the assistant director. "Scicolone, Sofia." he said, emphasizing the Sofia.

My mother pulled me forward, closer to the production table.

It was an unnerving way to get introduced to one's

stepmother. And the fact that she was made to look foolish when it turned out that she was not the Scicolone being called did not improve her regard for me. But thinking about it, I can appreciate how difficult it was for both my mother and Nella Rivolta. My mother only had one man in her life—the man who had married this woman—and my mother was faced with the difficulty of raising two of his children on whom he had turned his back.

Nella Rivolta, on the other hand, must not have been having an easy time of it herself or else why was she scratching so hard to get a meager job as a film extra? And she, too, had to bring up two of my father's children. I never saw her again after that day on the sound stage at Cinecittà. Not even when my father lay dying in the hospital—she didn't show up. Nor at his funeral. I thought perhaps we would meet there, for the second time. I think I would have looked at her with other eyes—more understanding.

My mother and I worked on *Quo Vadis* for several days, I as one of Deborah Kerr's clutch of slaves, my mother in a couple of mob scenes. We earned a total of fifty thousand lire (seventy-six dollars) and were exultant, but that was the beginning and the end of easy times in Rome.

Word reached us that my sister was gravely ill. My mother immediately packed up and left for Pozzuoli. For weeks we had been tramping from one movie office to another, but there were no calls for extras or bit players. Our capital had shrunk, but there was still enough to pay for doctors and medicine for Maria.

My mother was deeply concerned about leaving me alone in Rome, and I was scared to death. I had never been alone anywhere and, despite the fact that we paid them something out of our *Quo Vadis* money, our cousins were no friendlier. But at least they were tolerating me. And I had found work at the *fumetti*. That was the primary reason my mother left me in Rome. I earned enough from the *fumetti* to keep all of us going.

Before she got on the train, my mother repeated the litany I had heard many times before: "Remember, Lella, you must take care of yourself—all men are evil." Leaving me alone in Rome troubled her, but she knew that I was wise far beyond my young years. I would not repeat the folly of her first days alone in Rome; she could be sure of that. I had, too, developed a sense of being. By that I mean, too much self-respect to debase myself. But I still did not seriously think I would get anywhere in the movie world. I have always been a realist. I knew that despite my feelings about my ability, I really didn't have the physical attributes for success in films. I was too tall, too wide of hip, my nose was too long, my mouth too wide, my chin too weak. I simply didn't look like a conventional movie actress. Not even an *Italian* movie actress. And on top of all that, I had a pronounced Neapolitan accent, no contacts, and no training.

So as a movie actress my future was bleak, but not so in the *fumetti*. It's hard to explain the *fumetti*, which were panels of soap-opera photos that used small puffs coming out of the characters' mouths in which dialogue appeared. The *fumetti* were peculiarly Italian; they ran in the newspapers daily and were very popular. I would equate them with today's television soap operas in that they dealt with pretty much the same themes and heartthrobs. Somehow, during those first weeks in Rome, I had managed to get a *fumetti* audition. It was my training at the Naples acting school that got me the job, for what the *fumetti* people wanted by way of expressions was exactly what the professor had taught us. "What! You love another woman, John?" would appear in a balloon above my head while my expression—eyes wide, eyebrows arched, mouth in an *O*—was pure Naples acting school. At night I practiced my grotesque expressions in front of a mirror.

I was usually cast as the villainous girl of the strip, conventionally a gypsy or an Arab. When I began to receive a little publicity for my *fumetti* roles, the director decided that Scicolone was a rather comic and difficult name so he changed it to Sofia Lazzaro. It took about a week to make all the photos used in a single *fumetti* strip (the word means smoke, which is what the circle that contained the dialogue looked like—a puff of smoke), for which I was paid twenty thousand lire (thirty dollars). After I paid my cousins their rent money I sent almost all the rest to Pozzuoli.

Without the *fumetti* I'm sure I could not have stuck it out in Rome. Besides the money it paid, it also put me in contact with other young actors and in this way I developed a few friends. And it was on an evening when I went out with several of these friends that, by the purest chance, I entered my second beauty contest.

On this particular evening, my friends had taken me to the Colle Oppio, a big outdoor restaurant-nightclub overlooking the Colosseum. When we got there we discovered that a beauty contest to crown Miss Roma was scheduled as part of the evening's festivities. At that time, beauty contests sponsored by movie companies were commonplace, ostensibly to find new girls for the movies. Many of the girls in the Colle Oppio had come there to participate. Later in the evening, when the jury had assembled, one of the officials came to our table and invited me to enter the contest. I said no, it didn't interest me. I was, as usual, much too shy for that kind of spontaneous behavior.

A few moments later the official returned. He said that the members of the jury were all movie people and that one of them, a producer named Carlo Ponti, had noticed me and had specifically requested that I join the contest. My friends urged me to enter. You already start with his vote, they said, and anyway these are all people in the movie business, so it would be good for you if they saw you.

So I entered. And after the usual rigmarole of parading around and answering questions, the results were announced: Second place, Sofia Lazzaro. Always a bridesmaid. Afterward, Carlo Ponti came over to our table and introduced himself. He invited me to go for a walk in the little garden in back of the restaurant. I said to myself, Oh-oh, here comes the proposition. We walked around the garden and Carlo said, "I think I have a pretty good eye for talent. I have made a career for Gina Lollobrigida, Alida Valli, and many, many others. You have an interesting face. I was watching you. The expressions. I suggest you come to my office tomorrow and we run a test. Have you ever had a test? No? Good, we will see how you look on the screen. You can never be sure about a face until you see it on the screen." He gave me his address and bade me good-night. He couldn't have been more businesslike.

The following morning, nervous and apprehensive, I went to the address he had given me and found myself in a police station. I was so angry to have been duped like that that tears came to my eyes. One of the policemen came over to me. "Oh, just a dirty rotten trick someone played on me," I told him, and showed him the address. The policeman smiled. The address I was looking for was next door. In my anxiety I had gone to the wrong address.

Carlo's office was on the first floor and he received me immediately. He took me to a nearby theater where his company (he was in partnership with Dino de Laurentiis) was making a movie. A set had been built on the stage. Carlo turned me over to the director and cameraman, and left. My first screen test. I was so nervous I could feel the blood pounding in my temples. My breath was choked and I seriously thought I might faint. I was given a bathing suit to put on and told to make myself up.

Once I was ready, it took an enormous effort on my part to force myself to go back on that set wearing that bathing suit, to face the camera. The director handed me a cigarette and told me that the test would consist of my lighting the cigarette and then walking back and forth in front of the camera while smoking. A battery of blinding lights was turned on. I had never before in my life held a cigarette in my hand, much less smoked one. The camera started. Action. I was terrible. All thumbs. Ruinously nervous. Mercifully, it was over very quickly. Lights out. Disaster.

~~~~~~~~~~

Carlo Ponti

When I first laid eyes on Sophia, I was struck more by her personality than by her looks. Something played off her that gave her a kind of illumination. I couldn't believe she was a teen-ager. She was so mature, so focused in her desire to be an actress, so professional, yet at the same time timid and unsure of herself. It was an entrancing mix. I knew immediately she was someone remarkable. Shortly after our first meeting, at the beauty contest, she came to talk to me in my office; after I got her to tell me about her struggles during and after the war, and how poor she was, I began to understand about her. She was the man of the family, the provider, and everyone was dependent upon her. She spoke with deep feeling about her mother, deep love and gratitude.

Her mother was one of the most beautiful women I had ever seen in my life. She has a very difficult personality, and I don't easily get along with her, but the void between us acts as a buffer and we are always correct with each other. I respect her and admire her musical talent, but I don't think it possible that she could have succeeded as a pianist or an actress because she lacked a concentrated ambition. For herself. Her ambition for Sophia, though, was boundless, and she transferred to Sophia everything she had wanted for herself.

I honestly admit that I was first interested in Sophia as a woman, and only afterward as an artist. I use the word artist instead of actress because Sophia is not an actress, she is an artist. An actress is something you become, an artist is someone who is born that way. Like a singer who either has a God-given voice or hasn't, and no amount of training can change that. By the time I met Sophia, I had had considerable experience developing actresses for films. I had given many

of them their start—Alida Valli, Koscina, Lollobrigida
—but I had rarely found an actress who was a woman.
An artist is always a woman, an actress rarely is. Actually, I have only known two women who were artists in the sense of which I am speaking—Anna Magnani and Sophia. They had the same qualities.
Strangely, Marilyn Monroe comes to mind, but to
my way of thinking she was negatively influenced by
Arthur Miller. Not deliberately, but Marilyn had an
animal quality, the vitality of a beautiful animal, but
in trying to change her, in trying to intellectualize
her, Miller destroyed that quality. To change meta-
phors, Marilyn was a beautiful flower that had found
just the right soil, sun, and rain to nurture her, and
then was transplanted into a totally different soil and
environment with tragic results.

Not Sophia. She understood where and how she
thrived and what she wanted. Her screen tests didn't
succeed because the men who made them were con-
ditioned only to look for physical beauty, not inner
beauty, for the stereotypical little nose, big eyes, sym-
metrical face. They complained about the size of her
nose but they never bothered to consider the quality
that was inside her. I did. I sensed her potential; I was
impressed with her serious nature and the fact that
she wasn't on the make like most of the other young
girls who were willing to pay any price to get into the
movies. Sophia was determined to be an actress, but
she made it clear that she did not regard the casting
couch as a steppingstone.

Over the course of the following year, Carlo gave
me a number of screen tests, each time with a different cameraman, but each time the same negative reaction. The cameramen complained that there was no
way to photograph me, to make my face attractive, because my nose was too long—also, I was too hippy.
Carlo began each screen test with optimism that was

invariably squelched by the cameraman's pessimism
and by the results that Carlo saw on the screen.

But he continued to stay in touch with me, to find
out what I was doing, to give me words of encouragement. I told him some things about my life, about my
family in Pozzuoli, about the problems of struggling
alone in Rome. He always asked if I had enough
money to get by, and when I did not, he sent me small
amounts to tide me over. But this was the extent of our
contact. There was nothing serious between us. I had
just turned sixteen, Carlo was thirty-eight, married,
two children, and although we played around, we did
not have intercourse, not until later.

One day he asked me to come up to his office. We
had just completed a third or fourth screen test, I
can't remember which. He was tentative about what
he had to tell me. "These tests," he began, "I've just
had a meeting with the cameraman and he says the
same as all the rest. It's, ah, about your nose."

"What about my nose?" I knew what was coming.

"Well, ah, if you are to have a career in films, then,
you see, you should perhaps consider a little bit of
modification."

"You mean get my nose fixed?"

"Yes, and another thing: perhaps you could lose a
bit around your hips. You see, I am just suggesting this
from what all the cameramen say. It would not be
much of a thing with the nose, just shortened enough
so that they can photograph it, you understand."

I realized, of course, that I looked different from established movie actresses. They were all beautiful
with perfect features and I was not. My face is full of
irregularities but put all together they somehow
work. If I had had a bump on the bridge of my
nose, I wouldn't have hesitated to get it fixed. But
that my nose was too long, no, that was not a valid
reason because I knew that the face is commanded by
the nose, that it gives the face its character, and I
liked my nose and my face just the way they were. It's
true, I told Carlo, that my face doesn't resemble anyone else's, but why should I look like everybody else?

"I understand," Carlo said, "I too would like to keep your face as it is, but the cameramen—"

"I want to keep myself just as I am. I won't change anything."

"Well, we'll see," Carlo said, sorry he had brought up the subject.

"And about my hips," I said, "there's no denying I do have rather robust hips, but that's part of me, that's part of who I am, what I have to offer. I want to keep myself just as I am."

It seems rather remarkable to me now, looking back on it, that in the face of all those failed screen tests, I was so boldly confident about myself. But I guess you could say (I hope this doesn't sound pompous) that I was blessed with a sense of my own destiny. I have never sold myself short. I have never judged myself by other people's standards. I have always expected a great deal of myself, and if I fail, I fail myself. So failure or reversal does not bring out resentment in me because I cannot blame others for any misfortune that befalls me. At sixteen I already knew certain self-truths: I was a survivor; I relied on myself and no one else; I would get to wherever I was destined to go and it was futile to try to alter my fate.

Carlo never again mentioned my nose or my hips.

After my sister recovered her health, my mother brought her to Rome and we all three lived together in a cramped furnished room. Very difficult living conditions, but I was happy to be liberated from my cousins and reunited with my family. From morning till night my mother and I were out looking for work, but without much reward. Without my mother, I don't think I would have had the drive, the self-motivation needed to make those endless, fruitless rounds of producers' offices—with no encouragement anywhere. But my mother was a fury of ambition. It was, in effect, her career and she was determined to make amends for all that had been denied her when she was my age. She tried to see anyone and everyone connected with the film business, however remotely. She was constantly extolling my virtues. She had no reticence or modesty about me. I simply walked in her shadow. But despite her perpetual efforts, all I got was a few bit appearances in low-budget Italian movies bearing such titles as *Bluebeard's Six Wives, Hearts upon the Sea, It's Him, Yes! Yes!, The White Slave Trade,* and *The Dream of Zorro.* My part in *Hearts upon the Sea,* which was my first movie, will give you an idea of the extent of my participation in these epics. My entire footage consisted of sitting at a table and looking at the leading lady, who was Doris Dowling, an American actress whose Italian dialogue was dubbed. I didn't move, I didn't speak, I didn't change expression—I just sat and looked at Doris Dowling.

But these bits and pieces of movie appearances, banal though they were, kept us going. The popularity of the *fumetti* was waning, and aside from an occasional modeling job, there was no other work to be had. We were having a hard time in our tiny furnished room. My sister refused to go to school because she did not have a legitimate name to put on her certificate, and technically, the rules being what they were then, she could not take exams. She was too mortified to fill in the school forms, which would have revealed that she was illegitimate and did not bear her father's name. So she simply stayed in our room all day while my mother and I were out.

Early one morning during this bleak period, we were awakened by the police. They said they had already questioned the landlady about us, and they requested that we accompany them to police headquarters. We were taken to the office of a police official who started to interrogate us. What kind of work did we do? Where did we get our money? How much did we earn?

"Why are we being subjected to these questions?" my mother asked.

"We have a formal complaint," the official said, "filed by a Signor Riccardo Scicolone, questioning the legality of your status."

My mother was aghast. I looked at my sister. Her

face showed the pain of this stab to her heart. I simply couldn't believe what I was hearing.

"If you cannot prove satisfactorily to us that you are making your living by legitimate means, then we must give you papers and send you back in police custody to Pozzuoli."

Of course, I was able to prove how I earned my money, and, after much anxiety, the charges were dropped; but the humiliation was terrible. I have never in my life felt so degraded as I did that day in the presence of the police, having to face my own father's insinuations. Imagine if the police had forced me to return to Pozzuoli, denied me future access to Rome, thereby ending any chance at a career, and I had been forced to live permanently in Pozzuoli, branded with God knows what label by my own father. I was sixteen, my sister was eleven. Just imagine the life that our own father had tried to inflict upon us.

My only other brush with the law—and it was only that, a brush—was caused by a photograph which appeared on the cover of a magazine. It had been taken near the sea, and it showed me wrapped in a big beach towel with one bare leg pointed forward. The pose gave the impression that I was naked underneath the towel, but of course that was a matter for the imagination. It was a sensual picture, but in a healthy, outdoor way. Nevertheless, it was considered risqué by the guardian of Rome's public morals, and all copies of the magazine were confiscated and the publisher was hauled into court. I was fined a few lire for not appearing, as required, as a witness for the defense.

Much more revealing than that photo was a scene I played in one of my bit pictures, *It's Him, Yes! Yes!* In those days scenes were often shot specifically for the French version of a picture being made. Censorship was far less restrictive in France, so the scenes could be more revealing. During the shooting of the scene in which I appeared in *It's Him,* which involved several girls like myself in harem costume, the director asked that we do one take topless for the French version. The other girls obliged him and, after a moment's hesitation, I did too. It was a quick take, and that was that, but I learned something about myself from that incident. I don't feel seductive or sexy when I expose myself to the camera. I feel awkward and childish. I think exposure is a debasement of the acting process because it removes the element of mystery. The proper clothes are much more seductive than the naked body. That is not to say that I am opposed to eroticism, which can be beautiful and effective when it is natural and free of vulgarity.

In *A Special Day* I had a scene in which I had sexual intercourse with Mastroianni. It was a key scene which I worried about from the time I first read the script. It was a very difficult scene for me to do, the real difficulty being able realistically to involve myself, rather than pretending to go through the motions, which is mostly how this kind of scene looks on the screen. As it developed, Marcello and I played the scene with our clothes on, showing no nakedness, yet I feel the scene is much more exciting and sexual than if it had realistically portrayed two naked bodies writhing on a sheet.

Sex for me is an exalted act. It is private and mysterious and precious, and I have never denigrated its role in my life. Back when I was struggling for parts and recognition, it would have been unthinkable for me to go to bed with someone in order to further my career. Many girls did, thinking they could get parts that way, and perhaps they did, but I never believed in that. Most of those girls were destroyed by what they did. I believed only in myself. I tried to meet the right people, of course, to come in contact with those who were making movies and would employ me, but as far as getting sexually involved for this purpose is concerned, there was always a wall around me and the men I came in contact with were aware of it; actually, during that entire period in Rome, very few men indicated that if I were to accommodate them I would get a part.

Sophia's sister, Maria

When we first went to Rome, all three of us lived in one small room. Sophia was looking for work but she was very shy and my mother had to be with her all the time. They would leave early in the morning and not return until night, which meant that I, then eleven years old, had to spend the day alone in that room. I didn't have a friend, I didn't even know anyone in Rome. For two years I stayed in that room, all alone. I was mortally afraid of the dark, and when the shades of evening began to fall, I had terrible anxieties; when it turned night, I would sit in the dark and tremble with fear.

When I mentioned to my mother that I was terribly lonely and feared the dark, she said she couldn't cut herself in two and that it was more important that Sophia get work to pay the rent and the food than that I have someone to keep me company. Of course, I could have gone out. I could have gone to school. My mother had met a doctor, Hugo Cardone, to this day a good friend of Sophia's, who urged me to involve myself in some activity, to study, to learn English, but my whole life seemed *senza causa*, without form or purpose, and my anxieties and fears dominated everything else. Two long painful years, wrapped in loneliness, trembling in the dark, not knowing who I was or what I wanted to do, or even having a name of my own.

Eight

In 1952, when I was eighteen, I finally got my first
good part in a film, but I lost my name and almost
lost my life in the process. My mother had heard
about a low-budget film, *Africa Under the Seas*, that
had a role for a young lady who was required to do
most of her acting underwater in the seas around
Rome. Just as my mother had advised me to answer
yes when Mervyn Le Roy asked me if I spoke English, now she instructed me to answer in the affirma-
tive when they asked me if I was an accomplished
swimmer.

"But, Mammina," I protested, "you know I can't
swim a stroke."

"You'll learn. Just get the part and then we'll worry
about your swimming."

Even though Pozzuoli was on the sea, it was common for Neapolitans not to know how to swim. I had
often been in the water but my feet had never left
the bottom. However, when the producer asked me if
I could swim, my answer would have made my mother proud. "Like a champion," I said.

"All right," the producer said, "you've got the part,
but I don't like your name. Sofia Lazzaro is like too
many other names, and besides, it connects you with
those dreadful *fumetti*. We've got to change it."

"My name is really Scicolone."

"That's even worse—sounds like you belong in the
circus. No, we've got to find you a new name. Something not so Italian—short, clean, easy to remember."
This producer had just finished a picture with the

Swedish actress Marta Toren, and there was a large poster on the wall with her picture and her name on it. The producer's face lit up.

"That's it, Toren!" and he started down the alphabet—Boren, Coren, Doren—until he got to Loren, which struck him just right. Sofia Loren. "No," he said, "I don't like the spelling of Sofia. Outside of Italy they will think it's a misspelling of Sophia, so we'll change it to Sophia. All right with you?" I readily agreed, but in Italian, *ph* is not pronounced *f* but *p*, so for a long time the people I knew in Pozzuoli wondered why I wanted to be called Sopia.

Bravado in an office on the Via Veneto is one thing, but quite another on the bow of a rocking ship on the Tyrrhenian Sea. The director explained the first scene to me. I was to jump from the ship into the water. It was a sizable vessel, and as I leaned over the side to have a look, the water a mile away, dark and menacing, I panicked.

"I don't know how to swim," I blurted out, drawing back. "Send me back—please, send me back to Rome."

The director looked stricken. "We have all this equipment here, and all these people and technicians, you *can't* go back to Rome."

I was mortified, but in terror of the watery expanse below. "If you—if, well, if you'll have patience, I'll learn, I mean, you can give me lessons, everybody swims, don't they, so I'll learn as quickly as I can . . ."

"All right, fine," the director said, humoring me, "but right now we've got to make this shot."

"Which shot?"

"You jumping into the water."

"But I just told you . . ." I looked over the side again and almost fainted. "Oh, no! I'll go right to the bottom and never come up!"

"Now don't you worry. We have a man in the water who's an expert swimmer, and the minute you go under he'll be there to fish you out. Not a thing to worry about. When the cameras turn and I say jump, just jump, hold your breath, and don't breathe until

my man gets hold of you. All right, everybody—
places, we're ready to roll!"

The director was obviously a student of psychology,
for he knew that if I had had two minutes to straight-
en out my sanity I would never have jumped. But
there's a little animal in me that occasionally goads
me to take risks, and this time he gave me a shove. I
hit the water a few feet away from the churning propellers. Down under I went, my ears popping, but as
promised, strong hands immediately grabbed me and
guided me up to the surface. I took a deep breath.
On the deck high above me, the crew was applauding. The man holding me in the water was angry.
"Are they crazy? They made you jump where the
propellers were. You almost got chewed up. All they
care is where the light is better. You are lucky. You
are lucky."

This was the man who taught me to swim. He gave
me lessons every spare moment we had. Under his
guidance, I learned to swim very quickly. Since most
of the film was shot underwater, I learned to handle
an oxygen mask, swim with weights on my feet, snor-
kel, dive—the whole nautical works. By the time the
movie was over I was quite a good swimmer, and I
thanked my inner animal who had given me the
shove.

My appearance in *Africa Under the Seas,* a B-minus
picture at best, did not create a ripple on the surface
of the cinema waters. A large number of pinups of
me in bathing suits were distributed but I was still
seeking that all-important part that would give me an
opportunity to do more than dog-paddle underwater
with an oxygen tank on my back. So it was back to
the discouraging rounds with my mother, this time
with stills from *Africa Under the Seas* under my arm,
but producers did not jump at the opportunity of
signing me up for their new films.

"I've heard it said that it was Gina Lollobrigida
who, in 1953, without knowing it, presented me with
my first starring role, the one that set me on my way.
An Italian film company had mounted a lavish ver-

sion of Verdi's opera *Aida* and wanted Lollobrigida as the star. The part was to be sung by the great diva Renata Tebaldi, with Lollobrigida mouthing the lyrics, but at the last moment, I'm told, Gina reneged because she felt that serving as a stand-in for a singer was beneath her star status. Since the production was ready to roll, the studio desperately needed a last-minute replacement, and that's how I got the part. It was surely not an ideal role, for the voice was not mine, but I would have the opportunity to portray the wide range of emotions that the part required.

The first thing I did was to get a recording of Tebaldi singing *Aida;* I listened to it for countless hours of countless days, becoming so familiar with the lyrics and with Tebaldi's phrasing and delivery that her voice, and my miming of it, blended perfectly. By the time we went into production, Tebaldi and I sang as one person. I actually felt her voice coming out of me. The 1230 B.C. costumes had great beauty, and the dress style of that period well suited me. The afro-style wig, the ornamental jewelry, and particularly the dark makeup gave me a striking appearance. I would go to the set very early in the morning, four hours before my call, in order to have my entire body and face, from forehead to toes, covered with the sepia makeup that made my appearance so striking.

The movie was shot in an unheated studio in the middle of winter. Every time I opened my mouth to sing, puffs of steam would fill the air. To correct this, I chewed ice before each take, frosting my mouth, and an assistant stood just out of camera range with a powerful hair dryer which he aimed at my lips. In my scanty costumes, I was often blue with cold underneath my dark makeup, but the result was good and I received the kind of notices and publicity for my portrayal of *Aida* that I had secretly hoped for (but had prepared myself not to expect). The movie was widely distributed, and for the first time I was seen in England and the United States.

The salary I received for *Aida* was the first substantial amount of money we had ever seen. There were so many uses to put it to—a decent place to live, help for my grandparents, badly needed clothes, an endless lineup—but I felt that the most pressing need was to rescue my sister, Maria, from her withdrawal of shame. There was only one thing that would send her back to school, and that was her father's name.

My mother had talked to him several times about Maria but he always rejected her entreaties. "Why don't you give your name to Maria—she's your daughter, you know she's your daughter, you don't deny we conceived her, she looks exactly like you, what would it hurt you if she had your name, the same as Lella? She is suffering, she doesn't go to school, she suffers from disgrace." No words could move my father, because as a result of having given me his name, it had cost him money, and he was not going to repeat that mistake. My father had steadfastly refused to give my mother anything for my support, so at some point she had gone into court and succeeded in getting a decree requiring him to pay me a monthly stipend. I still have in my possession a receipt which I gave him:

Rome, 3 October, 1950

This note is a receipt for the amount of six thousand lire (6000), which my father gives me for: three thousand lire as legal allowance for the past month of September 1950, and three thousand lire legal monthly allowance for the current month of October 1950.

Sofia Scicolone

In those days, three thousand lire amounted to $4.60, which was hardly a financial burden, but nevertheless my father resented paying it to me, and was determined not to fall into the same trap with my sister. As long as he didn't recognize her as his child and give her his name, he could save an additional $4.60 a month.

But when my mother spoke to him after I had made *Aida*, he had a proposition: he would sell his name to Maria for the one million lire which he had found out I had been paid for *Aida*. He said he thought it was just compensation for his expense and trouble. My mother was furious. "He blackmails his own daughter for money! What manner of animal is he? He has never given a lira for her support and now he wants a fortune just for his name which is hers by birthright. He is an animal! An absolute animal!"

I didn't hesitate. As far as I was concerned, Maria must have her name, whatever the price. I suppose my father had fallen on very lean times and needed money. I don't know. What he was doing was wrong, of course, but I did not share my mother's anger. I had come to expect nothing good from my father. I gave my mother the one million lire (about $1500 in those days), and she arranged to meet my father at a notary where he signed the necessary papers in exchange for the money.

When my mother came back to our room we did not mention my father but only felt happy that my sister, who joyfully clutched the notarized papers to her bosom, had been given what in those days was generally regarded as her dignity.

~~~~~~~~~~

Sophia's sister, Maria

One year after Sophia bought my name for me from my father, he went into court in Milan and petitioned the judge to set aside the agreement—in other words, to take the name Scicolone away from me. I guess he wanted more money from Sophia. I don't know. I can only guess. The judge didn't allow it, but my father's conduct toward me had become so excessively unfair that somehow this act didn't bother me. So I cast his brutality away. I did not want to go through life with the stone of his cruelty in my heart.

I had come to realize that I alone was responsible for what was in my heart, and if I only filled it with feelings of love, given and received, and other such benignities, then it would never be blighted. That was not as difficult as it sounds. I have the heart of a child, you see, and children do not bear hate or grudges in their hearts—at least not for very long. Actually, in later years I saw my father quite often.

After *Aida* was released, Carlo Ponti suggested that I sign a personal contract with him. That meant that my contract would be with him individually, and not with the Ponti–de Laurentiis Company. My mother didn't like the idea. "You should not be tied down to a contract. You are just starting your career. You should be free to do what comes along. You should not be restricted to one man."

"That may be true, Mammina," I said, "but why don't I sign a contract for just one year and see what happens? I will get paid a little something every month and in the meantime I can look around and see how things go." So I signed with Carlo, but my mother was right. Time passed and all the good parts went to established "names." Whenever I discussed this with Carlo, at my mother's insistence, he urged patience. "Wait five minutes," he always said. "Just wait five minutes."

During this period I worked constantly in a series of quickly made, forgettable pictures, ten films within those twelve months. I mouthed lyrics in operettas like *Neapolitan Carousel* and *The Country of Bells*, and in two Ponti–de Laurentiis pictures. I played small supporting roles to Silvana Pampanini, another one of their contract stars.

They elevated me somewhat by casting me as Tony Quinn's wife in *Attila the Hun*, but it turned out to be a lump of a movie that did neither of us any good.

My spirits were lifted momentarily by the prospect

of an interview with the great Antonioni, but our meeting wasn't fruitful. I also had a meeting with Vittorio de Sica, who was charming and complimented me for *Aida* and said he was sure that someday we would work together; but he did not bring up any of the projects he was then working on.

So it was a hyperactive period in which I went from one inconsequential film to another, but it was a period of important learning for me. I am like a sponge in the way I absorb all the elements that suit me and reject those that do not. I had a natural instinct for such moviemaking basics as camera position, light angles, and finding floor marks without looking for them.

So this was not a period of frustration for me. I was busy working in films, I was learning, I was earning enough money for us to live in a decent apartment and eat well. I was the head of the family, the husband, going out to work every day, my mother was the wife, and my sister, now back in school, was the child.

Carlo and I began to see each other in a quiet, rather secret way. I was very much attracted to him —his open smile, the quality of his eyes, his diffident but forceful manner (I know that's a contradiction), and I trusted him right away—but it is difficult to explain the nature of our relation at that time. At eighteen, I still had the mentality of a Pozzuoli girl; none of the sophistication of Rome had rubbed off on me and my behavior was still influenced by the primitive mores of Pozzuoli. The strictures of my grandmother and the house I grew up in, and the severe, repressive influence of the nuns at school were still very much a part of me. Respect for the family was deeply imbedded in me, and for a Pozzuoli girl, an affair with a married man was unthinkable. Thou shalt not commit adultery was a fiery prohibition. The family was inviolate, and I was raised in a closed world where these prohibitions had forceful meaning. And, of course, my mother's early transgressions in Rome were a severe deterrent to any premarital involvement with a man. This does not mean that I did not "pet" with Carlo, but there is a vast difference between petting and real sex involvement.

Carlo was aware of all this, of my fears and reticence, aware that I wasn't just another accessible starlet (how I despise that word!) and he never tried to go very far with me. From what I gathered, Carlo had always had little affairs with actresses, and his wife didn't seem to mind as long as he didn't see the same girl very often and there was no threat of a serious relationship. That's why we saw each other secretly, so that his wife wouldn't become aware of me.

But when we did see each other, it was as if I were Carlo's fiancée in the Pozzuoli manner. I had family taboos and religious taboos to overcome before I could have an affair with Carlo. Eventually it was to happen, but not then, not until I felt the strength of his love and my deep need for him as my father figure. In the meantime, this was our period of courtship, very private, explorative, growing steadily in intensity.

To my surprise, Vittorio de Sica had not forgotten me. He phoned to say he had a project that he would like to talk about: *Gold of Naples*, an episodic film based on a novel by the Neapolitan author Marotta, that de Sica would direct. Another of the episodes, in which de Sica would also act, was to feature Silvana Mangano. The real surprise for me was that this was a Ponti–de Laurentiis film that Carlo had not even mentioned.

I had a very enjoyable interview with de Sica but we didn't discuss the film nor did he offer me a screen test, so when I left I knew there was nothing doing. I was quite disappointed because de Sica was one of the glamour names of Italian moviemaking, a man I greatly admired, and this would obviously be the kind of quality film that had proved so elusive for me. What's more, it was a part made to order for me: an explosive, earthy Neapolitan woman, a type I knew so well; she was even called Sofia.

One week after our interview, de Sica called and said, "Can you leave for Naples tomorrow?" What had happened in the intervening week was this: De Sica had gone to de Laurentiis and Ponti and told them that he wanted me for the part. He said that I had a quality of spontaneity, an outgoing impulsiveness, typically Neapolitan, that he wanted to capture in this part. He said that since he and I were both Neapolitan, and quite alike in temperament, he knew he would be able to work with me very well. De Laurentiis wanted de Sica to make a screen test so that he could see for himself if de Sica was right, but de Sica refused. He was sure of his judgment. Neapolitans go by instinct, they *live* by instinct, he told de Laurentiis, and my instincts about Sophia Loren and the instincts she will bring to acting this part are better than any screen test. I want her.

De Laurentiis still objected. He wanted a bigger name. But de Sica was very blunt, as Neapolitans are. What was needed was a wildcat with fire inside and Loren was it.

Through all of this, Carlo wisely said nothing. De Laurentiis knew of his personal interest in me and as long as de Sica was fighting his battle for him, it was smart of Carlo to stay out of it.

Finally, de Laurentiis gave in, but grudgingly. "You have always had good judgment, Vittorio, and I hope that you're right."

That first day in Naples, I came on the set congealed with apprehension, my voice constricted, my legs weighted. But by the end of the day de Sica had freed me of all my apprehensions and we were two free Neapolitan spirits, improvising, communicating, and enjoying ourselves. "You have juices running in you," he told me, "that have the force to carry you anywhere you want to go. Stay away from acting schools. Don't take lessons. You will teach yourself." By the time our episode was over, de Sica had become a force in my life. I liked him, I loved him, I admired him, and our "love affair" was to last for twenty years. We were destined to make fourteen

films together, and our method remained the same
as it was in that first film: de Sica standing behind
the camera, directly in my line of vision, showing me
with his expression, his gestures, his whole being,
what he wanted me to do; we rarely talked; words
were superfluous. He was a superb actor and he understood my shallows and my depths, but also he
understood how to make me go beyond myself, beyond where I thought I could go, or dared go, into
dramatic or comedic waters where the risk of over-
playing, of parody, of drowning is great and the per-
centage for succeeding is small. C above high C. That
was de Sica's great gift to me, his profoundest talent.
"Act with your entire body," he told me; "your body,
your toes, your fingers should be as involved as your
voice and your face."

In *Gold of Naples,* he helped me create an explosive, sexy, blowsy Neapolitan pizza girl who sprang
from a part of me I never knew existed. I trusted him
completely and that is the key to what I require to
function well, whether in movies or in daily life.
Trust, I must. If I don't, I become insecure and I
withdraw and revert to my shy self. But if I trust I
am a different woman.

De Sica

In making this film with Sophia, I discovered some
basic truths about her personality. She had built a
thick protective wall around herself, around that inner, secret part of her that emotions make vulnerable.
She hid behind that wall and was reasonably content
there. But her true nature was dramatic and tem-
peramental, typically Neapolitan, and her reactions
—joy, sorrow, anger, impatience, whatever—were excessive. So she kept them well contained behind that
wall. But when she acted, she could leap over that
wall and free her true inner feelings. She could

scream, laugh, have hysterics, seduce, demonstrate, and reach the most emotional heights. Acting in an emotional movie scene does for her what lying down on the couch at the psychiatrist's does for other people.

The most memorable scene in *Gold of Naples* was pure de Sica. A slow, long walk through the streets of Naples in a teeming rain, my soaked dress clinging to my body while the eyes of the men whom I passed followed me in carnal wonderment and approval. I caught pneumonia from the deluges of the rain machines and had to stay in bed for a month, but it was well worth it. I had found the step up for my career, and I had found myself as an actress. The dream of that skinny little girl, sitting in the dark in the Pozzuoli movie house, had finally come true.

Nine

When you are young and struggling, you cannot possibly know the precious value of the anonymity of the beginner. The beginner can take risks, make mistakes, experiment, because there is no image or reputation to maintain. Of course, the beginner cannot pick and choose what to do but must accept whatever mediocrity is offered to her, but she can bring to it the best that is in her in whatever way she chooses. She has nothing to lose; thus it is a useful challenge.

Success, on the other hand, does not tolerate mistakes; nor do journalists tolerate privacy for the successful. In the beginning, you welcome the glare of publicity because it leads to recognition and recognition leads to better and better roles and finally to the ultimate—stardom, which means you can be choosy and even originate what you do. So, for the beginner in films, publicity has unique value although its origin is often unpredictable and its effect erratic.

Such was the case in the blaze of publicity generated over the rivalry between Gina Lollobrigida and me. As I recall, it was 1954 when the matter first came up during a trip I made to London with a large contingent of Italian movie actresses to publicize an Italian film festival. Gina was there but I did not see her. At that time I spoke little or no English, so when it came my turn to be interviewed by the press, questions and answers were rather mismatched. The

subtle, discerning British press immediately went to
the heart of their interest in my abilities: they wanted
to know my measurements. I understood that question—38-24-38. I had heard it many times before.
"Who's bigger," one of the journalists then asked, "you
or Lollo?" That question was one I had never heard
before. And the rest of the questions were obsessed
with our respective measurements and comparisons
between them.

I have no recollection of just what I answered but
surely it was nothing like what appeared in the papers the next day. Under a banner headline, WHY
LOLLO WAS MAD WITH ME, there ran a verbatim interview in which I was quoted as saying that just
because I was bustier than Gina that was no reason
for her to be furious with me.

Of course I had said no such thing; I wasn't aware
that Gina even knew who I was.

After my success in *Gold of Naples*, Carlo, for the
first time, took me seriously. The "five-minute wait"
was up. He created a picture especially for me, although the project he decided upon bore a strong
resemblance to *Bitter Rice*, a film in which Silvana
Mangano had had spectacular success. Carlo's film,
to be called *Woman of the River*, was to be shot in
the same Po River location, and directed by Mario
Soldati, one of the best directors in Italy. The story
was co-authored by Alberto Moravia and no fewer
than six screenwriters worked on the script; one of
them was Basilio Franchina, who would become one
of my dearest lifelong friends.

This was Carlo's personal picture, not a co-pro-
duction with de Laurentiis, and that fact, plus the
fact that the script called for an enormous range of
emotions, culminating in a melodramatic scene when
I find my baby drowned in the river, put enormous
pressure on me. *Gold of Naples* was a short, lighthearted stint; this was a full-length serious picture,
and I was terribly unsure whether I could respond
to the demands it put on me.

I previously mentioned that I had caught pneumonia from the rain machines in *Gold of Naples*. On the evening of the last day of shooting, finally dried off for good, I had gone to have a celebratory dinner with de Sica and some others in a restaurant, but before the meal was over I collapsed and had to be taken home. What I had was bronchial pneumonia, accompanied by a high fever and a monstrous, racking cough.

By the time *Woman of the River* started I was entirely over the pneumonia, but on the first day of shooting I developed a condition which I thought indicated a relapse. At night, I had vexatious trouble breathing. My breath came in strident wheezes, thirty violins sawing away, and I couldn't sleep. In fact, I couldn't lie down because it worsened my condition. My doctor said it had nothing to do with the pneumonia I had had, but that I was now suffering from asthma. He was baffled as to its cause or how to treat it, but pooh-poohed the suggestion that it was psychological. The film was shot in June and July in one of the hottest parts of Italy but I wore double wool sweaters during the day in the belief that something was wrong with my lungs.

Every night, 7 P.M. to 5 A.M., my temperature shot up and the violins played. All through the night I relived how I had performed in front of the cameras that day. Every gesture, every movement, was subjected to minute examination. Was my performance too high or too flat? Was this or that gesture superfluous? Should I have played the love scene with more primitive passion? And on and on. At best, I managed to doze a little, sitting straight up. But in the morning, the minute I set foot on the set and got busy, the asthma rose off me like a mist and disappeared. During this time, Basilio Franchina, who was also the producer, became aware of my insecurity about the script's demands and my battle with the nocturnal violins, and he started to work with me on the script. Basilio had an empathy, a warmth, a sweet sense of humor, and a plain honesty that endeared him to me. He was intelligent and quite wise and I enjoyed the way his mind worked, what he said, and the manner in which he said it. I myself had had scanty education and I had read woefully little, but I recognized and admired educated people who were intelligent. I have a rather infallible instinct for choosing the right people to help me in my life, and who, in turn, I can help and trust. There have not been many of them, sad to say, but surely Basilio is one of them.

He was enormously helpful during *Woman of the River,* especially in my long-range preparation for the river tragedy. That scene was climactic and I had to infuse it with a wildness of tragedy and shock and pain and lament.

Some nights Carlo would sit up with me all night to keep me company while I battled for each breath. We had grown very close, Carlo and I—we were father-daughter, man-woman, producer-actress, friends and conspirators.

So intensely had I prepared myself for the big river scene that, complicated though it was, I did it in one take, with an exhilarated feeling of great accomplishment. And two important things happened on the last day of shooting. The first was that my asthma completely disappeared, and it has never recurred. Obviously, it had resulted from the weighty responsibility of the film on my young and insecure shoulders, and the asthma was my inner protest, exteriorized, against the pressure the film imposed on me.

The second thing that happened was that Carlo came on the set and, taking me aside, handed me a small box. In it was a ring with a small diamond. We had never spoken a word about where our relationship was heading and now, still without a word, Carlo had told me. I went off by myself and wept with joy. He was the only man who had entered my life and now I felt I could give myself to him completely. Of course, he was still living with his wife and children but my feelings were too strong now to be deterred by Pozzuoli's morals or anyone else's. I needed love.

It is not easy to tell if you are successful in a particular movie. Film performance is not the same as the theater, where the audience's immediate reaction and the next day's reviews give you a verdict. Even a television performance gets an immediate appraisal in ratings and follow-up reviews. But the takes of a movie, its bits and pieces, often shot out of sequence and spread over weeks and sometimes months of time, give you no real insight into your performance. And when the shooting is over, the actress has no way of knowing how it will all turn out. Months later, the finished product will be released at different times in different parts of the world, and even then it takes considerable time before a verdict is rendered—primarily in box office receipts. Of course, there are the day-to-day reactions of the director and producer, but they are heavily biased and actually they have no more perspective of the effectiveness of an actress's total performance than she has.

So, especially as a beginner, all you have as a measure of how well or badly you are doing is the fact that you are or are not hired for other pictures, and if you are, for how much increase in salary. Using those criteria, I was tasting success. I could not keep up with the demand for my services, and I went from one movie to another, finishing on a Friday and starting a new one the following Monday, as if I were starving and needed the employment to eat. I suppose the years of deprivation and struggle were catching up with me. Security was work. Security was money. Security was a big, sunny apartment with a balcony, a luxury car, and other such trappings. I was a far way from this level of affluence but I had made a start. When the time would come that I acquired these trappings, I would eventually discover that they were meaningless and divest myself of most of them. Success, I would find out, is interior. It has to do with self-fulfillment and the joy of living. But at nineteen, I was a light-year from such wisdom. I was a conformist.

Basilio Franchina

By nature, Sophia is not ambitious; left to her own devices she would probably be a schoolteacher in Pozzuoli today. It was her mother who supplied Sophia's ambitiousness; yet, paradoxically, once she is committed to a task she is fiercely and completely devoted to it, striving for perfection, working as hard and as long as she can to excel. If she had not had the talent to be an actress, she would have been the best teacher in Pozzuoli or the world's best secretary or a champion saleslady. That is because whatever she does, she does with concentration, love, and patience, and these bell ringers of her nature would have boosted her toward the top of whatever she undertook. It was simply born a part of her, along with her eyes, her walk, and everything else about her.

In the flurry of pictures I made in 1955, the year after *Woman of the River*, there was one called *Too Bad She's Bad*, which was directed by the very talented Alessandro Blasetti, and which brought me together for the first time with the two men who would figure so importantly in my life—de Sica, this time as an actor, and Mastroianni, who at that time was not a very well known screen actor. He had a good reputation as a stage actor but his films until then were not very distinguished and he had not had any significant success. And he had never performed in a film comedy before *Too Bad She's Bad*.

The rapport among de Sica, Marcello, and me was immediate. We all three came from the Naples area—Mastroianni was born in a little town a few miles from de Sica's birthplace—and we shared a conspiratorial bond reserved for Neapolitans. We shared a sense of humor, a rhythm, a philosophy of living, a cynicism that lurked behind our lines of dialogue and interplay. Our heritage was our repertorial experience. We played scenes with a kind of flair and fire that I had never experienced before. Freer. Nearer to life—in fact, magnifying life to the point of making a comment about it. De Sica and I played father-daughter petty thieves, with Marcello as the decent taxi-driver outsider who catches us filching from him and others. De Sica created a style which Marcello and I picked up, and we three performed together with a subtlety and verve that set the tone for the many films we were to make together.

As soon as a second script could be prepared, the three of us were reunited in *The Miller's Wife,* followed immediately by *Scandal in Sorrento* with de Sica, and then *Lucky to Be a Woman* with Marcello. Unfortunately, *Lucky to Be a Woman* substituted Charles Boyer for de Sica and our Neapolitan soufflé fell. I don't mean to detract from Boyer's great talent, but he was as far from the spirit of a Neapolitan as the Champs Elysées is from Mount Vesuvius. The film reflected the fact that without de Sica, Marcello and I were two sides of a triangle searching for a base.

I showed Mammina the ring Carlo had given me, holding my hand up in the sunlight, expressing my happiness, but knowing that she would not approve. She didn't. She viewed Carlo as an unwelcome intruder at a time when we had finally settled down comfortably in a nice apartment with a kitchen where we no longer had to cook in secret (as we had to in our furnished room, on an electric one-burner that we kept concealed in a bureau drawer when not in use).

"He's a married man with two children, he's twenty years older than you, and you will have nothing but heartache. You want heartache? That's what you'll get. You are a baby. You don't know a thing. It's so easy to start playing around, but then what? Then what?"

"I am in love with him, Mammina. He is so intelligent and cares so much about me. He's a doctor of law—did you know that?"

"Never mind law—it's a doctor of babies you will need. Don't you think I know what I'm talking about? Now is the time—before it starts—before it gets serious."

"Well, it *has* started and it *is* serious, but don't worry, I can take care of myself."

"Has he told his wife—is he leaving her?"

"No."

"You are a fool. He never will. Mark my words—*he never will*. Wait around for him and you will wind up an old maid lighting candles."

"No, Mammina, I don't think so. I love him, but I love myself, too."

Carlo was very concentrated on my career now and his eyes were on the future. He said that I must not limit myself to Italian films but that I had to learn English if he was to get me parts in international films, and eventually a deal with Hollywood. He also gave me a list of books to read—just left the list with me because it was not Carlo's style to demand, only to suggest.

~~~~~~~~~~

Carlo Ponti

I was trying to figure out how to get Sophia her first English-speaking role when an agent suggested that I try to get her the lead feminine role in *The Pride and the Passion*. I thought that it would be difficult since I knew that Ava Gardner was being considered for the role, and that Cary Grant had co-star approval. But to my surprise, Stanley Kramer came to see me and made me a take-it-or-leave-it offer of $200,000 for Sophia. It was one of the easiest decisions I ever had to make.

~~~~~~~~

I do not recall how Sarah Spain came into my life, but she was a linguistic angel with a soft Irish face who by prodding, wheedling, and bullying taught me to speak English. Very early every morning, Sarah came with me to the set of *Lucky to Be a Woman*, and for two hours before makeup, we would study English. And all day long, every minute I had free, between takes, during lunch, on the way home, Sarah Spain would hammer English into me. On days off she never left my side. Total immersion, and she taught me not as a parrot, but with an emphasis on grammar and comprehension. I knew a little French from school but not a word of English. Happily, I discovered that I had a good ear and an aptitude for language. That helped, but Carlo moved too fast for me. While I was still trying to make phrases like "Please pass the butter," and "November is a month for overcoats," sound more like English than like broken Italian, Carlo informed me that he had concluded a deal with the American producer-director Stanley Kramer for me to co-star in a huge period film, *The Pride and the Passion*, that was about to start shooting in Spain. When I heard the names of my co-stars I almost passed out —Cary Grant and Frank Sinatra.

I, little Sofia Scicolone, was to play opposite two of those romantic figures of my Pozzuoli dreams, in an English-speaking, multi-million-dollar spectacle film! —but (alas, reality!) at the same time, here was Sarah Spain berating me, scolding me, warning me that my English couldn't even be understood by sympathetic Italians on Mulberry Street.

I worked even harder. Sarah made me read T. S. Eliot and Bernard Shaw aloud, and my pronunciation benefited. I also benefited in other ways from the books suggested by Carlo and Basilio which I was beginning to read. At that time, most of the books I read were in Italian, but later, as my facility with English improved, I started to read books in English as well. As I previously said, I had never before read any literature. During my school days, the nuns would only allow us to read the pedagogical volumes approved by the church's pedants, and after I left school there had been no time nor inclination to read anything at all.

Now, however, I began to discover the treasures buried in those books by Chekhov and Tolstoy, Baudelaire and Stendhal, Shaw and Dickens. I started to keep a notebook in which I recorded sentences from the books which I found particularly enlightening; observations that affected my view of life and people. I have never stopped writing in that notebook, which I have in front of me now. Unfortunately, I seldom wrote down the author's name, just the quote. At random: "Self-justification is very common to people who have a troubled conscience, or to those who look for a philosophic reason to justify their failures in life." Also, "Her bad thoughts shone around her head like a black halo," and, "Science is the most beautiful woman and the most important woman and the most necessary woman in the life of a man—she has always been and always will be the supreme manifestation of love, and with her, and only with her alone, man will conquer nature and himself." Observations like that opened areas of reflection for me that were new and exciting. And I was never again able to look at the Mona Lisa with a straight face after reading, "Ah, yes, the Mona Lisa, that smile she has on her face, it looks to me like the smile of a woman who at that particular moment has just finished eating her own husband for breakfast."

It was a bursting time for me. I was simultaneously learning English, learning to read literature, learning the intricacies and refinements of being a good movie actress, and learning how to relate to a man. I was also filled with awe and trepidation at the prospect of performing in a multi-million-dollar American movie with two of Hollywood's glossiest superstars. I half expected a recurrence of my old nemesis, asthma.

What I didn't know at the time was that Carlo

and Kramer were faced with large obstacles to overcome before I could join the cast. First of all, the producing company, United Artists, wanted a star name for the part, not me, and secondly, Cary Grant, who had contractual cast approval, also was not in favor of playing opposite an unknown Italian girl who was still wet behind the ears. United Artists made an attempt to get Ava Gardner but she was committed to another film. So were the other stars whom they sought. But Kramer had seen *Woman of the River* and he kept the pressure on United Artists to let him have his way. Finally, they gave in.

As I recall, Cary Grant was still reluctant.

Stanley Kramer gave an elaborate cocktail party to commemorate the start of the film, and that's where Cary and I first met. I can't recall ever being as nervous as I was preparing for that event. I changed my dress a half dozen times. I knew that only English would be spoken and that, despite Sarah Spain's heroics, I was still a long way from fluent. Also, the very thought of having to face the judgment of Cary Grant—*Cary Grant*, for God's sake!—who had performed with most of the world's most glamorous screen actresses—well, the thought itself was paralyzing.

I had never been to an American-style cocktail party. Italian producers occasionally (but not often) sponsored a polite little gathering, but nothing like the lavish affair staged for *The Pride and the Passion*, with scores of reporters and photographers who had been flown to Spain especially for the event. I recall being introduced to the American columnist Leonard Lyons and another American writer, Joe Hyams, and to Donald Zec, who was a London journalist. They asked me questions which I partly understood, but it was a struggle for me to express myself in adequate English. And there was no one to interpret Italian.

Cary Grant arrived late, and Sinatra even later. When Cary and I were introduced by Stanley Kramer, Cary joked around with my name. "How do you do, Miss Lolloloren, or is it Lorenigida? Ah, you

Italian actresses, I can never get your names straight."
He exuded charm, and he was even more handsome
and debonair than he appeared on the screen. I immediately felt at ease with him and after a few
minutes of lively banter, I could tell from the look in
his eyes that I had passed muster.

While we were talking, Sinatra arrived and Kramer brought him over. Standing there with Cary
Grant on one side of me and Frank Sinatra on the
other, I said to myself, It's not possible that this is
happening. How do you do, Frank Sinatra, but it is
not happening to me but to somebody else and I am
having this dream and watching it happen. Again, as
always, I was looking at myself from the outside,
my nose pressed against the glass.

The Pride and the Passion was a long and arduous
movie, plagued with problems and delays. We were
in remote parts of Spain for a good six months, during which time the artificiality of the super-star image
wore off and I got to know Cary and Frank quite
well. Especially Cary. We liked each other from the
very first, and in that remote setting, with all our
languid time, we were constantly in each other's
company. And such wonderful company Cary was! I
was fascinated with him, with his warmth, affection,
intelligence, and his wonderfully dry, mischievous
sense of humor. I had never met a man remotely
like Cary before, and for him, I was a Neapolitan
first.

In the beginning he was very reserved with me,
and if our talk turned to something sad or introspec-
tive he would try to make a joke out of it, to keep it
from touching him. But more and more he confided
in me and trusted me. There were patches of self-
doubt in him which he disclosed—with reluctance,
but needfully. He was deeply disturbed over the fact
that he had never had a really sustained relationship in his life. He talked about his early life in London, his struggles, and the three women he had been
married to, but when he got too close to his center,
he would put up the mask he hid behind and turn to
joking.

At first I was puzzled by the way he hopped from one foot to the other, but as I got to know him I began to realize that he had an inner conflict of wanting to be open and honest and direct, and yet not make himself vulnerable. Of course, one cannot have it both ways. And slowly, as our relationship grew and his trust in me grew, he came to realize that trust and vulnerability went hand in hand; when his trust was strong enough, he no longer bothered with his mask. And I was just as open and trusting with him. He told me about his early life, and I told him about mine, and we found a bond in their emotional similarities. We saw each other every night; we dined in romantic little restaurants on craggy hilltops to the accompaniment of flamenco guitars, drank the good Spanish wine and laughed and were serious and confessional and conspiratorial.

And we fell in love.

But I was also in love with Carlo. How could it be possible? In love with two men? Well, it was, and I was very confused. Carlo was an enigma. He was still as solidly entrenched in his marriage as he ever was, and there was no sign that he intended to give up his wife and children for me. I could hear Mammina's words, "Wait around for him and you will wind up an old maid lighting candles." In a way, though, I sympathized with Carlo: it is not easy for a man to renounce his family, especially when the children are young. But my sympathy was intellectual, not visceral. In my heart, I wanted him to discard everything for me. I did not want to be an undeclared mistress, or any kind of mistress, no matter how much he meant to me. My whole sense of being rebelled at this role. I wanted the legitimacy I had sought all through my girlhood.

And now here was Cary Grant, ready to renounce everything for me. Wanting me with no strings attached.

Although Cary was my main concern, I managed to find time to work on the movie. Mercifully, I did not have a great deal of dialogue in the picture, and also, mercifully, I had Stanley Kramer's wife, Anne, to help me. Anne was a darling, considerate, bright woman. After each day's shooting, Anne went back to the hotel with me and helped me master my lines for the following day. She gave me a book of poems by T. S. Eliot, and I would read them aloud to her as exercises for my English. Anne helped me in so many ways. I was tempted to discuss my love life with her, but when it came right down to it I was too shy to reveal that much of my inner feelings. So in the night I would lie in my bed and try to think things out. Being young and spirited, although I fretted over this conflict it did not affect the euphoria I felt from working on the film.

Frank and I got along fine. That we were both Italian was a factor, I guess, but Frank doesn't speak Italian (or pretends not to) outside of a few words like *pasta e fagiole*. I learned a great deal about music from him. He always had music going but to my surprise he played nothing but classical records. Vivaldi, Respighi, but not opera, only classical concert music. One day I asked him who he thought was the greatest American jazz artist and without a moment's hesitation he said Ella Fitzgerald. I said I had never heard of her, and he was amazed.

The following day he had Fitzgerald recordings for me to listen to. "Ella Fitzgerald is the greatest thing your ears will hear during your entire life," he said, and then he put on the first record. He was right. He rhapsodized about her range, her style, her phrasing; musically, Frank taught me a lot.

On days when he was in a good mood, Frank told engaging stories about his early life, his mother's involvement in politics, his father's exploits. I recall one amusing anecdote he told about his father, who ran a bar in Hoboken, New Jersey, I think it was. His father had one customer who was a deadbeat, and he had put a lot of pressure on the customer to pay his bar bill, which was considerable. One evening, the customer came into the bar, leading a horse. He said he didn't have the money to pay the bill but that instead he was giving the horse to Frank's father. "My

Pa got so mad at the guy," Frank said, "that he got out his gun and shot the horse dead. But then he couldn't get him out of the bar. You ever handle a dead horse? There was my old man with that dead horse that he shot and he couldn't get him out of the bar. No way."

One day our location was visited by an American reporter who was doing a story about the film. He asked Frank how he would define the new girl who was on the picture. "Sophia?" Frank said. "She's the mostest." One of the nicest compliments I ever got.

During those perfect days in Spain, Cary and I shared much. He taught me many things quite wise, he opened my mind in many ways, and I learned a great deal just by observing his attitude toward life. And in some ways he learned from me. Aside from him, only Carlo has had this effect on me, no other man, before or since.

One day, while we were having lunch, a waiter approached Cary, who was deep in conversation with me, and timorously asked for his autograph. "Don't bother me," Cary said, and waved him away. The poor man recoiled and hurriedly withdrew.

I said, "Don't do that, Cary. Look how upset he is."

Cary looked at the man and called him back and apologetically gave him an autograph. "How nice you are," Cary said to me after the waiter had gone. "You really care about that man, don't you? I didn't mean to offend him, I just wanted my privacy with you . . ."

"But your autograph meant a great deal to that waiter," I said. "I know what it must be like for you, besieged by people all the time, but do you know how bad it makes people feel when they screw up their courage to go up to you and then you turn them away? You are their hero."

My reaction was a revelation to Cary. He said he had never really thought about the situation in quite that way. I do not know whether his reformation stuck, but from then on, when he was with me, he gave autographs. He used to kid around about it— that was Cary's way—but he had learned something from me, young as I was, about simple humanity.

That night we were dining in a little restaurant on a hilltop outside Avila. It was late. We were alone, but the waiters didn't seem to mind. An orange half-moon hung in the window and from somewhere below in the valley a singer's distant voice rose up to us.

Cary talked about getting married. With every passing day, he said, he was more sure that we belonged together, that finally he had found in me someone to whom he could totally relate. Finally someone to whom he could commit himself and to hell with being vulnerable. I trust you and love you and want to marry you, he said.

I never doubted for a second that Cary loved me as much as I could hope to be loved by a man. What he had said to me struck me like a jolt and took my breath away; I couldn't answer him. How could I explain to him the contradictions? The conflict between his image and Carlo's image? I told him that I didn't dare give an answer yet, that I still needed time and I needed to go back to my own environment and to be able to make up my mind away from the magic of those Spanish nights.

Besides, I was committed to a film, *Boy on a Dolphin,* in Greece and Cary was due to start work on a picture in Los Angeles.

The windup on *The Pride and the Passion* was hectic. Sinatra's patience abruptly gave out, and without finishing his final scenes, he packed up and flew back to Hollywood for personal reasons. Thus, when we finished the film, it really wasn't finished.

The last night, Cary and I had dinner together. There was a windup party scheduled for the following day but I had booked an early flight out in the morning. So this was our last time together.

We had been joking and laughing, but over coffee the talk turned serious. "Sophia," Cary asked, "what is going to happen to us?"

"I don't know, Cary. I really don't. And I wish I weren't so mixed up and confused. But one day I am pulled one way and the next day another. I don't know what's going to happen."

Cary's face brightened with a mock idea. "Why don't we just get married and discuss all this afterwards?"

I was so grateful to him for having released the tension and for having made a joke out of the serious turmoil of our souls.

On the airplane going from Spain to Greece, I was reading Tolstoy in Italian and came across this passage: "I put my foot in a school and see a big crowd of children, dirty, with dresses all torn and with frightened faces but with very clear eyes and with angelic expressions on their faces. It is then that terror takes over me, as if I see people who are close to drowning."

Its effect on me was overpowering. I abruptly closed the book and looked out the window, as if awakening from a nightmare. I felt Tolstoy's terror. The passage had struck some primordial nerve.

I was on my way to make a film that involved swimming underwater. Drowning—latent fear? No, too literal. Children? Yes, maybe—tattered and dirty and frightened, yet angelic—Sofia Scicolone? But why did I feel Tolstoy's terror? Why *terror?*

For several days the image haunted me. I am a witch, and visions like this affect all my senses.

Ten

After the enchantment of Cary Grant and what turned out to be the disenchantment of Alan Ladd and *Boy on a Dolphin,* I didn't know what to expect of John Wayne. My destination now was the oasis village of Ghadames, located in the Sahara near Timbuktu, where Tunis and Libya conjoin. Remote, primitive, completely isolated, scorching days, freezing nights. The picture: *Legend of the Lost.*

I was relieved to find that John Wayne was exactly as advertised. Big, authoritative, gruff but polite, and a pro through and through. He showed up right on the minute, knew all his lines and moves, worked hard all day long without letup, and quit right on the minute. There was no doubt that he was in command, the captain on the bridge of the ship. He did not have to exert his authority overtly because everyone automatically deferred to him. Even the director, Henry Hathaway. But he never abused his powerful position. He simply assumed his stance and kept it. With me, he was polite and pleasant, but distant. He did not show affection toward anyone but neither did he show any hostility nor make outrageous demands. But everyone was in awe of him, scared of him somewhat, and a great concerted effort was made to anticipate his needs. For example, a special, king-size bed had been trucked in and set up in his room before his arrival even though he had not requested it.

I played Dita, a much-abused urchin from the streets of Timbuktu, and John was a desert guide hired by Rossano Brazzi to help him find a treasure lode that had been discovered in a lost city in the Sahara by Brazzi's father, who had been a missionary. I recall a line of dialogue I addressed to Wayne: "I hate men!" To which he retorted, "And I hate loud chippies!" That kind of movie. Of course, after facing the rigors of sandstorms, tarantulas, rampaging natives, scorpions, thirst, heat, and a Brazzi gone mad, John and I fell into each other's arms as we were miraculously rescued by a desert caravan.

Physically, it was one of the most difficult pictures I ever made, and in the course of it I almost died. The only living accommodation in Ghadames was a flimsy, primitive, unheated motel. At night the cold was intolerable, and the only heat I had in my room was a gas space heater installed by the crew. My room was on the ground floor, and as is my custom, every night I carefully locked the windows and door. I have a fear of intruders breaking in that goes along with my innate fear of the dark. On the night about which I am telling you, I began to have ghastly nightmares, unlike anything I had ever experienced in my sleep before. I would half wake from a nightmare, try to rouse myself but then lapse into sleep again, only to have another horrible nightmare, half rouse, go back to sleep. I fought desperately to wake up, to use my voice, to open my eyes, but I simply could not. I was also aware that I was gasping desperately for air, as if I were having a suffocation dream.

Then, suddenly, a violent thump, and a sharp pain in my shoulder as my body fell from the bed and hit the tiled floor. I was awake, but still gasping, as in the nightmare. I tried to get up but I couldn't. All my strength was gone and my head was fogged with panic. The space heater had exhausted all of the oxygen in the room and there was nothing for me to breathe but the deadly fumes of carbon monoxide. I was asphyxiating. If I had not fallen from the bed, I would have never surfaced from my coma, but even on the floor, half awake, struggling for breath, I did not have the strength to move or to call for help.

I began to inch myself along the floor toward the door, constantly passing out and reviving. I do not know how long it took me to reach the door. Certainly a long time. By then I was virtually lifeless. I knew I was dying, strangling from lack of air, but instead of succumbing, from deep inside me there arose a pocket of strength. The enormous determination to live—my God, what it can achieve! The so-called superhuman effort. A miraculous reservoir. Slowly, slowly, slowly, little by little, I forced myself up until I could reach the knob and open the door. I pitched forward and fell into the corridor, unconscious. Luckily, Rossano Brazzi, coming in late, found me and frantically called the doctor. He said I was just about gone. Mouth-to-mouth resuscitation, injections, frantic first aid. I had severe headaches for a week. The doctor said I had been just seconds away from death.

Rossano Brazzi was the personification of the bigger-than-life Latin lover. Perfectly coiffed, impeccably dressed, he was a welcome relief, always performing, mimicking, prancing about, seductive looks in every direction, and always, *always* singing "Some Enchanted Evening." He had just completed the film version of *South Pacific* and an endless flow of "Some Enchanted Evenings" erupted from him. He was a splendid partner to work with.

The mayor of Ghadames had four wives, the eldest of whom fell seriously ill while *Legend of the Lost* was being made. Although the mayor's fourth wife was young and beautiful, he was very fond of his eldest wife, who was still his favorite. Her grave illness caused him great anguish. She needed immediate surgery but there were no medical facilities in Ghadames. It was nighttime and no plane could come in to get her on the unlighted, primitive airstrip, which was a steel mesh affair left over from World War II.

When I heard about the situation, I asked to be taken to the mayor whom I found in tears. I had become friendly with the mayor and this elderly wife, and I volunteeerd to help all I could. I got hold of the assistant director and got him to mobilize all the lights, generators, and vehicles which the film company had brought to Ghadames. I then arranged for them to be placed along the airstrip. By now it was midnight and the weather had turned freezing cold as it invariably does in the desert. Everyone maintained absolute silence in order to be able to pick up the sound of the small aircraft which had been contacted by radio.

As soon as we heard its motors, all the lights snapped on, enabling the pilot to make a landing. A stretcher bearing the sick woman was immediately carried to the plane. A doctor and nurse were aboard. The old woman was carefully lifted inside and strapped in place. There was no room on the plane for anyone else.

When the doors closed, the mayor's grief became unbearable and he broke down. I put my arms around him and comforted him as the plane taxied into position and took off. Before the picture ended, the sick wife, fully recovered, returned to the village. I seriously doubt that she would have survived the night if we had not mobilized the forces of the film company.

I had now made three American films in succession, in which I played a Spanish camp follower, a Greek peasant, and an Arab street girl. None of the parts or movies was memorable, but Carlo had adroitly used them as steppingstones toward his coveted goal, a Hollywood contract. It worked. Columbia Pictures made a deal with him for four films. The year, 1957—I was twenty-two years old.

I felt committed to Carlo, but uneasy because I had no answer when I asked myself, Committed to what? Almost three years had passed since that euphoric moment (it was my birthday) during the shooting of *Woman of the River*, when Carlo came to our location and presented me with that diamond ring. Until then, we had only seen each other secretly, but during the location shooting of *Woman of the River* Carlo stayed with me at my hotel, and certainly those working on the film knew about us. I didn't care. I loved him and wanted him, and despite my mother's dire foreboding, I felt it would turn out all right. If not, it would be a painful mistake. But the only people who never make mistakes are the ones who don't do anything. Mistakes are part of the dues one pays for living a full life.

My mother continued to lecture me about Carlo. She didn't like him. "Italian men do not leave their children," she warned. "They will play around but they will always go back to their children." The fact that Carlo had two young children did upset me. And that he was married continued to bother me, but how can I explain that I had the feeling that Carlo was someone I had known all my life, that I had as much right to him as anyone else, and that he had been my father and my husband for a long time? The thing I found most attractive about Carlo was his gentleness. I have my own peculiar yardstick for measuring a man: Does he have the courage to cry in a moment of grief? Does he have the compassion not to hunt an animal? In his relationship with a woman, is he gentle? Real manliness is nurtured in kindness and gentleness, which I associate with intelligence, comprehension, tolerance, justice, education, and high morality. If only men realized how easy it is to open a woman's heart with kindness, and how many women close their hearts to the assaults of the Don Juans.

I have another way to measure a man: with his bad qualities. Of these, I'd say that stinginess, arrogance, and cruelty are fatal.

From what Carlo told me about his relationship with his wife I knew that something vital had gone out of their marriage and that they had settled for a *modus vivendi*—living in the same house but not really as man and wife any more. So I felt that if Carlo did leave her for me she would not be as affected as she would have been if she were still in love with him.

I had never met Carlo's wife—Giuliana Fiastri was her name, daughter of a general—but the dignity and maturity which she exhibited all through this long, trying period elicited my profound admiration. She was a woman without a trace of bitterness or hostility in her, a woman who, having accepted the fact that her marriage was over, tried to make the transition as easy on herself and her children and on Carlo as she possibly could.

But in view of the fact that Italy did not recognize divorce, even with his wife's cooperation there was little Carlo could do to dissolve the marriage. He did apply for an annulment on the grounds that when he married Giuliana he had not believed in the sacrament of marriage, but the action was flimsy and the annulment quickly denied. The prospect of getting the marriage dissolved was bleak. But no matter how much I needed Carlo in my life, how incomplete I was without him, how desperately I wanted to furnish a home with him and have children with him and mingle my life with his, I nonetheless was determined that I was not going to get strung out as his mistress, naïvely abiding the dissolution of an indissoluble marriage. It was a severe conflict and one that troubled me deeply.

This was the state of affairs (no pun intended) when we flew to Beverly Hills, where Cary Grant eagerly awaited my arrival. Carlo knew that Cary was still in my thoughts. Instinctively I knew that Cary's fervid interest brought pressure to bear on Carlo. I didn't know exactly what Carlo could do about his dilemma, but the fact was that for three years he had had a good thing going for him, and as long as he could, he would probably be content to maintain that idyllic state.

Hollywood. *La patria del cinema*. That long-ago shy dream come to reality. Triumphal entrance. Glittering reception. A posh suite at the Beverly Hills Hotel, flower-laden, beribboned baskets of California fruit, a stack of invitations, publicity men by the dozens, bowing, scraping, limousine at the ready, couturiers dancing attendance, a cabana at poolside, the telephone operator saying, "Good morning, Miss Loren, what can I do for you, Miss Loren?" waved through at the studio gate, a queen-size dressing room newly decorated in royal colors—Hollywood.

Homage from the aristocracy—the stars, the unreal images on the screen of the Teatro Sacchino come to life, smiling, shaking my hand, speaking to me, calling me by name, but it is not me, for I am sitting shyly and invisibly in the corner watching Sophia Loren in her moment of glory, sitting apart from myself as I always do, letting the other Sophia, the now-star Sophia, the unbelievably lionized Sophia, bask in the starlight. A grand party in her honor at Romanoff's. And at Romanoff's, first taste of Hollywood mores, in the person of Jayne Mansfield. As photographers surrounded my table, precipitous arrival of Jayne Mansfield, whom I had never heard of, in a *very* low cut dress; she joined my table, and just by chance one of her ample breasts tumbled out of her dress as the photographers clicked away. Welcome to Hollywood.

Clifton Webb's party in my honor at his home. A storybook fairy tale: Danny Kaye, Gary Cooper, Gene Kelly, Jimmy Stewart, Fred Astaire (I first looked at his feet), Sinatra, Joan Crawford, Barbara Stanwyck, Cary Grant, Claudette Colbert, Merle Oberon, June Havoc, Fred MacMurray and on and on, a roll call of my heroes and heroines, but alas, Tyrone Power was doing a film in England. I never did get to meet him. He died so young.

Hollywood's bright promise, but the films not so bright. *Desire Under the Elms,* Eugene O'Neill's great searing drama, diminished and tepid because it was shot on an unrealistic sound stage instead of on location, and because as passionate lovers, Tony Perkins and I lacked chemistry.

Black Orchid with Tony Quinn, same problem. We had made an Italian film together, *Attila the Hun,* in 1953, a pointless, tasteless, trite affair that had in it my most unpleasant experience as an actress: a scene in which Tony passionately kissed me while eating a greasy lamb chop. I thought, though, that in Hollywood Tony and I would make amends, but splendid actor though he is, the sad fact was that audiences did not like to see us together on the screen.

Odd, because theoretically we should have been perfect together. Paramount tried us again a year later in *Heller in Pink Tights*, but the chemistry between Tony and me was no better. Also, in *Heller* the director, the renowned George Cukor, made me perform in a blond wig on the strings of a marionette. At least, that's what I thought at the time. He made me mimic his intonations, his gestures, his facial expressions, even his eye movements; every day on the set was a nightmare because I didn't feel as if I belonged to myself any more, and felt that I had been forced to subjugate my identity as an actress. It was a new technique, one I had not experienced before, and I was thrown by it. Cukor was not giving me suggestions to show what he had in mind; they were commands for precise imitations. I didn't have the courage to say, No, I don't feel right about this, Mr. Cukor, may I try it my way, please let me be creative —I was too new to the scene, and Cukor was a director of great stature and experience. Actually, later on I realized that I had learned a great deal from him, and the picture did have many good things in it, but not enough to make it successful at the time. Later on, though, the film was acclaimed, and it remains a favorite of mine.

I went to New York to make *That Kind of Woman*, with Tab Hunter as co-star, and that was the weakest pairing of all. Hopeless; negative chemistry, if such is possible.

The movie I made with Cary Grant, *Houseboat*, was the only one of my Hollywood endeavors that came off well. Of course, Cary and I did match up on the screen very well, and that was half the battle. But looking back on that Hollywood period—I have not made a movie there since then—I feel it was not Hollywood's fault that they didn't know what to do with me. American films at that time limited Italians to being gangsters and waiters. And they had never been able to accept a foreign actress for what she was. They felt they had to change her. That's what happened to me.

Carlo Ponti

As for leading men, Sophia's problem is that she comes across as a very strong personality on the screen, and consequently she is not easily partnered. (*Time* magazine commented that she could have swallowed her Hollywood leading men with half a glass of water.) There are only a few men who can compete with Sophia on the screen, who can exert domination when it's needed. Cary was one of them, and Mastroianni, Richard Burton, Peter O'Toole, Brando, Clark Gable, and Gregory Peck. Not many, considering that she's done over sixty films.

While I was in Hollywood, Sinatra completed the missing scenes for *The Pride and the Passion,* using studio backdrops for scenery. My sister and I saw him occasionally and he was always helpful and friendly. I had brought with me a recording I had made in Italy. Romantic, Italian songs. I sing quite nicely, and I enjoy singing. I took the record to Frank and asked him what he thought of it. He listened a few minutes, then turned it off. "No chance," he said. "Your sister's the one who should sing. With her voice, if she worked at it, she could move on out. Your sister's a *singer*."

That was high praise, coming from Sinatra, who doesn't give compliments easily, and for a while my sister acted as if she were going to try to make a career for herself. She could have been a wonderful comedienne with her vibrancy and her sense of humor; she's very pretty, she dances extremely well— all this plus her exemplary voice could have made her a star. But the pity was that she didn't have the temperament for it. She lacked the drive, the sense of dedication, the necessary concentration. Getting ahead in a difficult profession, singing, acting, writing, whatever, requires avid faith in yourself, in who you are, the talent you have, and what you want to do with it. You must be able to sustain yourself against staggering blows and unfair reversals. There is no code of conduct to help beginners. That is why some people with mediocre talent, but great inner drive, go much further than people with vastly superior talent. I'm convinced that this inner drive is something you are born with or not born with, and no one can teach you how to acquire it. When I think back to those first couple of years in Rome, those endless rejections without a glimmer of encouragement from anyone, all those failed screen tests, and yet I never let my desire slide away from me, my belief in myself and what I felt I could achieve. I was not a genius, just a hard worker; I wouldn't want to be a genius because, as someone once said, a genius has nobody to rely on but himself.

So after a brief time, my sister rejected her opportunities and her talent and returned to Italy. She said she was homesick and would return shortly. But she didn't. She eventually married and had two children and never did a thing with her voice.

"Who invented the heart? Just tell me and show me the spot where he has been hanged." Often my sentiment, because my doubts and conflicts over Cary and Carlo had come to a boil again in Hollywood. When I first arrived I had to do some pickup shots for *The Pride and the Passion* with Cary, and we saw each other quite often. His warmth and appeal were as strong as ever. Then after our work was finished, he called every day and sent flowers and it didn't matter to him or me that Carlo was staying with me. I often took Cary's calls with Carlo right there in the room. It must have mattered a great deal to Carlo but he didn't discuss it. Nor did he discuss his marital impasse. He had separated from his wife. But after his half-hearted try for an annulment, I was not aware that Carlo had any further plans for our future together.

But that did not mean that Carlo was able to take me for granted. Certainly the situation with Cary, which Carlo was fully aware of, was exerting pressure on him. And so was I. I know a woman can become very boring when she's pressuring a man, especially if he's married, but I had come to realize that if I did not reach a point of crisis with Carlo, nothing was ever going to happen. A married man wants to string along with the status quo—let's wait and see, have a little patience, dear—but if the man has strong emotions and ties to his family and believes in the things he has accomplished, then if pressure isn't brought to bear on him nothing is ever going to happen. I instinctively knew that pressure mounting to a crisis was the only way to get a response, but knowing that, I also knew that such a move generated the risk that Carlo might jump back into his old marriage rather than into my arms.

That was a risk I was willing to take. If I lost out, then his feelings for me weren't as strong as I had thought they were. So I told him, "Carlo, I love you, I have committed myself to you, but this is no life for me. I want a life of my own. I want children and a house we can call our own and I'm tired of hearing my mother's lectures. I want to feel pride when I'm with you and feel a nice wedding band on my finger. I met you when I was sixteen. I have lived with you, off and on, since I was nineteen. I am now twenty-three. That is long enough—more than enough of my life that I have spent this way. I am tired of being badgered by the press about you—of being coy with them and evasive. And sometimes dishonest. That's not me; I hate having to do that. It's really starting to get to me and the time has come to put a stop to it. I know it's not easy. I know the problems you face. But your whole way of life is overcoming obstacles and I know you could overcome this one if you *really* wanted to."

Now Carlo had a sharp, unequivocal crisis.

And so did I. Now that I was living in Hollywood

and experiencing the everyday life there, it was having an effect on my attitude toward Cary.

My first impression of Hollywood was precisely as I had imagined it to be. Beautiful scenery, expensive cars of dazzling colors, obligatory swimming pools rarely swum in, a plethora of motels, giant drugstores and giant supermarkets, so staggering in size and content that they could just as well have been on another planet. What I found most amusing were the drive-ins, and I adored having a food tray brought to the car and hooked onto the outside of the door. I was also enchanted with a dish I had never eaten before: cottage cheese with fruit salad.

It was all brand new to me, a unique *ambiance*, a different kind of living. The people all looked very relaxed and healthy, and their casual dress and informality were fascinating. A very appealing lifestyle, I thought—at first. But then I began to discover something else about life in Hollywood: it only ran on one track, and that track was the motion picture. Any and everyone was obsessed with movies. All you ever heard wherever you went were words such as grosses, below-the-line, above-the-line, percentages, negative costs, reruns, spin-offs, and scarcely a word to indicate that anything at all was happening in the real world other than the making of movies. Even if you were invited out to dinner, talk at the table would be limited to the latest Hollywood gossip, and immediately after dinner, a screen would miraculously appear from behind a Modigliani or a rare Flemish tapestry, and everyone would watch whatever not-yet-released film the host had been able to wrangle from a studio.

But my working experience in Hollywood was valuable. I learned about American movie technique and I was able to perfect my English and speak naturally rather than in the parrot fashion of *The Pride and the Passion*. So in that sense it was like going to school for a while. But I had also learned that in Hollywood I could not achieve for myself those goals as an actress which I aspired to. Parts for Italian women were infrequent and limited. If my career was to move forward, I knew that I would have to return to Europe, where I was more at home, and eventually to Italian productions in my own language.

From the start of our film, Cary sensed the change in me. We were not quite as easygoing with each other. Although we often had lunch together, and as always it was enjoyable, I suppose something had gone out of me and Cary, who is very perceptive, sensed it.

It was not pleasant for me. I still had not delineated my boundaries, so that I spilled this way and that, seeking but not finding identity. All I had established were my negatives: I would not go on indefinitely in that awkward situation with Carlo; I would not give up my European roots and make a permanent home in Hollywood. But what *would* I do? What were my positives? These were the only two men I had ever had any interest in.

Toward the end of *Houseboat* the situation was finally resolved by a totally unexpected event. Carlo and I were staying in a bungalow on the grounds of the Bel-Air Hotel. We were at breakfast. I picked up the newspaper, which had been brought with the breakfast, and there, the lead item in Louella Parsons' column, was the news that changed my life. On the previous day, Louella reported, two Mexican lawyers had appeared in a courtroom in Juárez, and within ten minutes had wrought a couple of legal miracles. First they had obtained a decree, officially divorcing Carlo from his wife, and, immediately afterward, with one lawyer standing in for me and the other for Carlo, they had exchanged marriage vows in a proxy ceremony performed by the judge. A marriage certificate had been issued. Sofia Scicolone of Pozzuoli was officially and finally married to Dr. Carlo Ponti of Milan.

I was stunned. It was scarcely the wedding I had dreamed of—two Mexican lawyers in a courtroom a thousand miles away pretending to be Carlo and me. But it was legal. We were man and wife. That was all that mattered. Mr. and Mrs. Carlo Ponti, not a fabrication for a hotel register, but the truth. We were. We really were.

Carlo came over and took the newspaper from me. He was as surprised at the announcement as I was. Of course, he had initiated the proceedings (after I had created our "crisis") but he had not expected anything so swift and final. He sat down beside me and took my hands in his, and he looked in my eyes and smiled at me—like a husband.

I wanted to share my moment of happiness, call someone, shout with joy, but we had no friends and there was no one to call. The grandest, happiest moment of my life and no one to tell.

That evening, we celebrated alone. We had dinner in our bungalow, by candlelight, and later I discovered that my secretary had put rice in our bed.

When I came on the set the following day, one look told me that Cary had read Louella's column. "I hope you will be very happy, Sophia," he said. Bravely, he kissed my cheeks. That's all he ever said about it, but finishing the picture with him was trying and upsetting.

One important scene remained to be filmed. Ironically, it was the climax of the film—my marriage to Cary—and it was precisely the wedding I had always dreamed of. A very unkind quirk of cinematic fate.

Seeing myself in a long white gown, a radiant bride, was a vision that went back to the darkest days of my girlhood in Pozzuoli. I used to cut bride pictures out of old magazines and paste them in my scrapbook. And now I was having that dreamed-of wedding with Cary, only a few days after my marriage to Carlo. A long white gown of antique lace, high at the throat, trim buttoned bodice, a sheer veil held in place with a sprig of white flowers, a bouquet of white roses, Mendelssohn's wedding music, a flower girl and bridesmaids, and Cary Grant waiting at the altar with a white carnation in his buttonhole. It is at a moment like this that playacting and real life touch each other and mingle.

I was so concerned about Cary, and about my own

wedding emotions, that I could scarcely keep my mind on the business of the film. I cared very much about Cary, as I do to this day, and I was aware of how painful it was for him to play this scene with me, to have the minister pronounce us man and wife, to take me in his arms and kiss me. It was painful for me, too, his make-believe bride. I could not help thinking of all those lovely times in Spain, of all the souvenirs I had in my memory. I am very romantic and vulnerable and I would cherish forever what Cary had brought into my life.

Eleven

My marital bliss was short-lived. Scarcely a month after our marriage, a thunderous pronouncement appeared in *L'Osservatore della Domenica*, the official paper of the Vatican. The article was written by a lawyer on the Vatican Rota, and although he did not mention me by name, he did identify the person involved as "a young, beautiful Italian film actress." The article stated:

"Civil divorce and a successive civil marriage are gravely illicit acts and have no judicial effect whatever before God and the Church. Those responsible are public sinners and may no longer receive the sacraments.

"The code of canon law regards as bigamists those who contract a new marriage—even if only a civil one—although they are bound by a valid marriage. It punishes both parties with the penalty of infamy (a stigma attaching, in canon law, to the character of a person). If they set up life in common, this is termed concubinage and may be punished even with interdict and excommunication."

Reading those words, my insides turned to ice. I had been raised a Catholic, and even though I no longer went to mass or confession or communion, emotionally Catholicism was my heritage and excommunication was a chilling threat. Of course, from the Vatican point of view, the article was absolutely correct; what we had done was indeed contrary to the strict canons of the church. But this denouncement of us had been totally unexpected. Many Italian Catho-

Sophia
Living
and Loving

Sophia at her communion.

In front of their war-damaged house just after the war.

Still called Sofia Stuzzicadente (toothpick) by neighborhood kids when she was eleven.

She adored the piano but had to give it up because of the headaches caused by her mother's banging her on the head every time she made a mistake.

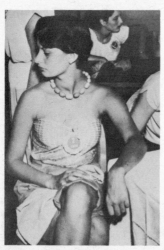

The beauty contest that sent Sophia on her way; a ticket to Rome was one of her prizes.

She even went topless for the French
version of this harem scene.

In 1932 Sophia's mother was
tested for a role in a film when
she won the all-Italy Greta
Garbo look-alike contest.

Sophia with her mother and sister during the struggle period in Rome. Their family roles were all mixed up: Sophia was the father, her mother was the wife-manager, and her sister was the neglected child.

Sophia as a sexy slave girl in *Two Nights with Cleopatra*.

The Miller's Wife was not much of a film but it marked the debut of what was to become one of the most successful film teams in movie history: with Mastroianni, top, and de Sica.

Carlo Ponti devised *Woman of the River* for Sophia and she responded with a sensuous, dramatic performance that finally established her as an actress to be reckoned with.

Sophia, a jewelless newcomer, with Yvonne di Carlo and Gina Lollobrigida. This was the only meeting with Gina, although the press war over their breasts was to go on and on and on.

During *The Pride and the Passion*, Sinatra introduced Sophia to the glories of Ella Fitzgerald's singing. Asked to describe Sophia, Sinatra said, "She's the mostest."

Boy on a Dolphin was a disappointing experience, but it did produce this dripping, clinging Sophia in a shot seen round the world.

A long stint in the Sahara with John Wayne in *Legend of the Lost* was a grueling experience that almost cost Sophia her life.

Whether to marry Cary Grant was a terrible dilemma for Sophia. They were wonderfully suited for each other and he brought a spontaneous quality to her life which she adored. But in the end, Carlo Ponti won out and this wedding scene from *Houseboat* was as close to marriage with Cary as Sophia ever got.

Life had her on six covers, this time to feature her new villa outside Rome, which can be seen in the background.

Photo by Alfred Eisenstaedt

No one has better captured the stunning beauty and pliant expressions of the Loren face than Alfred Eisenstaedt.

Getting smashed with Clark Gable in *It Happened in Naples*.

A Breath of Scandal was a
dismal film that
embarrassed Sophia and
Carlo, who made it , yet it
did produce a stunning
moment of graceful
beauty when Sophia,
playing the part of a
princess, managed to
capture regal splendor as it
has seldom been
captured before.

Two Women, above, was a triumphant re-creation of the agonies Sophia had suffered during the war, and her performance brought her an Oscar. Here she is being congratulated by de Sica moments after the good news had been flashed to Rome. That's Carlo at left, opening a celebratory bottle of Dom Pérignon.

After shooting a scene in *Boccaccio '70*, Sophia was joined in her dressing room by her mother, her sister, Maria, and Rachele Mussolini, who was about to become Maria's mother-in-law.

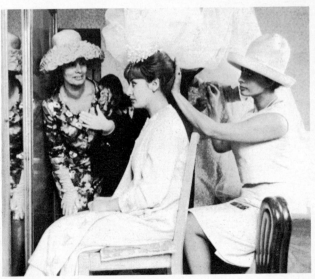

With her mother checking on her, Sophia primps her sister on the day of her wedding.

The baptism of Maria's first child. Next to Maria is her husband, Romano Mussolini; his mother, the Duce's widow, holds the baby.

Sophia wore a crown when she was presented to Queen Elizabeth along with Bill Holden, Jack Hawkins and other members of the cast of *The Key*, but the British press took a very dim view of two crowned heads at the same gala.

In *Yesterday, Today and Tomorrow* Sophia ran a magnificent gamut, ranging from the perpetually pregnant Adelina of the Naples slums to Mara, the voluptuous Roman call girl.

Here Mara, as one of her
more ardent customers,
Mastroianni commanded
her to "do a striptease,
with just the refrigerator
light on."

In Hollywood, Sophia
encountered Jayne
Mansfield, intent on
publicizing her
considerable cleavage.

Cary Grant ardently pursued the marriage he had first proposed in Spain.

In *Marriage, Italian Style*, Sophia and Marcello established their screen partnership as one of filmdom's greatest—to be ranked alongside Gable-Lombard and Tracy-Hepburn. The film detailed the relationship, over many years, between a rich playboy and his mistress, who eventually tricks him into marriage.

Brando was a deterrent to *A Countess from Hong Kong* in both temperament and performance, but Sophia adored Charlie Chaplin, who here has an antic moment during a surprise birthday reception on the set.

The Priest's Wife was a change of pace,
with the church acting as Sophia's
rival for Mastroianni.

Both Sophia and Peter O'Toole suffered vocal traumas when the time came to sing their big numbers in *Man of La Mancha*. With them is James Coco, who played Sancho.

The metamorphosis of
Sophia in *White Sister*,
before and after becoming
Sister Germana in a
missionary hospital in
Libya.

Sophia's father, at right, returned to live with her mother and sister after Sophia became successful. Note the furs and pearls which Sophia bestowed on them. Riccardo Scicolone tried to become Sophia's financial manager but she already had a very good one: her husband, Carlo.

Sophia's marriage to Carlo. The Mayor of Sévres is putting the wedding ring on Sophia's hand, which is the French custom.

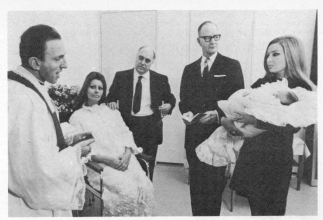

In Sophia's hospital room: Carlo, Dr. de Watteville and Maria have assembled for the blessing of Sophia's firstborn.

Everything they are to each other
is in this picture.

All the Pontis: Carlo's son and daughter from his first marriage, and his much more recent sons, Carlo, Jr., and Edoardo.

With an unhappy Richard Burton in *The Voyage*. During the filming of this picture, Elizabeth Taylor left Richard for good and Sophia tried to ease him over what was the most difficult period of his life.

Carlo and Sophia share the hope that someday they can return to their beloved villa near Rome.

When de Sica died, "a painful sense of loss
swept over me, loss of this man I loved, and loss of a
part of myself that would be buried with him."

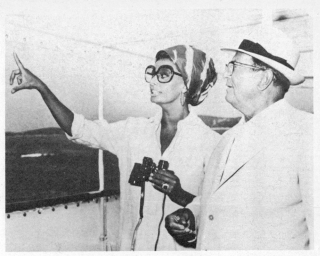

Tito and Sophia agree that the most difficult mission in life is to find someone you can completely trust.

Photo by Alfred Eisenstaedt

lics had procured divorces in Mexico and had remarried and were living their new lives in Italy without the church's molestation. But Carlo and I were the celebrity scapegoats whom they decided to hold up as examples. Public sinners, bigamists, infamy, stigma, concubinage, excommunication—what terrible words with which to be branded, what terrible scorn to heap upon us! Carlo and I had been happily planning a honeymoon voyage by sea back to Italy. Now we would have to forget all that. Italy was out of the question. My marriage, so long unresolved, was again unresolved. I hurled the Vatican newspaper to the floor and wept bitter tears. Why persecute me for wanting to be married to the man I love, to have children with him, a home with him, a normal, fruitful life with him? Does that make me a public sinner? For that do I deserve to be subjected to the church's scorn? The more anger and hopelessness overcame me, the more I wept. That was the saddest day of my life.

Others quickly jumped on the Vatican doomwagon. The Italian Men's Catholic Action organization demanded that all Catholics avoid going to Sophia Loren movies—and asked that they pray for my soul. Newspapers all over Italy took up the hue and cry against us. A magazine ran an article that recalled, with some regret, that if Carlo and I had been living in the Middle Ages we would have been burned alive in the public square. Another Italian paper quoted a Vatican spokesman as saying, "These poor people are not only victims of their lack of morals but also victims of their own ignorance. In the eyes of the Church, Ponti and Loren are living in concubinage."

When Carlo returned to our Bel-Air bungalow and found me in tears, he reacted forcefully. This is Carlo's way; when strength is required, he is strong. "Now listen to me, Sophia," he said. "We are married, and we are going to stay married. If this Mexican marriage falls through, we'll find some other way. This is all just a dust storm that will blow over. We are the ones who are the victims of ignorance, and it is the ones who are denouncing us who lack morals. We are the moral ones. Whatever has to be done, we will do. You are my wife and nobody will ever change that, and that's all there is to it."

Carlo's words were great comfort but the situation was destined to get far worse.

In my notebook, there is this quote: "Every great religion did nothing but prohibit, and enunciate a long list of things that you cannot do, but the things that you cannot do cannot arouse in you the desire to improve your condition."

Carlo and I were on an airplane, leaving Hollywood. I don't recall just what triggered it—I criticized the food or I said something silly—whatever it was, it was inconsequential. But suddenly Carlo turned in his seat and slapped me. A jolting whack across my right cheek. I didn't expect it. I didn't expect it at all. It hurt terribly because he hit me with the bad hand, the left hand which can't be controlled, as the right one can. It was a powerful slap, full force, and my head was wrenched by it and I burst out crying. I was so humiliated and incensed. I wanted to get off the plane. Of course the slap had nothing to do with the moment. Maybe it was because of Cary Grant. Maybe all those unspoken gnawings of jealousy that Carlo had endured so long.

Carlo didn't say a word, he just turned away and looked out the window.

I bent my head into my hands and wept. The stewardess, passing with refreshments, asked if she could do anything for me. I just shook my head. We never discussed it. We didn't talk for the rest of the trip or for several days afterward.

It was the only time in our twenty-seven years together that Carlo ever struck me. Or lost his temper, really. But even now I can feel the pain and the humiliation. My cheek was sore for several days.

Twelve

I had keenly anticipated doing my first picture in London, *The Key*, with Sir Carol Reed to direct and William Holden and Trevor Howard as co-stars, but on arrival I sensed something was wrong. This was confirmed when Sir Carol and Carl Foreman, the producer-writer, came to my hotel. They tried to be as amiable and gentle as they could in breaking the news to me.

Foreman said that although I had been signed for the role, they had come to realize that I was really too young for the part, that I just wouldn't be believable with Holden, who was much too old for me. They needed someone much more mature for the part, Foreman said, and Ingrid Bergman was ready to take over. He said my age would be a handicap I couldn't overcome. He hoped I would understand, that he thought the world of me as an actress and surely the first chance they had, Carol and he would like to line up a picture with me that would be more suitable. I got the impression that Sir Carol did not necessarily agree with Foreman's point of view.

My first impulse was to oblige them. But this was a role I very much wanted to play. Although the part was not very big, it had a certain quality to it that was challenging and intriguing. When I read a script, I never consider the size of the role, how many shots, any of that, I only consider the nature of the part and its possibilities. This role strongly appealed to me. I felt that it would help establish me as a serious actress. So, for the first and only time in my life, I overcame my impulse obsequiously to withdraw. "I'm sorry," I said, "but I don't agree with you. This is a part that I feel committed to. I don't think there will be any discrepancy with Mr. Holden. I have a signed contract and I want to do the film."

They were nonplussed by my attitude. They hadn't expected any trouble. After all, I was a beginner and by all rights I should want to stay on the good side of two of the world's most important filmmakers.

They had no choice but to go forward with me, but I knew that under the circumstances I had to give the performance of my young life. They arranged for a reading of the script, but I now felt so self-conscious that I knew I would do poorly so I feigned being ill and did not appear at the reading. Nor did I show up for rehearsals, again pleading illness. Psychologically, I felt somewhat compromised by their attitude and I did not want to expose myself to what I felt would be a negative situation. An okay-now-show-us trial run.

Actually, I have never been able to rehearse scenes before shooting them, not to this day. I walk through scenes for technical rehearsals, just mouthing the lines, but I simply cannot act when the camera is not turning. When I perform with actors who need rehearsals to warm up, I do the best I can, but it is never better than perfunctory. I feel so shy, so exposed when the camera is not going. It's an embarrassment for me. I suppose it's because basically I'm an amateur and not a professional. A professional actress should be able to rehearse, to give a full performance when necessary, but I have had no training and my acting consists simply of following my basic instincts. As I am in other situations, on the set I am two women, and the actress in me is only released at the moment the camera demands it. The word "Action!" frees me, I kick away my self-consciousness and I feel liberated, uninhibited, even reckless. The transformation that the living camera evokes in me is something I cannot explain. It is fragile and mysterious and too much analysis might destroy it.

Although I didn't show up for the readings and rehearsals of *The Key*, I assiduously worked on the script in my hotel room. I had put myself on the line and I was determined not to fail.

I didn't. After a tentative start, Sir Carol and I began to understand and respect each other. He was undemonstrative, very English, very much self-contained, taciturn, but at the same time supportive. He gave me complete freedom to demonstrate what I wanted to do, to express my emotions as I felt them, imposing nothing of himself on me unless he felt adjustments were advisable. Sir Carol trusted my instincts, and I had complete trust in him. To my mind, the perfect relation between director and performer.

I use the word "perfect" and yet de Sica was just the opposite. But de Sica was in a class by himself. No other director could do what de Sica did. He played every part, knew all the lines, and from behind the camera he acted out the entire film, doing my part, Marcello's, child actors, everyone. But he was an actor and that was his special technique. He did not want us to copy him, but from what he was doing we knew what he had in mind; however, he wanted us to use our own interpretation. Other directors might spend half an hour explaining a scene that de Sica would crystalize with a few moments of deft acting.

Before *The Key* was finished, Foreman told me how glad he was that I had refused to withdraw.

My father had suddenly materialized in my life, and I use the word "materialized" with a purpose. My mother informed me that he had decided to leave his wife and children and come back to live with her. I had established my mother in a fine apartment in Rome and I presume that he wanted to take care of everything for her, suddenly having become the husband he had never been. And he started to make suggestions for investments for me.

I made it clear to my mother that Carlo was handling all my business affairs, because I had trust in

Carlo, but no trust in my father. I didn't want any more disillusionment, any more heartache because of my father. Of course, there was the possibility that he meant well, that he might have made sound investments with my money, but the fact is that I don't care about money, I never have; what upsets me are the emotions that are involved when people are corrupted because of it.

The most upsetting thing in my life is when someone whom I trust violates that trust. My commitment to people I trust is total, how can it be any other way? Is there such a thing as partial trust? The very nature of trusting precludes any reservations, any suspicion, and the only way I know to find out if a person is trustworthy is trust him.

I have, on occasion, been taken advantage of, which has left me with emotional wounds that bleed for a long time. But on the other hand there are those I have trusted who have returned that trust and never disappointed me, and those are the most rewarding relationships in my life. But I couldn't take the risk with my father. I wanted to let old wounds heal and the memory of the hurts disappear.

After a combative three years with my mother, during which time they quarreled incessantly, my father deserted her for a young, attractive German woman. After he went to live with her, I never heard anything more from him about investments.

But a few years later, he again came into my life, this time through a lawsuit. I had stated in an interview with a German magazine something to the effect that when I was a child I had not received so much as a pair of shoes from my father. For this, my father sued for libel. He went into court and swore that my statements were false and asked for damages for having libeled his reputation. Even though the case was eventually dismissed by the court before coming to trial, it received considerable publicity which was painfully embarrassing for me. I suppose my father thought I would pay him some money to drop the suit. I don't know. It was an incident that caused me much pain.

Criminal law in Italy allows any citizen, even anonymously, to charge any other citizen with a crime. Thus, when the public prosecutor received a letter from a Milanese woman named Luisa Brambilla, whom I had never met nor heard of, charging Carlo with the crime of bigamy and me with being a *concubina*, the prosecutor was obliged to proceed against us. In her letter, Signora Brambilla stated that as a married woman and a mother she was demanding criminal prosecution of us in order to save the institution of matrimony in Italy. The condemnation of the Catholic Church had now escalated itself into a crime.

Once the newspapers got hold of the story, Carlo and I were assailed from all sides. The prosecutor received supportive letters of denunciation from women all over Italy; I was particularly upset by a letter, condemning me, sent by a group of Pozzuoli women. We were also attacked by lawyers, doctors, and government officials, and even the august Roman Catholic Morality League accused us of "bigamy and public adultery." I was not aware that a single letter was received by the prosecutor which defended us.

At a preliminary hearing before a magistrate, none of these accusers showed up in the courtroom to repeat their denunciations in person, but Italian law did not compel them to. The magistrate signed the prosecutor's warrants, which meant that if we set foot in Italy we were subject to arrest and jail. The basis for the bigamy charge was simple: the Church had declared the Mexican divorce illegal. Therefore, when Carlo and I were married in Mexico, he was still married to his first wife. Italy, our homeland, had now shut its doors to us. We were exiles.

But for me, no matter what they said about me, no matter how harshly they judged us, my reaction was a defiance of all of them. When I know deep down that I am doing something that is right (in judging my own conscience, I am the sole arbiter of what is right), then I do not brood about what is appearing in the papers or try to analyze why they are persecuting us or even try to justify myself. I am right and that's all there is to it. The courage of my conviction is what sustains me. I feel no guilt regardless of how sanctimoniously I am attacked. I do not bleed. I have no capacity for self-doubt.

I felt sorry for the Brambilla woman, that she lived so meager and shallow a life that she couldn't comprehend the strength of our love and our desire to live our lives together and enjoy the very matrimony and family that she alleged we were destroying. I was determined to live my life with Carlo and go through any necessary hell to sustain it and bear our children. I needed the strength of that determination because it was destined to take many years to achieve our goal, troubled, frustrating, sometimes perilous years until we could become man and wife.

Talk about irony! On the very day I was branded a criminal in Italy, I was presented to the Queen of England in connection with a royal performance of *The Key* in London. But even so simple an event as that managed to turn a bit sour for me.

It was my first royal event; I prepared for it carefully with the help of a member of the Queen's staff. I learned how to curtsy properly, and to oblige the request that I dress up formally for the occasion, I bought myself a lovely new gown. I spent the afternoon with my hairdresser, who created a stunning coiffure for me, topped with a small crown.

That evening, when we assembled to be presented to her Majesty, the people in charge were appalled to discover that I had a crown in my hair. They said that in the presence of the Queen, only her Majesty would be wearing a crown. I was dismayed, but it was too late; it was impossible to remove the crown without completely undoing my hair. There were but a few minutes before her Majesty's appearance and certainly no time to do anything about my crown.

～～～～～～

Sophia's sister, Maria

Queen Elizabeth was very gracious. While Sophia curtsied, the Queen's eyes flicked to Sophia's crown for an instant but the royal smile remained constant. The next morning, however, the British papers had a field day. "England now has two queens," they wrote, "Queen Elizabeth and Queen Sophia." A picture showing them with their respective crowns ran on all the front pages. "Last night the actress, Sophia Loren," another article began, "tried to upstage the Queen of England. . . ."

It was a howler, all right, and Sophia received more publicity from the crown incident than all the rest of the cast combined.

～～～～～～

The first time it happened with Clark Gable, I was really startled. We were in the middle of a love scene for *It Happened in Naples* when a piercing buzz erupted from the vicinity of his wrist. Clark immediately released me, gave me a pat and a see-you-tomorrow, and disappeared.

That's how it was with Gable. A thorough professional. He came on time, knew his lines and left the instant his wristwatch buzzed at five o'clock. It was a nine-to-five job for him and his watch was the equivalent of the factory whistle.

I always try to establish a friendly relation with my leading men because an audience picks up on things like that. And also because if you have to walk onto a sound stage at 7 A.M. and kiss somebody or get in bed with him, it's better to be friendly. Of course, it was easier to have such friendly relations with some leading men than with others, but of all the men I've acted with (other than Cary Grant), two had very special appeal for me. What first attracts me to a man is not his physical but his mental attributes, and I was utterly fascinated by the lively, witty, intelligent, humorous appeal of Peter Sellers and Alec Guinness.

I was making *A Breath of Scandal* in Vienna, with John Gavin and Maurice Chevalier, when an official invitation arrived to attend the Venice Film Festival. *Black Orchid* was in competition and I was a candidate for best actress award. But Carlo and I were wary of the possible consequences of entering Italy while under indictment as criminals. The festival invitation could have been a lure to capture us, confiscate our passports, and throw us into jail. Italian law did not permit a writ of habeas corpus, which meant that a prisoner could be held indefinitely without hearing or trial.

Carlo got in touch with the festival people and made a bargain: as the alleged bigamist, Carlo was the major criminal, and I, the alleged concubine, was the minor criminal; therefore only I, the minor criminal, would attend but with the assurance that the police would grant me free passage into and out of Italy. The festival officials gave us that assurance, but I can tell you it was a very apprehensive Sophia Loren who stepped off the train in the Venice railroad station. I half expected *carabinieri* to seize me and whisk me away.

My fears were groundless. Instead of *carabinieri*, there was a festive crowd of shouting, laughing, waving Italians to greet me, and a welcoming fleet of gondolas and motorboats in the Grand Canal, tooting boat horns and calling my name. It was altogether a triumphal return to Italy after an absence of four years —and my indictment as a public sinner did not seem to have dampened the ardor of the Venetians.

That evening, I was thrilled to hear my name called as best actress. As I stood on the stage in front of my applauding, cheering countrymen and received the Volpi Best Actress plaque, I had a difficult time containing my jangled emotions. The wholeheartedness of the ovation I received seemed to be the audience's way of telling me that despite the harsh accusations leveled against me, I still had my place in their hearts.

But be that as it may, when I left Italy that night, the criminal charges against us had in no way been altered and Rome was as inaccessible to Carlo and me as it had been before.

The sad fact was that Carlo and I had no place to live. We were without home and country. A rented villa on the French Riviera, a rented chalet in Switzerland, but our minds always on Italy, an incessant yearning to go back. In Switzerland, when my homesickness became unbearable, Carlo would drive all the way to the top of the Furka Pass or the pass at San Gottardo, where we had a magnificent sweep of the Italian countryside in the distance. There was not much to see, but it was Italy, and that in itself was gratifying.

Carlo constantly badgered his lawyers in Rome to find a way to invalidate his crime—that Mexican marriage—and finally, after five years of legal jousting and hearings, they did. But it was a matter more of luck than of astuteness.

Mexican law requires that the marriage vows must be exchanged before a notary, and the certificate signed by the bride, the groom, and two witnesses. In our case, however, the proxy lawyers who handled our marriage had neglected to provide the required two witnesses. By Mexican law, this oversight invalidated the marriage, which meant that Carlo and I had not legally married in Mexico, and thus Carlo was married only to his first wife and not a bigamist.

Before the Roman magistrate would consider this plea, he asked that the Mexican marriage certificate be presented in court. But when the court clerk in Juárez went to the files, he discovered that the Ponti-Scicolone document had been removed. Through some astute detective work, the missing paper was finally traced to an Italian newspaperman who had stolen it from the Juárez courthouse. After studying the certificate, the magistrate would only go so far as to say that he was taking the matter under advisement.

"The time has come," Carlo said to me, "for us to be bold. Let us go back to Rome and take our chances. I don't think they'll bother us now, as long as we don't live together."

"Not live together!"

"I mean openly. We may have to do some sneaking around, but it will be nice to end our exile."

Thirteen

Carlo Ponti

My original plan was to do *Two Women* with Paramount, with George Cukor to direct. It was Cukor's notion to have Anna Magnani play the mother and Sophia the daughter. But before casting, we wanted to get a screenplay. We submitted the Alberto Moravia book to some of the most celebrated Hollywood screenwriters, but one after another they turned it down. They liked the book but they did not see how they could make a film out of it. There's no story, they said, nothing happens; just these characters in a situation but it doesn't develop into anything.

Then Cukor flew to Rome to talk to Magnani. She had read the book but under no circumstances would she play the mother if Sophia played her daughter. "She's too tall," she told Cukor. "How can I perform with a daughter I have to look up to?" I had known Magnani for many years; we were close friends. I tried to make her change her mind but she was the most stubborn woman who ever lived. "I will play the mother," she said, "but not with Sophia as my daughter." And that was that. Without Magnani, Cukor had no interest in doing the film, and withdrew. That's when I bought the rights from Paramount and brought in de Sica to direct, and Zavattini to write the screenplay.

I don't think Magnani ever got over her mistake in rejecting *Two Women*. "Sophia Loren makes all of my films," she once complained bitterly. I had great

131

admiration and respect for Anna, who was my friend for a long time; if only I could have convinced her to act in *Two Women*, how different the end part of her life might have been.

⌐⌐⌐⌐⌐⌐⌐

De Sica had not approved of my English-speaking film odyssey, especially the Hollywood leg of it, which in the course of six years away from Italy had produced about ten films. But now Carlo had brought him a project which would reunite us, Alberto Moravia's novel *Two Women*. Set in wartime Italy, it was a recreation of some of the life and events I had endured in Pozzuoli and Naples during the war.

Although George Cukor had failed in his attempt, de Sica believed he could induce Magnani to play the part of the fifty-year-old widow who battles valiantly but fruitlessly to protect her eighteen-year-old daughter, with whom she is fleeing, from the ravages of the war. I was excited at the prospect of performing with Magnani, who at that time was the doyenne of Italian actresses. But when de Sica went to see her to discuss the film, she again rejected me as her daughter.

"Now, Anna," de Sica said, placatingly, "trust me to maintain the balance between you."

"You want me to play the mother? Fine, all right, then I have a suggestion for the daughter: Anna Marie Pierangeli. We would play together very nicely."

But de Sica held his ground, trying to cajole Magnani into accepting me, but the more he insisted, the more she hardened in her resolve not to have me in the part. Finally, intending only to needle him, Magnani said, "Listen, Vittorio, if you are so enamored to have Sophia in the film, why not let her play the mother?"

The idea had not occurred to de Sica until that moment, but once he heard it, he was intrigued with the possibility. As he said his good-byes at the door, he said to Magnani, "Have you given me your final word on playing with Sophia?"

"Yes. Final—*final!*"

"Well, then," de Sica said, "I just may follow your suggestion and cast her as the mother. Thanks for the idea."

De Sica sent me a telegram: How about you playing the mother with a daughter of thirteen? I consented immediately. The mother's part was magnificent and I had implicit trust in de Sica to be able to guide me through it. So it was Anna Magnani who gave me the role of my life and turned my whole career around.

After all the confectionary roles I had been playing, I knew I would have to work terribly hard in order to prepare myself mentally to get inside the earthy woman I would have to portray. "It won't be easy," de Sica warned. "You are not yet twenty-six and you will have to be convincing as a woman ten years older than that. You have a daughter of thirteen. You are a poor woman who has worked hard all her life but lived honorably and devoted herself to raising this young girl. You've had a very primitive existence and your whole attitude toward life is primitive, simple, direct. The war has been brutal and it has aged you even beyond your years. So we will shoot this with no makeup, and we will dress you as a peasant woman really dresses. You have actually lived through all this, Sophia. You know all there is to know about it. If you can become this woman, without any thought as to how you look, without trying to restrain your emotions, letting everything flow into this character, I guarantee you, you will have the role of your life."

To prepare for the part, I opened the sluices of my memory, letting the bombing raids, the nights in the tunnel, the killings, the rapes and starvation and inhumanity wash back over me. I particularly concentrated on my mother as I remembered her during the war, her fears, connivances, and sacrifices, and especially the way she fiercely protected us against the scourges of the war.

The climax of *Two Women* occurred in a deserted, bombed-out hull of a church where I had taken my daughter for refuge during our harrowing flight from the Allied bombers attacking our native village. Suddenly a group of Moroccan soldiers emerged from the shadows of the church and in a frenzied orgy savagely raped us. Afterward, they left us physically and emotionally battered among the church's ruins. My agony on picking up my ravaged thirteen-year-old daughter whom I had fought so hard to protect during the preceding months, the loss of the last thing left to me in life that had value and meaning—I knew this would be the most difficult scene in the film for me.

The night before we shot the scene, I stirred my emotions with my sharp recollection of the fears generated in me by the band of Moroccan soldiers who had been quartered on the ground floor of our place in Pozzuoli. I relived the terror that had seized me on those nights when they drunkenly pounded on our door, their gruff, unintelligible voices echoing through the flat.

With this vibrant background to draw upon, you would think that I would have had an easy time of it. But, in retrospect, it was the most difficult role of my life. For it was very hard for me to relive my girlhood terror and at the same time to transform the reality of my feelings into the role I was acting. In memory, I still looked at my experiences with the eyes and emotions of a girl, but the role demanded that I see them with the eyes of a tortured woman. In large part, I was portraying my mother, reacting as I imagined she would have reacted if, on one of those frightening nights in Pozzuoli, the Moroccan soldiers had succeeded in breaking down the door and raping me.

As the movie progressed, I drew constantly upon the storehouse of those war-years emotions, and I enriched my part with them. Behind the camera, de Sica's compassionate face and sharp eyes followed my every gesture, every word, the subtlest changes in my moods, constantly keeping me on balance, bringing down my performance when it was too high, turning it up ever so slightly if it needed it. Without de Sica, I could not possibly have performed the part as I did. He gave me the confidence to go far beyond where I had ever gone before, into an area where I would not have dreamed to venture. Thanks to his support, I even dared to play certain key moments out of control, as a skier will throw all restraint to the winds in order to achieve a new mark.

Before I made *Two Women*, I had been a performer. Afterward, I was an actress.

Carlo and I lived a strange life in Rome. We were constantly under surveillance and we had to invent an absurd existence in order to avoid being clapped in jail as public sinners—a move that the public prosecutor seemed eager to make. So our life was an exercise in studied confusion. Some nights we stayed in my mother's apartment. We regularly changed the apartments we rented, often renting them under assumed names. Sometimes we stayed overnight with friends. When we were invited to dinner, we always arrived and left separately, or with a group of guests. Of course, we never appeared together in public. It was a silly and strenuous way of life, but I must confess that the cops-and-robbers aspect of it made it rather exciting. We were like two lovers trying to avoid a murderously jealous husband. Whatever the cost, it was worth it, for we were back in Rome, exiles no longer, and I loved the city and being among my friends more than ever before.

However, the prospects for a marriage with Carlo were still bleak. The criminal charges against us had not been dismissed. Carlo was still technically married to his first wife. Carlo's lawyers were stymied. Six years had passed since Carlo had given me that fateful diamond ring during the filming of *Woman of the River*. It was a riddle without solution.

I begged my sister not to marry Romano Mussolini. I had nothing against the name. As far as I am concerned, the sins of the father are certainly not visited upon the son. No, it wasn't that. What bothered me was the fact that, knowing Maria as I do, I was convinced that she needed a stronger and more resourceful man than her husband. Romano was a very talented jazz pianist whom Maria had met at a jazz festival, and I suppose it was music that attracted her to him.

I found him to be a man filled with complexes and inhibitions, probably because of his past and his name. I considered him not at all the right man for Maria. I told her so when she asked me how I liked him.

But Maria disregarded what I had to say. She was set on this marriage and nothing could dissuade her. However, one good thing did result from her insistence: I got to meet Rachele Mussolini, Mussolini's wife all through his years as dictator of Italy. She lived alone in a small town in the north of Italy. She was one of the most beautiful and extraordinary women I had ever met. Frail, white hair, scintillating blue eyes, she was at first wary of me—fancy movie star arriving in expensive automobile—but by the time I left she had completely accepted me. In fact, she invited me to stay for lunch and the two of us had a wonderful time cooking pasta and veal in her kitchen.

Despite her age, she was full of life and energy, very intelligent and intuitive, interested in what she could do for other people, willing to fight for what she believed in. She referred to her husband as "Il Duce," but other than to say that he had been influenced by evil people, she offered no apologies for him. In her private chapel, she had interred some of Mussolini's remains. She loved him with a great and enduring ardor, and the way she talked about him was the talk of a woman still in love. I found her not at all Fascist, in fact still a socialist, as she was when she first met Mussolini.

My admiration for her was boundless. Her husband had been killed at the side of his mistress, Clara Petacci. He had spent his last night with her, and the two of them had been lured from their room at dawn and machine-gunned to death, with Clara throwing

herself in front of him, futilely trying to absorb his
bullets. And yet Rachele had no rankle toward him
because he preferred his mistress. Only love. She still
loved him for whatever it was that he brought to her
life. No one can love more than that, I thought. I
looked up at her lovely white head bent over her plate,
almost in an attitude of prayer. I was in awe of her.
She lived alone, a spare, impecunious life; the only
legacy she got from her husband, I thought, is a bur-
densome name—and yet she is consumed with love for
him.

~~~~~~~~~~

Sophia's sister, Maria

Sophia tried to discourage me from marrying Romano Mussolini by asking me questions: Is he a strong
person who can give you the things you need? Is he
not selfish and too interested in his own life? Have you
thought about what you want in a husband and if he
will be that man?

Actually there were two reasons I married Romano,
neither of which had anything to do with him. The
first was that I fell in love with his mother. She was
one of the most remarkable women I had ever met,
and from the first day I met her in her little Forlì
farmhouse which smelled of freshly baked cakes, with
strands of fettucine hanging to dry in front of the fire,
we hit it off famously. I love babies and old people,
and Rachele Mussolini was the most fascinating elderly woman I had ever met. She was wise and compassionate and considerate. She told me, "This will always be your house. No matter if you are married to
Romano or not, this is your house."

As for Romano, he was the weak, ungiving man of
Sophia's questions. He was even in love with another
woman when he married me. But I was very young,
and what mattered to me more than anything else was
that a man wanted to give me his name. The fact that

a man existed in the world who wanted to take me into a church and give me his name before God, overshadowed everything else. Also, Sophia at that very time was in deep trouble with the church and the public prosecutor. The name Ponti, which she had acquired in her Mexican marriage, had been stripped away from her. As illegitimate children we had dreamed of the day we would be married and have proper names of our own. But now Sophia had been publicly humiliated, the joy of being Mrs. Ponti having turned into the ashes of the Vatican's denunciation of her as a "public sinner." You can imagine what a grim ordeal this was for a woman who had suffered the painful arrows of illegitimacy as a child. I suppose, in a strange way, that I married Romano Mussolini as much to prove something for Sophia as I did for myself.

Maria's marriage to Romano was a circus. More than five thousand people jammed into the church in Predappio and spilled over into the piazza. It was ghastly. Paparazzi were everywhere, even snapping their pictures of the church altar. I'm told that while trying to force his way through the packed church to reach the altar, Romano fainted and had to be revived by a doctor. That very well might have happened, although I didn't see it. Or much of anything else. All through the ceremony a wall of snapping cameras in front of my face kept me from seeing anything. Nor did I hear very much. The noise of the paparazzi jostling for position, plus the noise generated by the people outside trying to get into the church, virtually obliterated the words of the ceremony. Afterward, I barely managed to force my way through the mob to get to my car. Going to the reception was out of the question. I told my driver to drive directly back to Rome. As he hurriedly pulled away from the church, he collided with a young man on a Vespa. It was a dreadful accident. The young man was killed outright.

It took me a long time to recover from the terrible effects of that day.

Maria's marriage with Romano lasted just long enough to produce two children. I'm sorry to say that my instincts about him had been right. He was a man who continued to live his life as he had before he was married. A married bachelor. Most Italian men are. In general, Italian women marry completely, Italian men only to the extent that it suits them. It suited Romano very little. He played with his jazz band and ran with the jazz crowd, and after a few years the marriage fell of its own dead weight.

When I first heard that I had been nominated for an Oscar for my role in *Two Women*, I ecstatically announced that I would attend the Academy Awards ceremony in Hollywood. I felt that just being nominated was an honor in itself and a rare one at that for an Italian-speaking actress in an Italian film. But then, upon reflection, I changed my mind. My competition was formidable: Audrey Hepburn in *Breakfast at Tiffany's*; Piper Laurie in *The Hustler*; Geraldine Page in *Summer and Smoke*; Natalie Wood in *Splendor in the Grass*. Besides the formidable opposition, the plain fact was that in its long history, an Academy Award had never been given to an actor or actress in a foreign-language film. Anna Magnani had won it, but for *The Rose Tattoo*, an American production in English.

So I decided that I could not bear the ordeal of sitting in plain view of millions of viewers while my fate was being judged. If I lost, I might faint from disappointment; if I won, I would also very likely faint with joy. Instead of spreading my fainting all over the world, I decided it was better that I faint at home.

I honestly had no real expectation of winning. But nevertheless, hope being the eternal rogue that it is, on the night of the Awards I was too nervous to sleep. The photographer Pier Luigi came to our Rome apartment to keep the vigil with me. At three o'clock in the morning (6 P.M. Hollywood time) I tried going to bed, but my eyes would not close and my heart would not stop pounding, so I went back to the living room to talk to Pier. There was no coverage of the Awards on Italian television or radio. By six o'clock I knew that the ceremony was over and I had not won. Pier Luigi bestowed his condolences upon me and I went to bed. At six forty-five the phone rang. It was Cary Grant.

"Darling," he said, "do you know?"

"Know what?"

"You won! You won the Oscar for best actress! I'm so glad I'm the first to tell you."

I didn't faint, but I went rather giddy. It was incontestably the greatest thrill of my life.

I know that some actors have recently deprecated the value and purpose of an Academy Award, but I'm certainly not one of them. As far as I am concerned, if you are a professional actor who has pride in his work, then the judgment of your peers should be important to you. I treasure each and every award I have ever received—and my Oscar is in a place of honor. It was stolen several years ago from the Villa Marino by thieves who must have thought it was solid gold. I sent the Academy sixty dollars and they mailed me a replacement.

Sophia's mother

In our relationship, Sophia is the mother and I am the daughter. She phones me regularly to keep tabs on me. When I'm not tranquil, she will try to steady me. My periods of loneliness, she reassures me. What a marvelous daughter she is! Such humanity. She has a sweetness I don't have. An understanding heart I don't have. A tranquillity. I have many shortcomings: I am too outspoken, too angry, not reflective. But that is how I survived, and Sophia understands that. I have no friends. I'm a strange character. Everything that I dreamed of for myself has happened to Sophia. I live in her image.

When we first went to Rome for her career, I knew not a soul, not a single person, but I made her keep at it. I took her everywhere. I devoted my life to her career. People in films used to call me "the Marshal" because I always had her in tow. It was not possible for me to help Maria with her singing career because I gave all of myself to Sophia and there was nothing left in me to help Maria.

But I have been compensated for all I did for Sophia, because everything that happens to Sophia happens to me. I am Sophia. When the Oscar was given for *Two Women*, it was given to me. The applause was mine. I was fulfilled. The night of the Academy Awards, Sophia had told me to wait by the telephone. I did. Early in the morning, she called with the news that she had won. I ran over to her house. The living room was ablaze with lights, television cameras, microphones, reporters, and I felt they were there for me. That's because Sophia had made me such a part of her career. Everything that I wanted for myself happened to Sophia. I live in her reflection, and it makes me happy.

My mother is tormented with the thought that she lost out on a movie career because she was not allowed to go to Hollywood when she won the Greta Garbo contest. I doubt, though, that she would have had the patience, the concentration, the passion for being a movie actress that one must have to succeed. Nor would she have *loved* acting the way I do. So she has lived her movie career through me, and I owe her a great deal, for in the beginning she gave me strength I didn't have on my own. She was my mouth when I was too shy to speak, my legs when I was too withdrawn to step forward, and my courage all those times when I was turned away without hope.

I have inherited some of her characteristics—especially her frequent changes of mood—but the difference between us is that she gives vent to all these moods, letting everyone know exactly how she feels at any particular moment (even to the point of telling people whom she doesn't like why she doesn't like them), whereas I have come to realize that if I showed all my moods the way she does the people I work with and live with would go crazy. What I do, therefore, is to make a mask of my face that hides what goes on underneath. I had to teach myself to do this, and at first it wasn't easy, but by now it's second nature and it has made my life much easier.

My mother and Carlo are about the same age, which, when I think about it, does make me feel a little strange. I don't really know how they feel about each other because they don't exchange two words when they are together; they seem a little uncomfortable with each other. Perhaps that's because my mother has never lived with us, or because Carlo is basically such an introvert. But I do know, from their comments to me, that they respect one another, and that's what counts.

Sophia's sister, Maria

I love to sing. Since I was five years old, people have responded to my voice and my personality, but I simply was not destined to have a career as a singer. I tried in Italy, singing American and Neapolitan songs, which I adore because Neapolitan songs are so full of feeling and marvelous words.

I had a chance at a career in America, but I simply could not grasp the opportunity. When I was in Hollywood with Sophia, she took me to a party one night and Frank Sinatra was there. I had met him in Spain during the filming of *The Pride and the Passion* and he had been very nice and friendly to me. At the party, I drank some champagne—I rarely drink, but when I do, it dissolves my inhibitions. Sinatra was asked to sing, which he did, and you know who went right up and joined him? That's right—me! Afterward, I could not believe that I had intruded my voice on Sinatra's. But Frank was very nice about it, and even encouraged me, and we sang several songs together for the guests. The next day he told Sophia that I had the makings of a first-rate professional singer and that he wanted to sponsor me. He found a very good voice coach for me and would have taken me under his wing, but unfortunately I was homesick. Italians, especially Neapolitans, get homesick very easily. My mother was writing me letters from Rome, urging me to return, so that was part of it but, more seriously, I am a person who is always in love, who *must* be in love, but in Hollywood I was not in love. And that made me miserable.

So I gave up my Sinatra-sponsored career and returned to Rome, where I promptly fell in love and got married.

But looking back on it, I really don't think I have a strong enough resolve in my character to sustain a professional career. I have seen what Sophia has gone through, what reverses, what sacrifices, what self-belief, what determination and concentration, the way she has struggled to attain her stardom, and the way she has fought to protect her privacy, and I honestly must admit I do not have those fires burning in me. An artist is a very special, dedicated person. Talent is not enough. Talent is only a rough diamond. The artist polishes it and cuts it and mounts it and refracts it in the light, and this calls for enormous confidence and resolve and dedication.

But in attaining her success, Sophia did not lose sight of the fact that both her mother and her sister had given up on possible careers; so to compensate for that, Sophia made my mother and me a part of everything she did. She took me with her to her movie locations, let me in on her secrets and dreams and disappointments—making me a part of her developing life, with the result that I was so identified with Sophia's career that on the night when she won the Oscar, I felt that it had been awarded to me.

~~~~~~

The phone rang. It was Carlo. "Did you hear about Marilyn Monroe?" he asked.

"No," I said.

There was a pause. "She's been very ill," he said. Carlo knew that I had an enormous admiration for Marilyn, that I adored her like a sister even though I had never met her. I identified with her. Perhaps because we both rose from ashes. "It may be fatal," Carlo said.

"Why are you calling to tell me this? What is it, Carlo?"

Carlo hates to upset me with bad news, and when he has to he always discloses it cautiously. He knew that I would take this news hard. "Well, to tell you the truth," he said, "she is dead."

"Oh, God."

Marilyn is dead. I knew her from all that I had read, from her film performances, from the stills and the pinups. Joe DiMaggio, an athlete, Arthur Miller, an intellectual, and the many rumors about all the others. But for a long time she had been alone, and I believe it was that loneliness that guided her hand to suicide. Maybe waiting for a lover who didn't arrive. Maybe desperate to be loved but no one even to expect. I thought about her, lying white-faced and dead in her lonely bed, and I wept for her. She was not at all what she had pretended to be.

And the sexy stills were mostly put-ons. Except for one series of stills I saw of her that were taken on a California beach. No makeup, no attempt to be a sex object, just simple pictures—she was truly beautiful; but the loneliness is there in her face. I think Marilyn was lonely from the day she was born until the day she died. Many people believe that she was obsessed with growing old and that that motivated her suicide.

I don't believe that. I believe she took her life because she could no longer endure the agony of being friendless and isolated. Without hope. The world had drained the life out of her. The leeching of the press, the men who stole her emotions without giving anything for them, and the insistent demand that she be the world's sex goddess. To oblige, she pretended sexiness all the time, but she didn't have to, because she generated sexiness without pretense; but she didn't know that.

I think the quality of sexiness comes from within. People have always considered me a sex symbol, but in playing those roles that conveyed that impression, I never once deliberately said to myself, Now, Sophia, play this real sexy, really set them on fire. I could not tell you what I did that made a particular role sexy; I simply played the character as I imagined her to be. I believe that if you play sexiness deliberately, the audience senses the phoniness and doesn't like it. It is something that is in you or it isn't and it really doesn't have much to do with breasts or thighs or the pout of your lips. Marilyn had great talent plus the fact that she had a natural, contagious sexiness. Nobody can teach an actress to be sexy, to play a scene sexy. Jayne Mansfield was a case in point. She had a good body but at best she was a caricature of Marilyn. And of sexiness.

On the screen, my fantasy provides me with the emotions a scene demands. If I am called upon to excite a man, then at that moment I am truly trying to excite him, not with tricks and invented business, but with whatever God gave me to arouse a man with. In *A Special Day*, there is a climactic scene in which I seduce Mastroianni, who plays the role of a homosexual. I prepared my fantasy for that scene for weeks prior to shooting it. When the camera finally turned, I was really and truly that housewife making aggressive love to the passive man Mastroianni was playing. No fakery; in my mind, I was completely that woman having sexual intercourse at that moment.

I don't think Marilyn had this kind of introspection about what she did, but instinctively she performed honestly. But she didn't seem to get joy from her work, or much joy from anything else. If, at seventeen, she had found a father, as I found Carlo, I think that would have been her salvation. In the end she was so lonely, so deserted, so bereft of a connection with life, that she chose the ultimate escape. She was my sister, and I wish I could have known her and brought friendship into her life. But on that day in Rome she was tragically dead. So I sat in the dark and wept for her, my tears a memorial to this woman I had so much admired.

Fourteen

For the comedy *Yesterday, Today and Tomorrow,* de Sica wanted me to do a striptease, so sexy, so arousing, so provocative, it would make a man howl.

"But, Vittorio, I've never even *seen* a striptease."

"Don't worry. You will do a striptease that will put all other stripteases to shame. First, I will get you a professor of striptease, then, between us, we will create a routine that will melt Mastroianni into a puddle of hot flesh."

De Sica's professor turned out to be the man who staged the numbers for the exotic ladies of the Crazy Horse Saloon. I had three or four sessions with him to learn the basic moves, struts, and teases. But then, using these routines, I had to mold them, with de Sica's help, into a striptease dance that was my own personal interpretation of how to excite my male audience of one.

On the day of the take, I was extremely nervous. In fact, I had been nervous for a week just contemplating this moment. The scene was my bedroom. My audience was a fully clothed Mastroianni stretched out on the bed. I asked de Sica to clear the set (a rare request on my part) except for the cameramen behind the two cameras which were recording the scene. Rhythmic music flooded the set from a record player. I smiled at Mastroianni. He smiled at me. And then I let him have it. Slowly, sensuously, tantalizingly, I removed my clothes, letting each article dangle provocatively in front of his eyes while my body undulated to the throbbing music. When I got down to my silk stockings, which I peeled off my legs in a graceful, languid manner, Marcello began to howl, braying at the ceiling like a lovesick coyote.

De Sica caught it all—the interplay, the timing, the sexiness, the carnal thunder my tease set off in Marcello. No scene ever gave me more pleasure. Marcello and I had finally found a script that let us open up, with insouciant, Neapolitan give-and-take. And Carlo had another script lined up for us that would give us even more opportunity to strut our stuff—*Marriage, Italian Style*—but abruptly, inexplicably, the euphoria of the film was snatched away from me. God knows I wasn't prepared for it.

Yesterday, Today and Tomorrow was composed of three segments, the first of which we shot in Rome, the second in Naples, the third in Milan. While I was doing the Naples section, I began to feel strange, not at all like myself. After several days of mounting concern, it finally occurred to me that I might be pregnant. I consulted a local doctor, who took tests which he said were negative. But my feeling persisted, so I asked a physician to come down from Rome. He came to my apartment in Naples bearing a frog he had brought with him from Rome. He injected my urine into the frog and we both watched anxiously for the result. If the frog dropped dead, I was pregnant—at least that's what the doctor said—and if the injection didn't faze the frog, then I was not.

After a little while, the frog began to act a bit strange. He listed to one side, and then to the other, and he appeared to be in a state of dizziness. When he jumped, he lost his equilibrium. But he did not die. After a few hours of frog observation, with the frog getting no nearer to the grave, the doctor solemnly announced that I might be pregnant—and then again I might not.

I thanked him and bade him good-bye. Afterward I took a walk and released the poor frog into a little pond.

That night I prayed that I was pregnant. Oh, God, please let me be pregnant. Please, God, I really want a baby. I am twenty-nine and it is high time for me to be pregnant.

My prayers were answered. Shortly before our shooting schedule ended in Naples, it was officially confirmed that I was indeed pregnant. It was a moment of great joy for me. The fact that Carlo and I were not married didn't bother me at all. If it worsened our situation, so be it. All that mattered to me was that I had Carlo's child in my belly. For years I had felt a strong, insistent desire within me to have children. When Carlo and I first started our relationship, I would talk to him about having children. I was just starting my career then and he was married, but that made no difference to me. I would have raised a child by myself. Of course, when a woman is sixteen, or even nineteen, she has no understanding of what it means to have a child, no understanding of the responsibility a child brings. When you are young it is easy to conceive a child and give birth to it, but it took Carlo's forceful advice to impress upon me the realities of raising a child. It certainly would have been wrong for us to have a child early in our relationship.

But by the time we went to Hollywood, our relation was better defined, so I was no longer careful about becoming pregnant. But I was making four pictures a year, working hard, so I had little time to brood about the fact that I had not become pregnant.

When we returned to Italy, my urge to be pregnant intensified. The actress part of me was happy and fulfilled, but the other half of me, the Neapolitan, childbearing, Mother Earth half of me, was fiercely unsatisfied. At twenty-nine, I had become obsessive about turning thirty without having produced a child. I think thirty is the big turning point in a woman's life, not forty, as many people think, because by the time a woman is forty she has formulated, more or less, her life plan. But at thirty, you feel suddenly old, although you are not old, and there is upon you a chilling realization that you must then and there begin to fulfill your dreams or else they are likely to remain just that—dreams. Every woman I've known has experienced a certain fear at turning thirty. If she is not married, then on her birthday she is a self-ordained spinster. If she is childless, she fears that she will be forever barren. I had never known a woman who happily greeted her thirtieth year, but it looked as if I was going to be the exception.

But, curiously, even when I was reveling in my pregnancy, I felt something was not quite right. Something about how I felt, a few little physical reactions, worried me. I didn't mention anything to Carlo, who shared my happiness over my pregnancy, but by the time we were finished with the Naples segment, I was deeply concerned over my condition. I knew that it was not normal for a pregnant woman to have the symptoms I was experiencing. So I went to Rome by car and saw my gynecologist. After examining me, he said I should spend two or three days in bed, after which I would be all right and could go to Milan to film the third and last segment of the film. But he cautioned me to be careful, to go to Milan by train so as to avoid the bumpiness of an automobile ride. I did go by train, but the trouble with his advice was that most of the Milan segment was to be shot with Marcello and me inside an automobile that would be mounted on a mechanically powered cradle, which bumps around much more than an automobile on a highway.

But my pregnancy never even got that far; it didn't even survive the start of the filming. The first night in Milan, I experienced great pain. Carlo wanted to keep my pregnancy a secret, because the press would have made so much out of it, so he called a local doctor to our hotel. The doctor gave me an injection, said that everything was going to be all right but that I must stay in bed and not work for the time being. De Sica, who was directing the film, came to see me; we were much too close for me not to tell him the truth. He knew how much I yearned for a baby; my anxiety over the possible loss of my baby upset him very much and brought tears to his eyes.

That night the pain suddenly intensified and I told the nurse, whom Carlo had hired to stay with me, that I had to go to the hospital immediately. She started to call an ambulance; although I could barely stand up, I insisted that we go by car so as not to attract attention. I just barely managed going down in the elevator, and I almost passed out getting into the automobile. At the hospital I was rushed to an emergency room, but I knew that my situation was hopeless, that the baby was gone and there was nothing anyone could do.

~~~~~~~

Sophia's sister, Maria

I went to Sophia as soon as she called from Milan. I went straight to the maternity floor of the hospital. The sound of crying babies filled the corridor. On every door there was a pink or blue ribbon—except hers. I went in. She was lying in bed, crying. I closed the door to shut out the sound of the babies but their cries came through the door anyway.

Sophia talked about adoption. She was terribly dispirited. There was no hope in her. I told her to be patient. To have faith. That she mustn't adopt until the feeling of motherhood had entirely left her. I don't know whether she was listening to me. Her grief was enormous. But I was sure she still had a deep desire to be a mother.

~~~~~~~

The doctor came the following day and performed a curettage, and the day after that I went back to work. Carlo, as shaken and depressed as I was, asked me to keep the whole thing a secret. I felt as if I had been physically beaten. As soon as I came on the set, Mastroianni came up to me and said, "What's with you? You look very strange." I tried to smile, and I gave him a little Neapolitan shrug.

"Now, don't fool around," he said. "Tell me what happened."

There was no way to pretend anything with Marcello. We knew each other much too well for that. So I said, "Well, I had a baby, and I lost it." I felt relieved to be able to tell someone. Marcello didn't say a word. He looked at me and then he turned and walked away. He never again mentioned it.

I worked every day, full days, and we finished the film on schedule. I had constant pain, but my physical pain was nothing compared to the pain in my heart. In all my years, I had never doubted myself. I had faced discouraging obstacles but always with a certain will, a confidence that I could overcome them. But now, facing the fact that for no apparent reason I had lost a baby that was three and a half months old, I felt a twinge of doubt about myself. What if I could not bear a child? What then?

Fifteen

There are certain moments which sparkle in memory.

"You are wanted on the telephone, Miss Loren. Mr. Charles Chaplin is calling." Charlie Chaplin? Me? The patron saint of laughter from my girlhood. As remote as a pinpoint star in the black sky over the Teatro Sacchino. Those dark, joyless days into which dropped the funny flares of Charlie on roller skates, running from policemen, wiggling his mustache and twirling his cane, eating shoelaces like spaghetti, making the tattered children of Pozzuoli laugh. For me, a demigod.

Now he stands at the door of my rented cottage near Ascot, and rings the bell. I am so nervous my throat is dry and the muscles of my face are frozen. He bears flowers in one hand and a script in the other. He is as shy as I am. And just about as nervous. He reads the script to me, performing all the parts. It is only a rough draft, but he would like me to know what it's about. I do not hear a word of it. I am captivated by his performance. I would do this film if what he was reading were the London telephone directory.

A Countess from Hong Kong had been in his desk drawer for twenty years. I heard tell that he had originally written it for Paulette Goddard, and that he had gotten it out and updated it after he saw me in *Yesterday, Today and Tomorrow*. To be directed by Charlie Chaplin—I would never have even dreamed it.

When Charlie had a finished script he invited me

153

and Marlon Brando, whom he had cast in the male lead, to his house in Vevey, Switzerland, for a reading. His wife, Oona, daughter of Eugene O'Neill, an exquisite woman, gracious and beatific, was there, as was Charlie's son, Sydney, who also had a part in the film. Charlie seated us comfortably and read the script in its entirety, again acting all the parts, playing my role coquettishly, then switching abruptly to the stern, befuddled American consul whom Brando was to play. Charlie even went to the piano and played a song he had composed for the film.

Through it all, Brando was half asleep, or pretended to be, his head down on his chest, his eyes closed. Charlie paid him no mind, and didn't seem the least bothered, but I found Marlon's behavior terribly embarrassing. This was Charlie's first film in almost ten years, a terribly important event for him, and Brando slept.

Marlon's behavior that night was simply a portent of his performance in the film. I liked Marlon, and still do, and I admired him enormously as one of the greatest actors who had ever performed in films, but he was obviously better suited to dramatic roles than to comedy. In all fairness, he was certainly not suited to the role he was asked to play in *Countess;* uncomfortable in it, he gave up on it soon after we started. He didn't feel right in the character's skin—that can happen, and to make matters worse, he and Charlie did not get along. There was no chemistry between them, no interplay, no carefree climate to encourage the inspiration and invention that comedy needs; they often knocked heads, and day by day the atmosphere on the set grew more tense. Marlon gave an interview in which he said, "Charlie's not a verbal man. Words at times are his bitterest enemy." Charlie's method of direction, like de Sica's, was not so much to explain as to demonstrate. As a superb actor, Charlie could much better convey his intentions by acting them out, and in a few moments achieve what another director would less ably describe with a torrent of words.

As for myself, I adored Charlie. I truly loved him. We saw each other often, even after the film was finished. He spent long evenings reminiscing wonderfully, especially about his boyhood in London. He knew about my beginnings: the slums of London and the slums of Pozzuoli had a lot in common. "I wouldn't want to go through all that suffering and unhappiness again," he once told me, "yet I wouldn't want it to have been any other way. I think of going back to the smell of cabbages and beans, and I could weep with nostalgia." When he said that, I could smell my own girlhood aromas of cheap white beans and pasta, and I shared his nostalgia.

He told me about his young years spent in a London workhouse, his head shaved for ringworm, his mother in an insane asylum; about his boyhood dreams. "Be careful what you wish for," he said, "because you are sure to get it." Then, speaking of his ambition, "It is desire that creates something desirable. But if the world and I don't get along together, then the world must change." I don't think he was being egotistical; I think he meant that conformity is undesirable for the artist, who must be true to himself and only himself. "Every art," he said, "contributes to the biggest art of all—the art of living."

I was often stimulated by his homespun wisdom. "Do not fear a confrontation," he told me at dinner one evening. "Even when planets collide, out of the chaos comes the birth of a star." He introduced me to one of the greatest delicacies I have ever eaten: a potato baked in a wrapping of aluminum foil, and then buttered, covered with caviar, and eaten accompanied by ice-cold vodka.

During one of our discussions, I confessed to him that I enjoyed solitude. "Well," he said, "when you are alone you are in good company." I told him how much I admired the love that he and Oona had for each other. So unselfish. So deep. "One of the things I have found out, Sophia," he said, "is that you have to have had meaningful experiences in life before you can truly love." He also said, "As I get older, the more I see, the more I don't want to see." On one occasion, when guests asked him to play the piano, he refused, and afterward I asked him why, in the presence of a group, he became so shy, pointing out that I was the same way. "But why wouldn't you play for your friends?" At first he didn't answer me, and then he said, "I get shy when I don't know how to do something very well."

The last time I saw him, he had some gentle advice for me. "You have one failing you must overcome, one thing you must learn if you are to be a completely happy woman, maybe the most important lesson in living: you must learn to say no. You do not know how to say no, Sophia, and that is a serious deficiency. It was very difficult for me, too, but once I learned to say no, life became much easier."

He was right, of course. It is certainly a serious failing on my part. But I don't want to upset people. I don't like to disappoint. If I were to force myself to say no, it would be harsh and unnatural. I must somehow make it a part of my nature. As it is, I only say no when I have turned a thing over and over and have developed a strong feeling that has swept away all doubt. Then nothing can deter my decision. Until then, I have great patience, I make compromises; when finally I do come to a decision, I can be very dangerous. If only I could make those decisions sooner. If only no came easier to me. That's what Charlie was saying.

The movie didn't do very well. The critics called it old-fashioned, the box office was poor, and the movie's failure was heartbreaking for Charlie. It was his last film. Perhaps it if had succeeded, he would have made more. As far as I was concerned, what I learned from him as a director, and as a man, made the experience, for me, a triumph.

And now he is gone. There will never be another like him. I carry his words of wisdom in me, and often listen to them, as a miser takes out his gold and counts it.

In a moment of melancholy, if I close my eyes I see Charlie walking away, as in his films, twirling his cane, with feet splayed apart and his bowler hat perched on his head, the image slowly receding into the distance.

Sixteen

Of all people, it was Carlo's wife who at last found a solution for our troubles over the Mexican divorce and marriage. The bigamy prosecution was still active, but nevertheless, Carlo and I had risked a resumption of living together in Rome; there was no hope, however, that in the face of the Vatican's condemnation we could ever find a solution in Italy. For eight years we had been bigamist and concubine, and it looked as if we were going to be eternally condemned to that fate.

Carlo's wife, Giuliana, proved to be a better lawyer than all of Carlo's high-powered attorneys. Her solution was simple: move to France and apply for French citizenship. Once that was achieved, then as French citizens she and Carlo could be divorced, thereby enabling Carlo to marry me (a Frenchwoman) without fear of political or religious persecution.

We did just that. And with a flourish. By government decree, Carlo and I were invested with French citizenship as a way to honor us for our contributions to the cinema art of France. Giuliana Fiastri, who had automatically become a French citizen by virtue of her marriage to Carlo, was granted a divorce on the grounds of adultery, and Carlo and I set our wedding day in April, 1966. We were determined to make the wedding ceremony as private as possible. Despite the fact that we had an apartment on the Avenue George V, Carlo engaged a large suite in the Lancaster Hotel and stayed there by himself on the night before the wedding. He had arranged for the ceremony to be performed by the mayor of Sèvres, a Paris suburb. The mayor had been sworn to secrecy. We phoned my sister in Rome, and Basilio in Cannes, and told them to come to Paris as secretly as they could.

I was in London doing *A Countess from Hong Kong* at the time; Oona was the only person I told about going to Paris to get married. I trusted her completely and I wanted to share my happiness with her. I spent the eve of my wedding at a friend's house in Paris. We were confident that our subterfuge was succeeding, but the next morning, when it was time to leave for the wedding, I looked out the window and saw a photographer outside the front entrance. I knew we had to act fast if we were going to preserve our privacy. My friend was as tall as I, so I suggested that she put on my coat, scarf, and dark glasses, and rush out to the chauffeured car that was waiting. I would leave five minutes later with my friend's husband, who would drive me to Sèvres in his car.

The ruse worked. The photographer dashed after my friend, and the only outsider present at our wedding was a photographer friend whom I had invited to take pictures for our family album. It was not the wedding of my dreams, with a white gown of old lace and a long train like the one Edith Head had designed for *Houseboat*, but I felt quite all right in the yellow dress and coat I wore, set off by a small bouquet of lilies of the valley.

The ceremony was simple and brief. Strangely, it was both meaningful and meaningless. To be finally married after eight years of struggle and abuse, certainly had importance, but standing there, as the bride, I couldn't help but feel that Carlo and I had been married a long time. Our marriage was like reading a newspaper account of an event that had occurred in the distant past.

I phoned my mother in Rome to tell her the good news (she wasn't at the wedding because she refuses to go up in an airplane). "Well, Mammina, you were always pessimistic but it's happened. We are Mr. and Mrs. Carlo Ponti."

"Ah, yes," she replied, "but not in white, and not in the church."

My mother only sees the dark side of the moon.

Moscow Film Festival. Best actress award for *Marriage, Italian Style*. Our film was presented in a theater that seated six thousand people, the biggest movie audience I had ever seen anywhere. The film was presented in Italian but without subtitles. The sound track was kept low and an interpreter, standing beside the screen, spoke all the dialogue in Russian. That's the Russian method; they rarely use subtitles.

I had anticipated little or no recognition on the Moscow streets; movie stars, I had thought, were deprecated and ridiculed as figments of the sick Western culture. To my surprise, though, I found Moscow fans just as ardent, as star-struck, as movie-oriented as they are anywhere else. I was in Russia another time, to make the movie *Sunflower* with Mastroianni, and both times people on the street reacted with greetings, and with that special surprise and happiness that appear on people's faces when they see someone from the screen in the flesh. Russians do not request autographs very often; they are much more inclined to present flowers, or an offering of fruit or candy in appreciation of what you have brought to their lives. They put you on a pedestal and look upon you as a demideity of some exalted order.

It seems to me that adoration of a hero figure is universally as basic as hunger. Muscovites do not have access to fan magazines and they are not reached by the Hollywood publicity mills, but they are just as affected by the superstar personality cult; they share the universal need to escape from drabness. As I always do, I tried very hard to keep my feet on the ground. I feel uncomfortable on a pedestal (I'm afraid of heights), or anywhere other than on terra firma along with everyone else. I think people who meet me feel that, feel that I am one of them, a member of their family who has returned after a long absence. I personally answer all my fan mail, and not with a form. Otherwise I would feel that I was cheating the people who care enough about me to sit down and write me a letter. I get hundreds of letters a week; it sometimes takes an entire weekend just to autograph and send off photographs which have been requested. But I accept that as part of my existence. Just as I accept the fact that I am a prisoner of press photographers.

However, I do not share the sentiments of celebrities who proclaim that the price of fame is too high, and publicly yearn for their days as unknowns. They are either lying or pretending modesty. For is not recognition, fame, success—call it what you will—what we strive for when we begin a cinema career? Although we resent their intrusion into our private lives, we owe a great deal to the people who go to see our pictures, and who put us on our pedestal, expose us to the world, and rob us of our secrets. It's true that loss of privacy is a painful price to pay for our success, but it would be more painful if an appearance in public did not arouse a response from the people who come in contact with us.

Sometimes popularity can have frightening repercussions. A few years ago, when we were still living at the Villa Marino outside Rome, a madman suddenly appeared on the grounds, holding an ax over his head and shouting for my son Carlo. The man assaulted the front door with his ax, chopped it apart and came storming into the house. It was one of the most terrifying experiences of my life. The man had escaped from an insane asylum. Apparently I had once given him an autograph, and now he was loudly proclaiming that he had had sex with me and that Carlo, Jr., was his son, not Carlo's, and demanded that we hand him over. He was finally calmed down and gave up his ax without too much of a struggle. He had been in and out of a dozen asylums. He writes me letters all the time. While we lived in Rome, we had to keep close tabs on his whereabouts.

This kind of incident, for movie people, is not as unusual as it sounds. I get some rather terrible mail, some threatening, some pornographic, and the predictable gamut of deranged phone calls, often at three or four in the morning. My policy now is to throw away unsigned letters without reading them, and to disconnect the phone as soon as the sick telephone calls begin.

So publicity is a tiger, as they say, easy to jump on but very hard to ride; a loss of privacy is the price of the ride. But if you have a giving nature, as I have, there are some unusual compensations in being a public figure. I have been able to reach out and to help people by investing them with the special attention that is the prerogative of those of us on the pedestals. For instance, there was the time when a priest whom I knew came to me and told me about a little nine-year-old boy named Paolo who had a serious heart condition. He was not expected to live much longer. "I know you have met Dr. Christiaan Barnard," the priest said. "Perhaps he could do something to save this boy's life."

I had been introduced to Dr. Barnard during one of his visits to Rome. Of course, I was enchanted to make his acquaintance. After the priest's visit, I phoned Dr. Barnard in South Africa and arranged for him to see Paolo. I then arranged for the boy's immediate flight to South Africa. He was having great difficulty breathing—a sickly, half-dead little boy who was half the size he should have been. I arranged for a bed to be installed on the airplane and for a nurse to travel with him. All this was made possible only because I was Sophia Loren. But I had made a pact with the priest that there was to be no mention of my name in connection with this project.

The boy was flown to South Africa, and after examining him, Dr. Barnard decided to attempt a heart operation he had never performed before. He later described it for me, but I do not have the kind of head that retains such details, although I do recall that the main artery to the heart had to be replaced with a plastic substitute because not enough blood was reaching the heart. After the operation, I telephoned Paolo many times while he was in the hospital, and each time his voice was a little stronger. But then came an unpleasant development: the priest, who had given me his word not to reveal my identity, gave a magazine interview which revealed that I was the mystery benefactor who had arranged for the operation. I suppose he meant well, but I was furious.

I saw Paolo when he returned. He had cast off the color of death and there was a glow of life in his eyes that hadn't been there before. Since then, over the years, he and his family send me messages and photos, and lately I heard from his mother that Paolo, who is a big, strapping youth of twenty now, is engaged to be married. The price of riding the tiger may be steep, but I don't mind paying it in exchange for the life and happiness of a Paolo.

I have digressed from my observations about Russia. One of the most unexpected surprises was the intensity of religious feelings I found among the people of the Ukraine while we were on location there. Virtually every home I visited had a little table with a white cloth on it, on which stood a sacred image with a candle burning beside it. I suppose both motion pictures and religion, in their different ways, inspire fantasy and belief, and that these are as basic to living as bread, wine, and political philosophy.

My last day in Moscow, an elderly woman shyly approached me as I emerged from my hotel. She spoke to me in Russian, which by then I somewhat understood, words of admiration and gratitude. She handed me a small etching. It was a scene of wild flowers, the colors softly faded with age, an etching which had probably been in her family a long time. I was very moved. I have received many awards and tributes but I don't think I ever felt more gratified than I was at that moment, receiving that exquisite little gift from an anonymous Russian woman.

Seventeen

While making a fairy tale called *Happily Ever After,*
a title which should have augured well for me, I discovered I was pregnant for the second time. I had
been feeling rather strange for several weeks, but
only toward the end of the filming did I have pregnancy tests made. I had been away from Carlo on
location for a long time and since I did not get pregnant easily, I regarded it as rather miraculous that I
had become pregnant again.

After my first miscarriage, my doctor had said that
my trouble was that I had been working too hard,
that I was fatigued and filled with the anxieties that
filming generates, and that that was what had caused
me to abort. "Some women can go on working after
pregnancy," the doctor had said, "but you are not one
of them. You lost the baby because you were so
active."

I went to another doctor, my sister's gynecologist.
Then pregnant with her second child, she swore by
him.

He looked at the test results and said, "I want you
to go right home, get into bed, and stay there."

"I haven't finished the picture I'm making."

"Do you want this baby? Then do as I say. You are
not to get out of bed. I don't want you to move at all.
The more quiet you are, the better your chances."

I went straight home and got into bed. I was not
going to make the same mistake I had made with my
first pregnancy. I phoned Carlo, who was producing
the film.

"Carlo, guess what. I'm pregnant."

"Oh, my God, no!"

"I feel rather strange, sort of the way I did the first time, but the doctor says I have a good chance if I stay in bed. So even though I have only three days left to complete the film, I can't finish it. Get a stand-in and do long shots that I'll dub in later—or whatever else, but there's no way that I'm going to move from this bed. *I am going to have this baby.*"

Carlo was not upset over the unfinished picture, but he said he had no confidence in that doctor and wanted me to get someone else. I felt, though, that by following orders I was going to be all right. I said I felt I could trust this doctor.

I stayed in that bed for three months, absolutely immobile. I didn't even risk sitting up to eat my meals, and taught myself a technique for eating flat on my back. I focused my mind on one thing and one thing alone: having this child. I didn't read, I didn't look at television or listen to the radio, I tried to talk as little as possible, I kept plugs in my ears to shut out any noise that might disturb me, I didn't take phone calls or read my mail. My mind was free of everything except this baby. I thought about my insides constantly, about what was happening to me. I didn't even dare touch my stomach for fear I would disturb something. I have never been in prison but surely no prison confinement could have been worse than those months in bed. I felt a constant uneasiness, an anxiety about my condition, despite my efforts to be tranquil. The doctor was giving me hormonal injections and telling me that everything was going along fine, but that inner voice of mine kept saying, "No, Sophia, it isn't. Look out."

Charlie Chaplin phoned and beseeched me to go to London for the gala premiere of *A Countess from Hong Kong*, but I begged off. Early in the morning, after the premiere, Brando called to say that I had been right not to have gone. "The critics," he said, "just destroyed all of us." He wished me well with my baby, told me not to worry and to take care of myself.

The night it happened, Carlo was in London. I was at our place outside Rome. It was snowing. Basilio was keeping me company. We were talking when abrupt, stabbing pains assailed my stomach. Basilio immediately called the doctor, and urged him to hurry out to see me. The doctor said not to worry, a visit wasn't necessary, nothing unusual was happening, but I knew better. In my condition I was not going to stay at our rather remote villa. Basilio wanted to call an ambulance but I didn't want to attract attention. A makeshift bed was arranged for me in the back of our car and somehow I managed to get down the stairs and to the hospital. I was having contractions every ten minutes, as if I were in labor. The pain was intense. Ines, my faithful Ines, was at my side. She is my secretary, but she is my sister, too.

When I arrived at the hospital I was rushed into the emergency room. My face had drained to a yellow color. My mother and the doctor were already there and Carlo was on his way. The doctor examined me and said, "It's just a little crisis, it will pass, you have nothing to worry about."

My mother was furious. "Don't say she has nothing to worry about because I know she is in trouble and you must do something!"

The doctor tried to calm my mother down but when she has worked up a full head of fury she is not easily managed. "Do you want her to die? Look at the way she suffers! Look at the color of her face! Her blood is draining out of her and you say not to worry! You must do something—you must!"

"Now, now, my good woman, calm down," the doctor said. "I have given her something for the pain and something strong to sleep and we will see what is going to happen. I am going to a dinner party now, but I will leave my number with the nurse, and in any event I will come back and see her when I leave the party."

"But she is having contractions. She is in false labor. She is having a miscarriage. Can't you give her something so she has it over with and the pain goes away?"

The doctor stiffened. "That is out of the question. It is against the law for us to interfere in any way. If she is going to miscarry, then she must do it naturally, no matter how long it takes or how painful it is. I shall return later."

And that was that. As the night wore on, the pains became unbearable, but suddenly, around 4 A.M., they ceased, and I could feel the life drain out of me. Ines called the doctor. She told him to come right away and not to say everything was all right because I had already had a miscarriage and I was hemorrhaging. The doctor eventually arrived and around six in the morning I was taken to the operating room and a curettage was performed on me for the second time.

Carlo had returned and was with me. My three and a half months of inactivity had left my legs so thin and weak I could barely stand. This was surely the lowest point of my life. And to make matters worse, while I was still on the operating table, a Rome newspaper already had a detailed account on their front page of how I lost my baby. This terrible moment of private grief, spread luridly before the eyes of the world.

"Well," I said to Carlo, trying to sound bright, "now I can finish those three scenes for *Happily Ever After*." Then I broke down and wept as despairingly as I had ever in my life wept before, and Carlo wept with me. We had lost something precious, a fatal irreplaceable loss, and we felt diminished by it.

Carlo Ponti

Sophia's miscarriages were the worst experiences of my life. The greatest shock I ever had was the first miscarriage. She had been so happy to be pregnant, I had felt so euphoric, and then this sudden, unexpected plunge into bleakness and dejection. For the first time I suffered a disillusionment about Sophia's unassailable control of her own destiny.

The second time was even worse. It wasn't as shocking as the first time, but it had a finality to it that drained me of words of encouragement, the ultimate in helplessness. The way Sophia suffered—I had never seen her in such agony, most of which was spiritual, not physical. After the first miscarriage, I had begged her to change doctors; even though her doctor was a famous professor I didn't trust him, but Sophia has a strong sense of allegiance and she wanted to give him another chance. All I could do was sit beside her hospital bed and hold her hand and feel her racking sobs pass through my body.

~~~~~~~~~~

Sophia's secretary, Ines Bruscia

I have worked for Carlo Ponti for twenty-eight years. At first, I was the script girl on the films he made in Rome, and I was there when Sophia, who was then fourteen or fifteen, came to make her first screen tests. She was serious, very grown-up, really not much different from what she is today. She had never before faced a camera but she had very good instincts about what to do, how to move, where the chalk marks were. She made an impression on me.

Then, in 1958, when Sophia was making *That Kind of Woman* in New York (I had left Ponti's employ temporarily and was living in New York), Ponti asked me to become Sophia's secretary. That was twenty years ago. I have devoted my life to Sophia and her family since then, and she has brought love and caring into mine; I consider it an even exchange. We have lived very closely. When she has suffered, I suffered, when she has triumphed, I was exalted. The worst times, by far, were the miscarriages. Her spirit and vitality disappeared. Her whole philosophy of living was damaged. After the second miscarriage,

the light in her eyes extinguished and I feared for her.
I think it hit Ponti just as hard. He wanted that child
very much. I didn't realize how much until the miscarriages. It was the only time in all those years I saw
him depressed, but a deep depression so that for some
time he could not properly work or eat or live his
everyday life. We Italians have an affinity for *bambini*
that consumes us.

After the second miscarriage, Sophia became extremely nervous and could not control her emotions.
Sitting at the dinner table, she would suddenly burst
out crying and go to her room, never to return. After a
while, Ponti recovered himself and he talked to Sophia about the baby. Underneath he was still as disturbed as she was, but he had control of himself and
tried to pick up her spirits. It is my opinion that if
Sophia had not been able to get pregnant again, it
might have destroyed her. She was obsessed with
those miscarriages. It was the only time she had failed
in life, and she didn't know what to do about failure,
certainly not as final and tragic a failure as the loss
of those two babies.

I threw myself back into work, trying to keep my
mind off what had happened. Up to that point in my
life, despite formidable obstacles, indomitable will
and self-belief had never failed me. Now I grew more
and more obsessive over the fact that apparently I
could not carry a child for more than three months.

"Sophia, you must not care so much about having
this baby," Carlo said. "What does it matter? If it
comes, fine, if it doesn't, it doesn't. We can always
adopt a child if you want one that much. But to eat
yourself up over this—"

"How can you talk that way?" I got really wild.
"You don't care because you've had two children with
another woman. But I don't have any. No, I don't
want to adopt, I want a baby out of my own belly. I

have not given up. Not yet. And I don't want you to give up for me."

It took a good five or six months for the pain and defeat of the miscarriage to fade far enough away to allow my strong natural feelings to return. A friend of mine, who had had a great deal of trouble getting pregnant, had been telling me about a wonder doctor in Switzerland who had solved all her problems. He was Professor Hubert de Watteville. He told me to come to Geneva for a thorough examination, bringing all my medical records with me.

Dr. de Watteville was a very thin, tall man in his early sixties, face like an aristocratic bird, pronounced nose, on first meeting rather distant, and I felt disappointed that I wouldn't be able to talk to him easily, as a friend. But later, when we got to know each other, he emerged as one of the most understanding, generous, caring people I have ever known. His own marriage was childless and he seemed to compensate for his lack of children with the babies he helped his patients bring into the world.

Dr. de Watteville injected me with Pentothal, which put me out, and thoroughly examined me, testing my tubes to make sure they were open, giving me another D and C to be sure I was perfectly clean, testing my uterus, but finding nothing that could account for the fact that I lost my babies around the third month. He said there were several factors to consider that might have caused the miscarriages. But under the circumstances, he could do nothing until and if I got pregnant again. I was by then thirty-two years old, and after two miscarriages pregnancy might be difficult. I found Dr. de Watteville's prescription for my getting pregnant rather peculiar, to say the least. He gave me a four-month supply of birth-control pills. "When they are used up," he said, "we will see what happens."

What happened was that when I started to take the pill, which I had never taken before, my entire body seemed to go into hibernation. I had never felt less capable of having a baby.

I could not lift myself from the valley of my depression. Certainly not by my own bootstraps. I was in a desperate situation, my whole sense of being threatened, and there was nothing around me that offered even a thread of hope or uplift—except my strong belief in God. My alienation from the Catholic Church did not at all affect my allegiance to the Almighty. I have never expected miracles or sought superstitious help from religion. I feel that a pure religious feeling has very little to do with the machinery of the church—going to mass, taking communion, blindly obeying its stringent dos and don'ts. Most people, I feel, deposit vows in the church as one deposits money in the bank, and in this way they think they accumulate a religious capital, which will pay them enough interest in paradise that they will never have to work any more. I have always believed in the existence of a supernatural force that I could reach through prayer. But not normal prayers, by rote out of a prayer book, or spoken aloud and addressed to the heavens. My prayers are inward, silent, directed to God, who dwells within me. I do not ask for miracles or even overt assistance. What I seek is the strength of believing in myself and the people around me. I firmly believe we can make our own miracles if we believe strongly enough in ourselves and our mission on earth. So I spoke fervently to the God within me, the God who is within all of us, and my spirits rose.

I also spoke to my grandmother. When she died, I am convinced her spirit entered my body. When I need her, she is there to succor me. She is my guardian angel. So my thoughts turned to her and I spoke to her, and her words further strengthened my forlorn spirit.

I don't believe in the traditional rigmarole of church ritual. Incense and wafers and goblets of wine do not touch my spirit. But the quiet sanctity of a church is welcome to my meditations, and often when I am near a church, especially if I am working on a film, I find time to visit its peaceful interior if there is no service in progress, and feel comforted by its spiritual silence. But I don't get on my knees and pray. I don't cross myself or anoint myself with holy water. I have found my own religion and I relate to God directly instead of through the intermediaries of church and priests. I suppose this makes me a failed Catholic, but I feel I am a religious person, and for me that is all that counts.

At no time did I lose faith in de Watteville, but my desperation prodded me to get additional advice. I heard about a New York specialist whom I engaged to fly to Rome, but after examining me he seemed more interested in locating the best restaurants in Rome than in discussing my condition and what to do about it. So I gave him a list of my favorite places and never saw him again.

When my four-month supply of pills ran out, I went to Geneva to see de Watteville and spent several days undergoing tests and getting hormonal injections to induce ovulation. I worried constantly. Obsessively. Finally, Dr. de Watteville said, "Now, listen, this is not the way to have a child. I want you to go back to Rome and get your mind off your problems. We've done all we can to prepare you, now nature must take its course. But nature will better take its course if you put yourself at ease."

My sister said the same thing. She suggested that the two of us spend a couple of weeks at a spa in the north of Italy, which featured hot sulfur springs and mud baths. It turned out to be a rather depressing place, for most of the people there were suffering from rheumatism, arthritis, bursitis, and the like, but I stuck it out for thirteen days, immersing myself in the spa's spartan rituals. My body relaxed and I felt relieved of much of my physical tension, but my mind was much more stubborn and it was only toward the end of my stay that I felt less anxiety.

Exactly one month after I returned to Rome, I got pregnant.

First I called Carlo, who was in London. "Oh, no!" he exclaimed, and I could see him slapping his palm against his forehead. I knew he was apprehensive of the terrible effect a third miscarriage would have on

me. Then I phoned Dr. de Watteville, who took the
next plane to Rome.

~~~~~~~~~

Ines Bruscia

When she did become pregnant for the third time,
Sophia had an anxiety about it for the entire nine
months. I stayed with her; I was the only person, and
I still marvel at the way she sacrificed herself to have
that child. Nine months in bed, no activity at all,
not even talking on the telephone, and not one word
of complaint. Never once did she say to me, Ines, I
am so bored or so tired of lying here—not once. She
read and slept and looked at television a bit but that
was all. Only Ponti came to visit, and, as I recall,
Basilio was there once or twice. From the way she
isolated herself within the cloister of her determination, I felt confident that nothing could interfere with
the birth of Carlo Hubert Leone Ponti, Jr.

~~~~~~~~~

I immediately went to Geneva and settled down in
a little hotel on the lake, close to Dr. de Watteville's
office. He ran a twenty-four-hour urological test; from
detailed analyses he discovered that I was suffering
from an imbalance of hormones. He said the imbalance was primarily caused by a shortage of estrogen,
with which he planned to inject me regularly.
Twenty-four-hour urine tests would be run every
week to monitor my hormonal balance.

"Would the shortage of estrogen be the reason I
lost my first two babies?"

"I think so. But let's not dwell on the past. Let's get
this little fellow through his nine months and out into
the world. Unfortunately, because of your history, I

am going to have to ask you to remain in bed, in as quiet a state as possible."

"For the entire nine months?"

"I think it's best. We're going to produce this baby, you and I, and we want to give him every possible break."

That is precisely what I did. I wrapped myself in the cocoon of motherhood and hibernated. Dr. de Watteville gave me tranquilizers, primarily Valium, and since I had never taken tranquilizers before, they had a strong effect on me. I slept a great deal of the time. Only Ines stayed with me, although Carlo visited regularly. During the third month, I became apprehensive that I might again suffer my former fate. I experienced a recurrence of the strange, light-headed, drained feeling that I had had prior to my previous miscarriages. Dr. de Watteville, or one of his assistants, had been visiting me daily, so they were aware of this change that was coming over me. I felt a sickening sort of panic that once again I would lose my baby.

But Dr. de Watteville gave me a special injection that contained, among other things, an extra-strong dosage of estrogen, and within twenty-four hours the crisis miraculously passed and I felt all right again.

During the fourth month, I changed to more spacious quarters on the eighteenth floor of the Intercontinental Hotel, but it really didn't affect the monotony of my existence, which was spent flat on my back, twenty-four hours a day. But there was a second bedroom for Ines at the Intercontinental, and a kitchenette where meals could be prepared for me when I tired of hotel food. My memory of those months is hazy. I do recall that the newspapers were full of accounts to the effect that I had not emerged from my room because I was keeping a pregnant Neapolitan girl there, waiting for her to have her baby which I would then proclaim as my own.

The most emotional moment for me occurred in my thirteenth week, when Dr. de Watteville brought a machine to my room with which to listen to the baby's heartbeat. The machine had an amplifier on it, so that I would also be able to hear the heart. It was a terribly exciting moment for me, the first concrete evidence that a living thing actually existed in my belly. Dr. de Watteville rigged up the machine and then, with a sounding cup, started to probe around on my stomach. Five minutes passed. Ten. Nothing but silence. Not a sound. Dr. de Watteville checked the controls on the machine. Everything was in order. But as the cup moved slowly across my belly, it did not pick up a heartbeat. A balloon of anxiety rose in me and stuck in my throat. Another five minutes passed with no response. My breathing became difficult. I was prepared for the worst. The sounding cup had by now covered my entire stomach and picked up nothing. Panic words like "false pregnancy" and "breech birth" filled my mind. Then, suddenly, there it was. A miracle of sound. The steady, rhythmic, beautiful music of my baby's beating heart. I cried with joy as little involuntary chirps of relief came out of me. I could have listened to that lovely tattoo for the rest of the day, and I was disappointed when the doctor finally disconnected the machine and carted it away. It had been one of the grandest moments of my life.

I was also very affected by the first time I felt the baby kick. And yet it wasn't a kick at all, which was what I had been led to expect, but a flickering, like a little butterfly alive in my belly. The exhilarating thing about motherhood, I discovered, was that it was not the perfunctory process the books would have you believe. Each stage of development was, for me, a unique experience, beyond words.

Dr. de Watteville took me secretly to the hospital at five in the morning to avoid the hundreds of journalists from all over the world who were staked out in the lobby. He accomplished his subterfuge by having an automobile driven directly into the ballroom of the hotel through a large rear door. The baby was to be delivered by Caesarean section; thus the time of the delivery was set by the doctor rather than by nature.

I had never seen Carlo, ordinarily the calmest of men, as nervous as he was before the operation. The night before, he paced the room and carried on a nonstop, disjointed conversation. At one point he went down to the lobby, where there was an exhibition of primitive paintings; he returned shortly afterward, lugging canvases into the room, having bought *all* the pictures in the exhibition. At that moment, Carlo was only thinking of my need to have that baby, with no thought given to what fatherhood, at age fifty-three, would mean to him. He had had two children, but at a time when he was young and distracted by the demands of his career. Often, immersed in their work, men lose their sense of proportion. They don't seem to realize that they have just as great a need to have children as women do. Usually a man discovers this only after the child's birth, so that the woman, by her earlier drive to be pregnant, anticipates her husband's later-blooming desire. Thus it was with Carlo, who for the first time would find deep joy in fatherhood.

A Caesarean, I discovered, is a terrifying operation. In the operating room, with needles in my arms, all prepped, my stomach covered with tape except for the part to be cut, the blinding lights above, all surgery conversation clearly heard and adding to my anxiety, instruments being readied, oxygen mask held ready, no anesthetic given until the very last second for the sake of the baby. Dr. de Watteville was already leaning over me with his scalpel, and I thought, My God, are they never going to put me to sleep? My body contracted in anticipation of the cut of his knife, but mercifully I went under the anesthetic at that very moment.

But not far enough under. The anesthetic was too mild, and I felt everything toward the end of the operation when I was being stitched up. The pain was ghastly, and I tried to scream out but I couldn't.

I was gripped by a nightmare in which I kept hearing, over and over, "Your baby is dead, your baby is dead," the voice a series of echoes. "It was a girl, a nice baby girl, but your baby is dead, your baby is dead."

The first person I saw when I came to was de Watteville, who said, his face all smiles, "You have a fine baby boy." I embraced him, this man who had helped give me this most precious gift. Then there was Carlo embracing me and whispering joyful things in my ear. The baby was in the incubator, but a few hours later he was brought to me and placed in my arms. He had a little bandage on his bottom where de Watteville nicked him with the scalpel (he must have been as nervous as the rest of us). The baby had the beautiful round face of an apple, an apple inset with perfectly round blue eyes. What a strange moment that was, that first moment with the baby. A stranger put in my arms, feeling not at all that he had come from my body, a moment of bewilderment for me, until he turned his pink mouth to my nipple and put his tiny hands on my breast and sucked his first milk. Then we were joined as mother and child, and that special happiness, so long postponed, was mine forever.

The problem of what to do about the hundreds of journalists from all over the world who were clamoring for exclusive interviews was solved by staging a huge press conference in the hospital amphitheater, where normally students watched operations. The day after my delivery, four hundred and fifty reporters and photographers packed the amphitheater. My bed was wheeled into the room, with the baby beside me, and I had the unpleasant feeling that I was playing a scene in a movie. I felt rather disgusted at having to disturb the quiet enjoyment of my first moments of motherhood with this clicking, flashing, noisy disturbance. I was too weak to talk. Carlo and the doctors answered the barrage of questions and I managed wan smiles for the photographers. "This child," Carlo told the assembly rather grandly, "is a triumph for women all over the world." Carlo Ponti, Jr., the baby was named, with middle names of Hubert, in honor of de Watteville, and Leone, after Carlo's father.

Now comes the embarrassing part: my postpartum nuttiness. When the time came, I refused to leave the hospital. It was January, cold and snowy, and I was afraid to expose the baby to the outside world. Ten days had passed, but no, I wouldn't go home. The baby stayed in the room with me and I looked after his every need—much too well. Anytime he cried, night or day, I picked him up and walked him. As a result, he cried a great deal, since that got him immediate attention. During the night I diapered him repeatedly, whether he needed it or not. And I constantly fed him, even though the doctor asked me not to. I had very little milk, because of the Caesarean, but I fed the baby as much and as often as I could. I had the windows of the room taped shut, so that no fresh outside air could possibly find its way into the room. Whenever anyone entered the room, even the nurses, I made them put on antiseptic masks. It was really a ridiculous performance on my part, but I had gone through so much to have this baby that I couldn't bring myself to risk the cold and microbes of the outside world.

For a month and a half little Carlo and I stayed snug in our hospital room. I spent much of my time answering the hundreds upon hundreds of letters I received from women everywhere, congratulating me, asking advice, pleading for my help in their own infertility. I discovered that thousands of women shared my problem, and some of them wrote so movingly about how much joy my own triumph brought to them that it made me weep. They wrote to me as their sister, their daughter, the child they never had. I answered every one of them.

Finally, on my fiftieth postpartum day, the hospital threw me out.

Four years later, when I had my second son, Edoardo, I couldn't wait to leave the hospital. I had again spent almost eight months in bed, but as an accomplished mother I was relaxed and secure and knowledgeable. As a consequence, motherhood was much more enjoyable. In that respect, motherhood and film acting had much in common: sound instincts are essential but are made all the better by experience.

Eighteen

I said I was a witch and indeed I am. I have acute extrasensory perception. Eerie premonitions. Haunting superstitions. I always have something red on me, even though it may be out of sight. Ever since I was a little girl—witch's red. Never a day of my life, without something red on my body. I have always believed that red would bring me good luck and ward off negative, evil forces. Many other superstitions. On one occasion I was making a film, *The Miller's Beautiful Wife*, with Mastroianni and de Sica, when, after a very animated scene, I dropped the mirror which my makeup man had handed to me after the take, and it broke. I was as stricken as I would have been if the set had fallen on me. All day long I waited for the violent disaster which the shattered mirror presaged. By the end of the day, I was a wreck. I had barely been able to perform. The effect of my superstition actually was the bad luck I had anticipated!

My premonitions. I was once invited to a gala charity ball in Brussels. The day before I was to leave, I had an overwhelming feeling of impending disaster. I immediately canceled my appearance. My place was taken by Marcella Mariani, a former Miss Italy, who was a rising young actress. On her return to Rome, the plane I would have been on crashed, killing Miss Mariani and all aboard.

Just last year I had an eerie fire premonition. In the evening, I often light a candle in the living room, which my secretary routinely extinguishes before she

goes to bed. On this particular night, after I had gone
to bed, I felt impelled to go to the living room. The
candle was still burning, my secretary (for the first
and only time) having forgotten to put it out. As I
snuffed out the flame, I had a terrifying vision of a
raging fire. I put it out of my mind and went to bed.
In the predawn hours of the following morning, I was
awakened by cries of "Fire!" The lower floors of the
building where we live in Paris were in flames, and
dense smoke was pouring into our apartment. It was
terrifying. Carlo was out of town. Since descent was
impossible, the governess and I wrapped the children in blankets and climbed the smoke-filled stairs
to the roof. I broke a window with my shoe and we
somehow managed to get out on the roof, where later
we were rescued by firemen. I had to spend the day
in the hospital, where I was treated for smoke intoxi-
cation—smoke from the fire I had clearly seen seven
hours before it broke out.

On another occasion in Paris, Carlo and I were
having dinner together when I felt impelled to ask
him if our villa in Rome had insurance. He was startled by my question since ordinarily I have no interest
in such things.

"Are we insured against theft?"

"Yes, of course, but why are you asking?"

"I don't know. It's just something that has suddenly
come into my mind. Our getting robbed at Marino."

"Well, don't worry. We are insured, and we are
protected."

The next morning we received word that the Villa
Marino had indeed been robbed by a band of thieves
who stole, among other things, my Oscar and a prized
collection of antique boxes which Carlo had gathered
from all over the world.

Several years later, I had a dramatic extrasensory
warning about another robbery in New York, a premonition which I also ignored but with much more disas-
trous consequences. This was actually our third robbery. The second had occurred while I was filming
The Millionairess in London. I was living in a rented

house in Hertfordshire, and I had gone to the London airport to pick up Carlo, who had been in Italy. There were visitors and staff in the house. When I returned and went upstairs to my bedroom, I found the drawer to my vanity table standing open; my jewel box, which had been in it, was gone. The window beside the table was open, obviously the means by which the thieves had entered and escaped. They had taken with them all my prized possessions, every piece of jewelry that I owned. After each of my pictures, Carlo or I had commemorated the event with jewelry, and those jewels had great emotional value for me. Also, it was a source of enormous satisfaction to me, considering how my life had started in Pozzuoli, that I had amassed such valuables. I was particularly attached to the necklaces, one of diamonds and sapphires with matching ring of sapphire, another of antique diamonds with ring and earrings to match, a three-strand necklace of white pearls and another with alternating white and black strands, an exquisite ruby necklace, pins, bracelets, antique watches, gold chains, and belts—perhaps a million dollars in value, and all of it uninsured.

That evening I tried to be as British about the loss as I could, keeping my upper lip as stiff as I could, but the next morning, while I was in makeup, my stiff upper lip dissolved and I broke down in tears. I hadn't realized, until they were gone, how much I had prized those pieces of jewelry. Each piece evoked a lovely memory of my life with Carlo and also reinforced my resolve never again to go hungry. Their pilferage was a death in the family. De Sica, who was performing in the film with me, came into my dressing room and shut the door. He sat down, handed me his handkerchief, and told me to blow my nose.

"Your uncle Vittorio is about to give you a little lecture on wasted tears. Who are we, you and I? We're a couple of penniless Neapolitans who have struck it rich. As for me, I make it, I lose it gambling, I make some more. How many times they have wiped me out at the roulette wheel or the chemi box. So what? A couple of movies and I have it all back. So will you."

"No, no, it isn't that. You don't understand what that jewelry meant to me. It was a symbol of how far up in the world I had come from the hardships of Pozzuoli."

"Listen to me, Sophia. I am much older than you and if there is one great truth I have learned about life, it is this: Never cry over anything that can't cry over you."

We were staying at our apartment in the Hampshire House in New York when Carlo received word from Milan that his father had died. Carlo was deeply attached to his father and he was terribly shaken by the news of his death. I drove him to the airport to take the next available plane to Italy.

When I returned, I sat in our living room for a while, talking to Ines and Carlo's son Alex, who had come to our apartment upon hearing of his grandfather's death. Carlo, Jr., then four years old, was in his room with his governess. Around nine o'clock I excused myself and went to my room to go to bed. Immediately upon entering my room, I was aware of a "presence," a distinct feeling that someone was in my room. Then a sinister black moving shadow cast its length across the room, causing me to gasp and rush back to the living room.

Alex and Ines laughed at my upset over the "sinister black shadow," but good-humoredly went back with me to my room and gave it a thorough search, closets, bathroom, and under the bed. Needless to say, no sinister presence revealed itself.

Early the next morning, I heard distant muffled screams in my sleep. I woke, wondering if the screams were in a dream or real. I took out my earplugs, which I always sleep with, and again I heard the screams, immediately followed by a pounding on my door. Before I could respond, the door opened and in came a man carrying what I first thought was a stethoscope; my reaction was, He's a doctor, and little Carlo is ill.

But when he came a few steps closer, I could see that what I had thought was a stethoscope was really a large brass ring with keys on it, and the man bearing it was the concierge from the hotel desk.

Right in back of the concierge was a second man who had a gun in his hand. He came right up to the bed and pointed the gun at me. "This is a holdup," he said.

I pretended not to understand. "What do you mean?" I asked.

This irritated the bandit. He put the muzzle of the gun against my forehead. It had a silencer on it. "Don't kid around," the man said. By now I was trembling with fear. The man was wearing a wig and a false mustache. He had olive skin and wore dark-tinted glasses. He resembled Ringo Starr. His face was close to mine now, and I could see that he was as scared as I was. I could also see that his eyes, beautiful, piercing blue, were precisely Paul Newman's eyes. He ordered me to get out of bed and get my jewelry. I hesitated, primarily because I sleep in a very short nightgown that stops at the top of my thighs.

The thug was at my dressing table, ransacking it. He rifled through my wallet and took the two thousand dollars he found there. He also pocketed a ruby ring that was beside the wallet. In the other part of the apartment, I could hear Ines crying. I realized that it was she who had been screaming. What I found out later was that three men with guns had held up the desk and bound up the five or six people they found there, with the exception of the concierge and the manager. They had demanded a list of the hotel's safety-deposit boxes, which the manager had given them. Not finding my name there, they knew that what they wanted was in my suite and demanded to be taken there. The concierge and the manager could have easily taken the thugs to an unoccupied suite, since they did not know where I was located, and pretended that we were gone, but instead they brought these three armed men directly to us.

When Ines saw them enter with their guns drawn she immediately started to scream. One of the men pistol-whipped her across the head and face and told her to shut up. The governess picked up the phone and told the operator to call the police. The hotel operator said, "Now, take it easy, don't panic, honey."

"There are men here with guns, call the police," my governess entreated.

"Now, honey, everything will be okay, don't you worry."

As far as I know, the operator did not call the police. I later found out that the Hampshire House, like other hotels, had been plagued with many burglaries (since then security has been tightened).

The two holdup men in my bedroom were getting tougher and more nervous by the minute. I had gotten out of bed, as ordered, not caring any longer about my shorty nightgown. In my mind, as if in a nightmare, I saw flashes of violent images, even a graphic image of Kennedy being shot in the head by that assassin. The thug with the blue eyes demanded the "real" stuff. I had asked the jewelry house of Van Cleef & Arpels to lend me some jewelry to wear to a big Rockefeller party I was going to attend that night —an exquisite diamond-and-ruby bracelet, with matching necklace and earrings; I told the bandit the jewelry was in a bag in the lowest drawer of the dressing table. Instead of being satisfied, the leader got more angry and more irritable as he examined the jewelry and then stuffed it into his pocket.

"This is junk," he said. "We want the ring, not this junk." I had never heard the word junk before. "We want the ring you wore on TV with the David Frost guy."

Not until then did I realize what had been the magnet for this robbery. I had been interviewed on television by David Frost, a ninety-minute interview during which I had worn a fantastic diamond ring which, again, had been loaned to me by Van Cleef expressly for the telecast. The ring's value was around a half million dollars.

"That wasn't my ring," I said. "That was loaned to me by Van Cleef and I've already returned it to them." Which was the truth. The thug grabbed me by the hair and hurled me to the floor.

"God damnit, I told you not to look at me. Now give me the ring, not this junk!" Now that he was getting physical with me, my fear intensified. I would certainly have given him the ring if I had had it. Then he said, "Where's your baby?"

I panicked. The second thug, who had been in the living room guarding Ines, now came to the door and said, "Let's go!" All I could think of was my baby's welfare. I ran to a hall closet and grabbed a bag off the shelf. It contained every piece of jewelry I owned. I thrust the bag at the thugs as they were moving by me and out the front door. The leader snatched the bag and they ran off.

I learned my lesson. One can pay very dearly for vanity and it is a price I hope I will never again have to pay, because from that day to this I have not owned a serious piece of jewelry, an expensive fur, or anything else for which someone might pull a gun or threaten my family.

The second those thugs disappeared, I ran to my son and squeezed him to my breast. At that moment I realized that the most exquisite strand of diamonds or emeralds around your neck is as nothing compared to the loving arms of a child. The police had me look through books of mug shots, but I didn't see Ringo Starr with Paul Newman's eyes. If only I had heeded my premonition. So many premonitions, only a few of which I've cited here. If I had heeded more of them, I could have avoided robberies, fires, and assorted disasters. But I suppose I never shall, and so, you see, I shall never amount to much as a witch.

Nineteen

Richard Burton came to Rome in the summer of 1973. Carlo had signed him to co-star with me in *The Journey*, which de Sica was to direct. Richard and I had never met before, but he telephoned me from Hollywood and asked if he could come to stay with us in Marino a month early, in order "to get in shape" for the film. He explained that he did not want to stay in a hotel (which I could understand), because he would constantly be surrounded by paparazzi and find no peace. From newspaper accounts, I knew all about the troubles he was having with Elizabeth Taylor, to whom he was then married but estranged. In the press there had been graphic accounts of boozy tirades and public spats, private reconciliations and formal separations of the famous couple. I told Richard we would be delighted to have him come and stay in the guesthouse.

He arrived with an entourage that consisted of a doctor, a nurse, a secretary, and two bodyguards. What I didn't know was that Richard had started a detoxification program to cure his drinking habits, and that that was what he had meant by getting into shape for the film.

We got along fine. He was still very much in love with Elizabeth, and when he wanted to talk about her, which was frequent, I was glad to listen. He swam a lot and never once went out in the evening. He would often have lunch on the terrace beside the pool with me and the children. He was witty and vibrant, and dazzling words and quotations tumbled from him as from a literary cornucopia. He was rather nervous, which I attributed to the detoxification pills he was taking, plus the fact that, after a lifetime of heavy drinking, he was not drinking at all. He was also on a special diet. Sometimes in the afternoon we would play Scrabble, and despite his range of vocabulary and knowledge of literature I would invariably beat him, which caused him to cast a howl to the heavens loaded with Welsh swear words—how could he be beaten in his native language by an illiterate Italian peasant? Peter O'Toole had the same reaction when I also took his Scrabble measure. The fact was that neither of them could spell very well, and with my background in Latin I had a good feel for words in English, which I spelled more accurately than they did. Winning at Scrabble in English over these two amusing, literate, educated adversaries gave me much pleasure.

Just before the film was to start, Carlo came to me with the sad news that de Sica would have to have an operation (he suffered severely from emphysema but refused to stop smoking), and that our film would be delayed at least a month. Carlo knew that Richard adored de Sica and asked me to break the news to him. It upset Richard very much, but he said he would like to stay on at Marino and continue with his cure if that was all right with me. In our talks, Richard always took full blame for his troubles with Elizabeth.

In these discussions my role was that of psychiatrist, comforter, and ego masseuse. It wasn't difficult. I had become genuinely fond of Richard, and when I praised him I did so with conviction.

When we were finally ready to begin *The Journey*, Richard received a phone call from Elizabeth. It was their first communication since his arrival. She was in a hospital in Los Angeles and wanted Richard there for an impending operation. She was scared and she wanted Richard, the one and only Richard, her husband. He must come. This was on a Friday and filming was to start the following Monday. Carlo gave

Richard permission to go, on the assurance that he would be back in Rome two days later.

Friday night Richard flew for twelve hours over the pole to Los Angeles, stayed with Elizabeth on Saturday when she was operated upon, and, true to his word, returned to Rome on Sunday night. It was an arduous, emotionally disturbing trip; shortly afterward he moved all of his people to a hotel in Rome so that he could be alone.

Elizabeth was also scheduled to start a film in Rome, and soon after her operation she arrived. Richard met her at the airport with high hopes of reconciliation. She came out to Marino for lunch. Richard was tense, she was amusing and charming, but it was apparent that she was tentative and ambivalent about Richard. She stayed at Marino with him once or twice, but all of us, except Richard, could see it was going to end. His personality underwent a disheartening change; he became much more aggressive, and sometimes even rather violent in his reactions.

In the middle of one night my telephone rang, waking me from my sleep. It was Richard. He had just had a long talk with Elizabeth and she had made it clear that it was finally, completely, irretrievably finished between them, and that she would never come back to him. "She talked about divorce, Sophie," he said, his speech a bit slurred, "and she means it, it's over. She's never coming back and I am all alone here and I don't know what to do. I need help, Sophie, I really need help." I said that I was in bed and alone with the children, that Carlo was away, but that he should take a sleeping pill and try to get through the night as best he could and we would talk in the morning.

As soon as I hung up I phoned Richard's secretary at her hotel. She said she would immediately come out to Marino to be with Richard. I looked for him the following morning but he slept all day and did not show up at the pool. I tried to think of how I could help him, but what could one say or do?

Richard was appreciative of his sojourn at Marino

and the relationship we established. A year later, we did *Brief Encounter* as a television special.

I have not seen Richard since then, but he seems finally to have triumphed over himself. He had great success playing in *Equus* on Broadway, and his new marriage seems to have done wonders for him. I certainly hope so. I have great fondness and admiration for him, and consider myself his friend. During the sad period when I knew him, however, he was a tragic figure, the way kings in Shakespeare, once grand, are broken upon the wheel of preordained tragedy.

Twenty

The last time I saw de Sica was on the final day's shooting for *The Journey*, which he was directing. Unfortunately, he had had his ups and downs during the picture, having not fully recovered from his operation. He was lacking in the old de Sica energy and *joie*, and only fitfully sparkled behind the camera with the vitality and inventiveness that we had always shared. On this final day of photography, however, shooting a scene between Burton and me in a cabaret, de Sica was his happy self. The day before I had done something which I had never done in my life before: I had asked for an autographed picture. Now on that last day, he presented me with a handsome, smiling picture of himself on which he had inscribed: "When you were fifteen, you told me, 'I do.'"

I loved that inscription, for indeed we had had our cinema marriage when I was fifteen. After Richard and I completed our scene, we all said fond goodbyes. De Sica had to stay on the set to complete some shots of the dancers on the stage of the cabaret. I embraced him, and he said, "I'll see you soon in Paris." I walked off the set toward my dressing room, but inexplicably I felt impelled to turn around and have a last look at de Sica. He was sitting on the apron of the stage in a characteristic pose: legs apart, smiling, joking with the girls on the stage while he waited for the camera setup. Then he threw back his head and laughed at something one of the girls had said, as only de Sica could laugh—and that's my last vision of him, sitting there on the stage, roaring with laughter.

A month or two later, I was reading one evening when I suddenly felt impelled to read a play, *Filumena Marturano*, written by Edoardo de Filippo fifty years before. I had been urged to do it on the stage, and I took it off the shelf to see if I could memorize some of the long speeches. If I could, and de Sica would direct it, then perhaps . . .

The witch had had another of her premonitions, as I found out two days later when Carlo called me from Rome. I immediately knew, from the tone of his voice, that he was trying to break bad news to me gently.

"Did you know that de Sica is in Paris?" he asked.

"No."

"Yes, and he was very sick."

"Where is he now?"

"Well, still in Paris. They took him to the American Hospital yesterday—"

"Then I must go right out and see him."

"—and this morning, today, you see, he is . . . oh . . . dead."

I had no reaction. None at all. I couldn't speak. I felt nothing. My mind was congealed. Actually, my reaction was too big for my senses. My mind could not comprehend that de Sica, *Vittorio de Sica,* was dead. I did not cry. I felt no need for commiseration. I went to my bedroom and locked the door. I sat down on a chair at the window and looked far across the Paris housetops to the white gleaming towers of Sacre-Coeur. Then in my mind, like a reel of film, a cavalcade of our relationship over the years began: our first meeting in Rome when I was fifteen, and then our first film, *The Gold of Naples,* which really started me on my way; de Sica going through my part with me from behind the camera . . . The tears began to come and great sobs rose from within me as we relived our film adventures, from *Two Women* to *Marriage, Italian Style.* "How the years can fly away, and how little one forgets."

I called the American Hospital. I was burning with a desire to visit de Sica before they moved his body

to Rome. But his family had given strict orders that
no one was to visit the coffin. All day long I called, I
must have phoned fifty times, but no one would speak
with me on the telephone. At a time of severe grief a
family is entitled to its private reactions, but my need
to visit de Sica's body was overpowering.

The following day, I was again on the phone. I
discovered that the coffin was still at the American
Hospital. Finally, I found a sympathetic ear. I cajoled,
I entreated, I promised to come alone and stay only
a few minutes. Finally, reluctant permission was granted. At times like those, I am grateful for what my
name can achieve for me.

I went to the hospital that night, accompanied by
Ines. I was taken to the end of a long, dark corridor
in the basement of the hospital, where a door was
unlocked for me. I went in by myself. It was a tiny
low-ceilinged room, illuminated by a single candle
that burned beside the coffin, which was already
closed. Next to the coffin was a cot on which remained
the impression left by de Sica's body when it had lain
there, prior to being transferred to the coffin. On the
pillow was the indentation left by his head, and a
little smudge from where his hair had been. The
candle flickered. Somewhere far off a dog barked incessantly. There was no other sound. It was the saddest place I had ever been in. So unlike de Sica. I
put my arms on the coffin and bowed my head on
them and meditated about him. A painful sense of
loss swept over me, loss of this man I loved, and loss
of a part of myself that would be buried with him. I
thought about many things, and I prayed for his
beautiful soul. Some of my tears fell on his coffin.

I went to Rome for the funeral, which was an
agonizing experience. It was held in a huge cathedral
before a densely packed crowd. Photographers were
everywhere. When de Sica's coffin was carried into
the church, the crowd applauded, as they had applauded my entrance. (There had also been applause
at Magnani's funeral, a tribute to the artist.) I suppose they applauded me because of what de Sica
and I had accomplished together during his lifetime.

I had a terrible time keeping my grief from the photographers. During the service, when I started to cry, they pressed near me to get their shots, but I tried to hide my face behind the man in front of me. How awful it is, at times like that, not to be left alone. No respect for grief, or for the church. No respect even for the dead. Not to be granted a private moment to say a proper farewell to a man I loved.

Twenty-One

A police official in Rome

We have on record two attempts to kidnap Carlo Ponti. Actually, the first kidnaping attempt was instrumental in foiling the second attempt. The first kidnaping incident occurred late at night on the Appia Antica outside Rome. Mr. Ponti was alone in his car, going from his office, where he had been working late, to his house on the outskirts. En route he was forced to stop because there was a stalled car across the road in front of him. As he came to a halt, he looked in his rearview mirror and saw that a car had pulled up in back of his. The door of the car opened, and a masked man jumped out with a gun in his hand, and started to run toward Ponti's car, which was a fast Alfa Romeo. Immediately upon seeing that masked man in the mirror, without a moment's hesitation Ponti put his car in gear and went careening around the stalled car, which had obviously been planted there to stop him. The gunman opened fire. Ponti crouched low in his seat but managed to keep his foot all the way down on the gas pedal. The Alfa Romeo spurted away. The gunman kept firing. One of his bullets shattered the rear window. When Ponti got to his house, he summoned the police. Mr. Ponti's Alfa Romeo was riddled with bullet holes. We advised Mr. Ponti to call for police protection whenever he was driving that route late at night.

That is how it happened that Mr. Ponti had a police escort on the night of the second kidnaping attempt. When he called in, we were just dispatching a police car to investigate a fire and explosion near his home, so we assigned that car to follow him.

On the way, a car pulled alongside Ponti's car and started to force him off the road, but at that very moment the driver spotted the following police car and he sped away. At the Ponti house, the police discovered an unmarked van parked in a hidden area just outside the entrance to the villa. The engine was running, and in the rear of the van they found rope, tape, hypodermic needles with drugs—all the appurtenances needed for a kidnaping. If Mr. Ponti had not called for a police escort, this was the fate that awaited him. Afterward, we ascertained that the nearby explosion and fire had been deliberately set off to distract the police from the intended kidnaping.

<hr>

A friend of Sophia's

Two years ago, Sophia came to Rome on a short visit, and I accompanied her to the airport for her return to Paris.

She was scheduled to leave Rome on the eight o'clock night plane, which was the last one to Paris. We got to the airport in plenty of time but when she presented her passport to the control desk she was asked to step aside. I went with her when she was taken to an interrogation room. She was scrupulously searched; her handbag, wallet, and briefcase were turned inside out; some budget and production papers which she was bringing to Carlo were given particular attention. Sophia asked the airport officials to hurry because she was in danger of losing her plane, but they said not to worry, there was plenty of time. I learned later that all her luggage had been taken off the plane and was undergoing meticulous inspection.

At eight o'clock Sophia pointed out that her plane was leaving but they said they were sorry, she would have to await the arrival of an official from Rome who was going to personally interrogate her.

After a wait of two hours, the Rome functionary arrived. He began to question Sophia: What did you do in Rome today? Tell me every place you went, whom you saw, give me straight answers. Sophia said that before she answered her lawyer would have to be present.

Sophia's lawyers eventually arrived. They entered into animated discussion with the official: the technical and financial matters they discussed made me think I was listening to a foreign language. Of course, if there had been a vestige of evidence of wrongdoing on Sophia's part, the smallest infraction, the official would have pounced on it, but eventually he returned her passport, and without a word of apology for what he had put her through, returned to Rome.

By now, word of Sophia's predicament had reached the outside world and several hundred journalists, photographers, television people and the like had jammed the corridors outside the interrogation room. Sophia had no choice but to remain in the interrogation room, virtually a prisoner, until she could get on the first morning plane for Paris, which happened to be a Japan Air Lines flight at four-thirty.

It was a long night. Nine hours elapsed from the time we had first been brought into the room to the time the JAL plane departed. The press mob continued to wait outside the door. There were calls from newspapers and wire services from all over the world, trying to get a line on what had happened. There was no one to help Sophia get from the room to the plane.

I held Sophia's arm tightly, and we pressed forward as best we could. The press had spent eight hours in that hallway and they wanted something to show for it. They grabbed at Sophia, shoved microphones in her face, and tried every which way to get her to talk, but she looked straight ahead, as if in a trance, looking at no one, saying not one word, moving forward as best she could until, after a lot of pushing and shoving, we got to the JAL counter.

But her silence didn't achieve its purpose, for the following day the papers were full of her "verbatim" statements, condemning Italy, calling it a dreadful place, saying that she would never go back again; the reporters regaled their readers with graphic accounts of how the customs inspectors found millions of lire in her possession, and how valuables were found sewn in the hems of her dress; there was even speculation on how long a prison sentence she would get for her crimes. Of course, all these accounts were false and completey invented by the journalists.

Carlo Ponti

I live in hope that someday things may turn for the better and we can all go home to Italy. Perhaps it is a foolish dream, but I am by nature an incurable dreamer, and during the life I've lived I have grown quite fond of foolish dreams.

Twenty-Two

I don't believe I ever went into a project with higher expectations than I did with *Man of La Mancha*, my first and only musical, but it ran into trouble right from the start. First of all, the indecision of the producer as to just who would direct the film, and then the indecision as to whether it would be shot on Spanish location or on sets in Rome. It was ultimately decided to shoot everything in Rome, thereby losing that realistic quality that the magnificent Spanish countryside could have brought to the story. There is no substitute for moving clouds and rolling countryside, and no wind machine has ever stirred a breeze like the soft wind that blows across the Spanish plains.

But the film did have its compensations for me, the chief of which was the advent of Peter O'Toole into my life. Gay, witty, ribald, outrageous, and crazy—but crazy in a lovely way. A nocturnal carouser, he was always punctual and sober on the set. We played poker incessantly and I was amazed to discover that he cheated more than I did. He is awesomely educated and literate and always stimulating. When I am with people, especially those I don't know very well, I am litmus paper; I do not act, only react, so when stimulated I happily rise up to the level created. I loved to talk with Peter, whose conversation was constantly elevating. We really *talked*, we really communicated, exchanging ideas, touching on feelings, laughing at silly, wise cockeyed observations. Stimulating conversationalists are rare and Peter is in a class by himself. He provoked me to say funny things, pushed me to limits that surprised me, and most importantly, often, with his erudite sense of humor, made me see things in a different light.

Since neither of us is known for our singing ability, we were both scared to death at having to sing the songs required of us. I had sung a few times in films —a song in *Woman of the River,* a song with Gable in *It Started in Naples,* and another with Peter Sellers in *The Millionairess,* but those were incidental songs, not at all the same as singing in a musical which carried with it the burden of having been enormously successful on Broadway. Although most of the music was recorded in the privacy of a studio, I was required to sing one song live on the set because it was interwoven with the action. I showed up on the set that morning, opened my mouth to sing, and found I was absolutely voiceless. I was panic-stricken for a moment but O'Toole took me aside and assured me that all I had was "psychological laryngitis." But the nurse on the set took my temperature and found I was running a high fever. I pointed out to Peter that a temperature was certainly not psychological. I was really alarmed, but Peter would hear none of it.

"It's all in your mind, Sophia. You heat up and lose your pipes because you don't want to sing in front of all these people."

He was perfectly right. Two days later, in the private confines of a little recording studio, my voice was fine, and I recorded the song which my larynx had refused to perform in front of all those people on the set.

Peter was just as nervous about his singing. When the big moment came for him to go to the recording studio to do "The Impossible Dream," the only memorable song in the film, he demanded that I be there just to hold his hand while he tried to get through the song. When it came out on the screen, half the song was composed of Peter's voice, and the other half was a spliced-in professional singer.

At the very end of the picture, I found out I was pregnant with Edoardo-to-be, and immediately took to my maternity bed. Peter still had scenes to shoot, but he called every day with a warmth and affection that only a true friend could display. When the movie was over, before Peter departed, he came to say good-bye; as a present he brought me an enormous ostrich egg on which he had written, "With all my love, Peter." I truly love Peter, and whenever we see each other, no matter how much time has elapsed, our conversation picks up from yesterday. I must confess how delighted I was with a statement Peter gave an interviewer about me: "The more I was with Sophia, the more edible she looked."

I love to be considered a dish; I suppose it's the cook in me. And no one will ever put me on a menu more enticingly than did Noel Coward. We spent several evenings together when I was making *Lady L* with Paul Newman in Switzerland, where Noel had a house. I'll never forget the first time I went there for dinner with Peter Ustinov, who was directing *Lady L*. Noel insisted on introducing me to the bullshot, a fascinating blend of consommé and vodka that fogged my mind for the rest of the night, but not so much that I couldn't appreciate the volley of wit between the two men. As for his epicurean remark about me, Noel subsequently announced, "Sophia should have been sculpted in chocolate truffles so the world could have devoured her." I have never been more flattered.

Long after *Man of La Mancha* had been completed, and I was in bed in Geneva awaiting the debut of Edoardo, I received the record album made from the sound track of the film. I had not seen the picture but I knew that it had not been very well received and would not be a commercial success. I put the disc on the record player; what I heard made me burst out in tears. Hearing our songs washed back those five months of hard work, all the anxieties I had endured, all the problems and fears and hopes and frustrations. What I heard sounded so good to my ears, so full of life and entertainment, and I cried for the unrewarded efforts of Peter and Jimmy Coco as well as for my own. The cruelty of our profession, to demand so much from us, to take so much of our enthusiasm and belief, and then to cut us down with a few words of dismissal, the most painful of which are "write off." How do you "write off" five months of your life? So I wept for all of us, but as mercurial as the gods of failure are, so too are the gods of success, and a professional actress really shouldn't cry over a spilt film. But as I said before, I am not a professional. I am an amateur and always will be, and when I hurt, I cry.

I am still in awe of how difficult it is to be good on film, insecure about my ability to pull out of myself the emotions that are needed, anxious to cooperate with the talents of all those who are there to assist me, from the grips to the directors. I always seem to be working as if I were starving. I learn all my lines weeks before the film starts, to enable the dialogue to marinate in me and become a part of me. I could never do what Marcello does. He doesn't look at his lines until he comes on the set in the morning. No matter how difficult the dialogue, he memorizes it just before doing the scene. He is always scared to death when the scene begins, but this is his way of acting and certainly, for him, it is very effective. I could no more do a scene like that than fly.

When I make a film I really live what I do. I am not acting, in the sense of pretending. I am undergoing that experience. When I perform with an experienced actor who knows all the tricks of his trade, especially if he has been on the stage, it always makes me feel somewhat inferior, but as far as I am concerned, that kind of acting precludes the emergence of the unexpected when the scene is being played, and it is the unexpected that gives acting its creative thrust.

In the theater, gestures, voice, mannerisms are more effective than they are in films. When the camera comes in on the actor for a close-up, it is totally revelatory, and if the actor doesn't truly feel what he is performing, if real emotions are not there, but only technique, nothing will come off that screen that will touch the emotions of the audience.

That's why I suffer so much before doing difficult scenes. I am totally insecure; I have enormous self-doubt. It is harder for me to do a difficult role now than it was ten years ago because I am more critical, I expect more of myself, and I want to give more of myself. But the danger in going so close to the line is in losing control. No matter how much emotion I give —anger, grief, passion, hysteria—no matter how deeply I immerse myself in that living moment, I must nevertheless keep a firm grip on the throttle so that I control what I am doing, rather than the other way around. Intimate sexual moments must be played with the imagination, not real sexual response, or I could not possibly adhere to the technical demands of the scene. Also, the nature of film acting is such that scenes have to be repeated several times from different angles, in close-ups, in a master shot, and the performance must each time be identical to the previous rendition or the shots won't match. This is one of the most difficult aspects of film acting—to control emotions that look out of control.

During the shooting of *A Countess from Hong Kong*, there was one scene where Brando had a long speech to which I had to react. The close-up was on me during the entire speech, which required an emotional reaction from me that wound up in tears. I knew that this was going to be a very difficult scene for me, and that I couldn't do it many times, so I asked Charlie Chaplin to stand off camera where I could see him, and to direct me as if he were a musical conductor, pacing me so that my emotions were not too big too soon, leading me to the climax with his hands as a conductor would indicate what he wanted to the violins. It worked very well, and we shot the close-up in one take.

But producing tears and their accompanying emotions is often difficult because the atmosphere on a set tends to be lighthearted, with lots of distracting by-play going on, and it is often not easy to get myself into the necessary mood for the scene. I don't like to close a set or try to put a damper on the people I work with. Instead, I have found that by concentrating I can shut out everything around me and create in my mind the isolation I need for the tears I am about to shed. I even pretend to be listening to people around me, but actually I have shut them out and in my mind I am living whatever tragedy I need to create the mood that will carry me through the approaching scene.

Of course, comedy scenes thrive on a flip, jovial set, and in that case I am grateful when the atmosphere contributes to the performing—although playing American comedy is totally different from playing Italian comedy. American comedies are written to be funny, funny lines and situations that are played for laughs, whereas Italian comedies are serious, and the laughs come from a tragic or dramatic moment that points up some funny foible of the characters, the locale, or, with great good luck, of the human race itself. *Marriage, Italian Style*, with Mastroianni, was a perfect example of the seriously funny Italian comedy.

Marcello and I share an Italian point of view, of course, but there's much more to our partnership than that. We are interchangeable parts of the same body. Our impulses are on the same frequency. We first met in Pompeii in 10 A.D. when he was a chariot driver and I was selling statuettes on the Via Dei. When we act together, our souls join hands. There is no hyperbole too extravagant for describing the cohesion we have before a camera. When I perform with Marcello, I am the full moon. And he is the ring around me.

We also share an outspoken honesty. Neither Marcello nor I have any artifice, which, by the way, isn't always a blessing. We recently went to the United States to help promote *A Special Day*. We made an appearance together on the Dick Cavett show, in the course of which Cavett began asking Marcello questions about the reputation of Italian men as great Latin lovers. After several such questions, designed to identify Marcello as one of those great Latin lovers, Marcello, in his painfully honest way, said, in his heavily accented English, "Well, to tell you the truth, Dick, I'm not a great fucker."

The studio audience gasped. I said, "You must excuse him, Dick, because he doesn't know the language very well and he thinks he can say anything in America. What he really wants to say is that he's not a love machine. That he's fallible like everyone else."

Marcello gave me a look. "No," he insisted, "I said what I wanted to say: I'm not a great fucker."

There was a long pause, then Cavett said brightly, a rather sick smile on his face, "Do either of you have any hobbies?"

And that's how the program ended.

Twenty-Three

"How long is it going to last, this love? I don't know—three weeks, three years, three decades. You are like everyone else, wanting to shorten eternity by using numbers."

This is my answer to those who question my relationship with Carlo. We are married too long. Our ages are too far apart. Our looks are too different. We defy the system that prefers to think of marriage as "a desperation, legally authorized, and every kiss the conquest of repugnance." I admire Carlo's intellect, his tenderness, the way he kneads himself into my problems. He is, above all else, a helpmate, not just a mate. I cherish Lawrence Durrell's observation: "A helpmate surpasses a lover, and loving kindness surpasses love, even passion."

The foundation that Carlo and I built, on which we based our life together, was firm and it has admirably supported our life. I do not ever think of Carlo as older or in any way except as the man I need in my life.

That doesn't mean that Carlo doesn't have his shortcomings. He doesn't talk much, so that I have to guess most of the time what he's thinking about, what he wants from me, or what he'd like me to do. I have to take words from his mouth with a pliers. Also, he works too much, but this is intrinsic to people from the north of Italy: if they don't work, they die, so I have learned to accept this as a fact of life.

And I have learned to accept the telephone. Life

for Carlo without a telephone to talk into and movie scripts to read is intolerable. He has worked twelve to fifteen hours a day ever since I've known him, and I've come to the conclusion that his mania for work must have a Freudian origin.

I have also adjusted to the fact that Carlo is antisocial. It wasn't a big adjustment for me since I too am not very social. But certainly one of the reasons that I don't accept invitations is that I know Carlo will be bored. He does not like any form of social life. He doesn't like theater or music, and if somehow I were to induce him to go to a concert or an opera he would fall asleep during the overture. He is just as bored in a nightclub, and everyplace he is bored, he sleeps. If we go to the premiere of a film and he doesn't like the film, he promptly drops off. I must then nervously try to keep him awake: "Carlo! Carlo!" Actually, Carlo's napping doesn't annoy me; it's been a fact of life for such a long time I'm amused by it. But it seldom happens now because I long ago decided to protect him from his boredom, which is easily achieved simply by avoiding social events.

It really isn't much of a sacrifice for me since I myself am anything but a social butterfly. In the six years we have lived in our Paris apartment, we have rarely had a dinner party or any other social event. At the most, I enjoy having dinner with two friends in my own dining room. But sometimes when I am forced to go to some social event, despite my protests I have a good time. But it's not worth the agonizing I experience before going. Even on those rare occasions when I'm in the mood to go out on the town, the overattention I get in public takes most of the fun out of it, although once in a great while I enjoy dancing at a good discotheque or going to Maxim's for a campy evening. But if I do have an evening like that once in a blue moon, friends take me, and I go without Carlo. Most of the time when he goes out, other than the once or twice a month when we go to friends' houses for dinner, is when he has to entertain someone for business. I go along if he wants me to, and I converse and I never fall asleep. I always find something of interest even in the most difficult situations, because I look for it and I am patient.

Carlo, on the other hand, is terribly impatient, volcanic inside, although outwardly calm. His face appears expressionless, but I know just by looking at him when he's bored or irritated, although other people haven't a clue. Perhaps he sees the same things in me, for he knows me as well as I know him, and he respects my moods and reacts to them perceptively. He is a considerate man, but the only thing he can't really deal with is boredom. He deals with me adroitly. When, for instance, he notes that I am a bit depressed, if he thinks it is for something he has done he never mentions it; but if he thinks I'm depressed for something that doesn't concern him, then he brings it up and discusses it helpfully.

But I rarely bring to Carlo my problems about the children or my family or anything else. I like to solve my own problems because he spends his day solving problems. That's the nature of his work life, and he rarely involves me in those problems. I don't know anything about our money or our investments or the nature of contracts or any of that, not because Carlo wants to keep these things to himself, but because I am totally uninterested in any of this and prefer it to be Carlo's exclusive domain. He tries to insulate me from all bad news; he is my shock absorber.

Carlo Ponti

People don't understand our aversion to social life. In fact, we are called antisocial. But what they don't understand is that because we are public people, we prize our privacy. We cannot, on the spur of the moment, decide to have a pleasant dinner in a restaurant or a night on the town. The moment we put our feet out of our apartment, we are molested by the press and the public. The social pressure on us is overwhelming. We have a dozen invitations every day from all over the world. State occasions, good causes, glittering balls, and commemorative affairs. How many people are there in the world who are internationally recognizable? Sophia and I happen to be two of them, and being married to each other doubles our attraction. When we go out, we are public curiosities. The press assaults us and outrageously distorts what they write about us. I guess we sell copies, and in certain journalism, selling copies rates far above integrity.

We mostly avoid parties because if we go to one person's house, then everyone else we know is miffed if we don't go to theirs. Some people feel that Sohia does not have fun, is not enjoying her life, because she stays home so much. But they don't realize what an ordeal it is when she does go out. The public and press never give her a moment to herself. She must be constantly aware of what she says, what she does, whom she talks to, the look on her face. The fact is that she is a prisoner when she goes out, and free to be herself only when she's behind her own four walls.

Carlo rarely displays his emotions. Only a few times have I known him to weep. A couple of years ago, while he was attending an important film meeting in Cannes, his sister called with the sad news that their mother had died. I decided not to call him right away, to let him finish his meeting, for how does expediency help the dead? So I waited three hours, although I must confess that I felt a sense of guilt in doing so. When I finally told him, Carlo broke down and wept over the phone.

Another time he wept was when news reached him in New York that his father had died. He adored his father and held him in great respect; Carlo wept then, letting the sadness seep quietly out of his soul.

And then there was the time that Carlo wept with joy. After so long an agony of bigamy and miscarriages, tainted happiness and threatened miseries, so many, many torturous years, and then that precious moment when he walked into my hospital room and I handed him the little blanket that contained his son. The tears sprang from his eyes and his cry of pure joy filled the room as he took his new little son in his arms. This is a side of Carlo that he shows to no one but me. People who don't know him very well think he's a cold, aggressive businessman. But actually Carlo is a very emotional man, as sweet and empathic a person as one could hope to know, generous to a fault, involved, and anxious to please. But his personality is such that he never makes a show of these qualities. How often he has performed unrewarded favors for friends of his in the film business. He once induced me to perform in a friend's film (the friend was a producer who was down on his luck) against my better judgment, for I was sure, from the looks of the script, that the film would be a disaster; also, I didn't like the producer, who was a man of little humanity. When it was indeed a disaster and the producer proved to be ungrateful, Carlo was not bitter about it, for it was the act of generosity that mattered to him and not the churlishness of the recipient.

Carlo travels a lot and is away from the children and me more than I would like, but this is the nature of his business and it has been like this since I first knew him. In the beginning, when I was very young, I used to resent his absences, but once my own career got under way I was away on films for extended periods myself, and we both adjusted to absenteeism as a facet of our lives. Then, too, I found out something important about solitude.

I have been leafing through my notebook, and to my surprise I find that I have written down more observations about solitude than almost anything else. "True happiness is impossible without solitude." I devoutly believe that. I need solitude in my life as I need food and drink and the laughter of little children. Extravagant though it may sound, solitude is the filter of my soul. It nourishes me, and rejuvenates me. Left alone, I discovered that I keep myself good com-

pany. "How do you defend yourself against solitude?"
my notebook asks. "Mister, I am solitude," it answers.

In solitude, I read and experience what I read. And
in solitude, I deal honestly with my feelings, and with
myself. I test new ideas. I redress any missteps I
have taken; solitude for me is a house of undis-
torted mirrors. "The peace and contentment of a person," I once read, "are not outside of him, but inside
of him." Solitude is guardian of my peace and contentment. When I am alone, I am never lonely. I
have the company of what I am thinking and what I
am reading. Recently, I read a passage of Chekhov's
that haunts me: "Probably my destiny, since I was
born, was not to understand anything, and if you
understand something, I congratulate you. I have
darkness in my eyes. I don't see a thing."

I think about Chekhov and his world. I think about
his despair and sensibility. I wonder if, as an actress,
I can convey an emotion as powerful and haunting
as these words of Chekhov's have affected me.

Carlo Ponti

It is difficult to know Sophia. She is a good con-
versationalist when she wants to be, but she does not
like to talk about herself. Or reveal her inner thoughts
and feelings. Even I only see occasional flashes of what
lies deep within her. She is a profoundly honest woman, completely so with me, but there is a part of her
that she is determined to keep to herself and that's all
there is to it.

I know that she has anger in her, but I have never
seen a demonstration of it. In twenty years, she has occasionally been angry with me, but she has never
raised her voice or thrown anything or in any way
given vent to her anger. She is simply too controlled.
I have never seen her really angry with the children.
Those times when I know I have provoked her anger,

she has always contained it. If it started to get the better of her, she simply went off and stopped speaking to me. Since I am a very controlled individual myself, we are well suited to each other's temperament. I sometimes raise my voice in business, but never in the home.

The English people are the most jealous in the world but they don't show it. Sophia is Neapolitan but in covering her jealousy she is more English than the English. But she cannot cover up with me and I know from the look in her eye when a jealous spark has ignited within her. She never provokes a scene, or raises her voice, but when she's jealous she knows I'm aware of it and that by itself achieves its purpose. I myself am devoid of jealousy. It is simply not in my makeup.

One of the most important things that Sophia contributes to our relationship is her unique way of looking at life. She has an inviolate set of values, and an innate sense of what is truth and what isn't. I rely on her judgment of people, which I have found infallible—sometimes to my sad regret when I have not listened to her. There is no point in playing games with Sophia. She is about as easy to fool as Fort Knox.

The most outstanding thing about Sophia is her fantastic ear. It gives her balance, such an infallible equilibrium that not one phrase escapes her that is out of place, not one gesture that is excessive. Thanks to her ear she never says a thing she will have to regret, that is out of tune with her nature. She picks up languages effortlessly and with their precise rhythms. Her ear is the key to understanding Sophia. It has been largely instrumental in making her the star she is. As an example, in 1969 I produced a movie in Russia, called *Sunflower*, with Sophia and Mastroianni. After we had been there for two months, Sophia was the only one in the entire company who had managed to understand and to express herself in Russian, one of the world's most difficult languages. When the film was completed, the Russians gave an official dinner in honor of the company. The highest-ranking Russian official proposed a toast to us, and then Sophia rose to her feet, and raising her glass, extemporaneously answered in Russian with a toast to our Russian hosts and the Russian people we had met. That an Italian woman had cared enough for them and their culture to master their language made the Russians very emotional. At the end of her toast, everyone rose and applauded, and once again, Sophia's ear had triumphed.

Anything Sophia wants to do can reach perfection.

~~~~~~~~~~~~~

We quarrel infrequently. They are very polite quarrels; in fact, most of them should be called disagreements, not quarrels. We do not raise our voices or throw objects or slam doors. What upsets me most are the times that Carlo won't respond. But when Carlo decides to sit out a quarrel and say nothing, I finally get upset and go to my room. Sometimes we don't talk for several days. That constitutes a major quarrel.

When I am upset like that, I get in bed. I am a firm believer that the bed generates only good. When I am upset, despite my perturbation, I can descend into sleep with ease, like a deer or a baby. All my life, from early girlhood on, I have taken refuge in sleep. Misery and hunger never found my dreams.

But sleep does not cure my suffering, only postpones it. When I suffer, I lose my ability to think and reason, so I stay mute until my suffering abates and I can again coordinate my thoughts. The silence between us is broken when one of us speaks to the other, not about the quarrel itself, which we never again discuss, but when one of us just resumes talking—about children, house, help, work—husband-wife small talk. Sometimes, if Carlo is the one who decides to make up, he phones me long distance. Of course I never refuse the call; he is away and whenever he is away, quarrel or not, I miss him.

Ines Bruscia

I do not think that Sophia has fun in the ordinary sense of the word. She is too serious. What she likes is to stay in her house and take care of things. She looks after her dresses and shoes; is meticulous about answering the mail; goes over shopping lists and menus, sometimes doing the cooking herself; devotes much time to the children, sometimes playing games with them and telling them stories; talks to a close friend on the telephone; reads, but not as much now as before she had the children; she even helps out with the cleaning, especially in the kitchen.

She invariably gets up very early. When she is working, she rises about five o'clock. When she was working with Charlie Chaplin, it was every morning at four-thirty because the studio was so far from the apartment. She rarely goes out when she is making a film. For Sophia, work is a religion. When she is not working, she gets up around six or six-thirty. She eats lunch at noon with the children and Ponti, when he is in town, and the meals are exclusively Italian.

Weekends are spent casually in the apartment with the children. The children often invade their bedroom in the morning and play in their bed with Sophia and Ponti. It is a close, loving, enjoyable atmosphere. But people don't want to accept their lives as a fact, especially the press. They accuse me of painting a false picture. The problem is that people don't understand love; they understand sex, but not love. They do not understand the Pontis' mutual dependence, their importance to each other. When Ponti is away, he calls Sophia three, four times a day. They need each other. I can't imagine Sophia without Ponti or Ponti without Sophia. He needs her vitality and smartness, she needs his reflective mind and common sense. She is Neapolitan south, where they tend to exaggerate things, and he is Milanese north, where the tendency is to minimize, so in this way they balance each other.

The twenty-two-year age difference doesn't mean a thing. I am never aware of it. Ponti never brings his business into the house. They never discuss money or deals or any of that. Their talk is about the children, schooling, help problems, travel plans, the everyday talk of married people. I have rarely seen Sophia angry, but her anger flashes and is gone, a quick flame that burns itself out. Another Neapolitan trait. The people who work for her have worked for her a long time—me, Ruth Bapst (the governess), Sophia's make-up man, the maid, the housekeeper. Ponti's people too have been with him forever. It is a testament to their qualities as human beings.

The only times I have heard them quarrel is in the car. Ponti drives too fast and Sophia always complains about it, but he refuses to slow down. He says that's the only way he knows how to drive—fast.

For as long as I can remember, the press has been writing lurid obituaries for our marriage. On the rare occasion when I go to dinner or a nightclub with a friend while Carlo is out of town, I'm cheating. If I stay home and confine myself to family life, I'm fighting to save my failing marriage. If I don't perform in one of Carlo's pictures and he hires another actress (I may not like the part or it may not be right for me), I suddenly read that I'm crying myself to sleep because my husband is having a red-hot affair with this actress.

This is what I most resent about being in the public eye. I cannot have any life of my own. Carlo and I have inured ourselves to these attacks, but the conscienceless worms who write them and take the pic-

tures are always around us, no trick or disguise too
mean for them, no fabrication in print too wretched.
Their constant harassment occasionally does get to us,
although we never respond to anything they print.
The very continuance of our marriage is the best answer to all these cheap stories, which die aborning
because they are baseless.

Carlo Ponti

In the press, I am always having an affair. I'm not
saying that I'm pure as the driven snow, but if I had
all the affairs that the press inflicts on me, I'd never
have time to produce a movie. But they operate on
the principle that good news is no news so they are
constantly hacking away at our marriage. Our names
in print sell copies, I suppose, and they readily try to
destroy our marriage and our family life if they can
peddle a few copies more on the newsstand.

It's been like this since the very beginning of our
relationship. During the filming of *Boy on a Dolphin*,
in 1956, I got word that an Italian magazine was
planning to run a big scandal piece about Sophia
and me. The publisher was an old friend of mine with
whom I had gone to school. I phoned him and told
him that I knew about the piece, but begged him not
to run it because my mother was terribly ill (which
she was) and that such an article might have a grave
effect on her. I was married then, and this article was
the first revelation that Sophia had entered my life. I
asked my friend to postpone running the article until
my mother was over her crisis. He said he would
look into it. The next week the magazine came out
with the story, a vulgar account of the relationship between Sophia and me. I sent the publisher a scorching
letter which he neither published nor answered. I
saw him once, after that, and told him off, but he just

laughed and said that the culprit was the editor, not him. When Sophia and I were married, however, to my surprise he sent us a flowery cable of congratulations and good wishes.

That early experience taught me never again to trust the press, or to respond to the press, or to be upset by malicious exploitation. The fact that Sophia and I have survived over twenty years of these daily assaults seems to incite the press all the more to do their damnedest and their dirtiest to get at us. In the world of show business, where relationships change like the seasons, we are a phenomenon that's beyond their belief. It's almost as if they resented us.

〰〰〰〰〰

I am a free woman, a *liberated* woman on my own terms. I have an independent career. I make more than enough money to be self-supporting. I could leave my marriage at any time without fear of being alone. So you see, I freely choose to preserve the life I have.

But this does not diminish my approval of the main objectives of the women's lib movement. I have never joined a women's lib group, although many times invited to, but I agree that women should be as free to deal with their lives as men are with theirs. Being female should not limit employment, earnings, or opportunity for advancement. Young mothers must have a chance to prepare themselves for their later lives. A woman, married at twenty, suddenly finds her children gone and her life her own when she's forty. Then what? Surely she should be properly compensated for those "mother years" of her young life. I personally think there should be a provision in the marriage contract that gives her twenty-five percent of her husband's annual net income.

I approve of this goal and others for which women's lib groups are fighting, but I think that lately these groups are getting too aggressive, too bullying in their tactics, and that is a grave mistake. No matter how hard they fight for these rights, women should never forsake their natural qualities, not in their actions, nor in the concepts they are fighting for.

Also, I find that recently too many of the women in the movement have lost sight of their important goals and have splintered off into inconsequential caterwaulings, strident bayings at the man in the moon. Too often what now poses as important conclaves and meetings are merely "a sniffing of bottoms raised to the degree of official ceremonies."

I do not sympathize with those women who want to fully emancipate the young mother from the home. I recognize that it is extremely difficult to run a house and take care of little children while at the same time trying to prepare for a future, but we must never overlook the deep need that a young child has for its mother. Nor should we forget that the love of a little child is a greater reward for a woman than any job can bring her. Of course, I am speaking from the snug perspective of a woman with young children who leads a very privileged and special life. I pursue a career that only puts occasional demands on my time, thereby providing me with considerable free time to exist intimately with my children. And when I am working, I have Ruth Bapst, a young Swiss governess, to look after them. She has been with us since Carlo was born. She was a nurse at the hospital and by now she is an adored member of the family.

But even mothers who don't have my privileged life could begin to prepare themselves for later careers if they were provided with an income from their husband's earnings. And this, I think, is the most important of the goals which the women's liberation movement has set for itself, one that I heartily approve of. But one goal that I do not approve of is that of free-will abortion. My struggle to have children, and the emotional scars left by my miscarriages, caused prejudices that I cannot overcome. I can't help thinking that a fetus taken from a woman might have developed into a little boy as bright and winning and rewarding as either of my two sons. To my mind, abortion kills a fetus-child as surely as does an automobile that might run over him in the street.

But I must confess that I just as strongly believe that women must not be forced back into the dark ages of illegal abortions performed in dirty back rooms by charlatans who hack out their insides. Certainly women who are impregnated as a result of rape should be afforded legal abortions. And young, unmarried girls who do not want their babies, and who are not able to care for them either financially or emotionally, should have the right to eliminate that child. But that is an intellectual observation on my part, not an emotional one, for emotionally I cannot countenance the life-ending aspect of abortion.

The pill and other modern contraceptive devices are an effective means of preventing unwanted babies, and I am all for such methods, but unfortunately too many people, because of ignorance or religious taboos, do not use them. Certainly an educational campaign to increase the use of birth-control devices would be a big help, but I honestly don't know what we can do about the rising incidence of pregnancy in young girls between the ages of thirteen and eighteen. I certainly don't approve of birth-control pills being given to thirteen-year-olds, even though I am aware of how difficult it is for the parents of these girls, who are, in effect, given the choice between nonpregnant and pregnant promiscuity. What experiences are left for these young girls who have had active sexual lives so early? No matter what anyone says, they are not prepared to deal with the emotions that are involved in their acts, so they turn to drugs and the other excesses that are now overwhelming teen-agers. A philosopher once wrote, "Adolescents must go through the fury of purity"; somehow the parents must prepare their children for this fury and then help them through it.

But the family as a group, as a meaningful presence, is a lessening force for young lives. When I was a teen-ager, my family and I lived as an entity, and I faced them and their morals, their wisdom, their strictures, their approvals and disapprovals, every day. They cared about me and it would have been unthinkable for me to have done anything that would have brought disgrace upon them. I pity these young girls today who do not have such a positive family force in their lives. Neither the pill nor abortion can help them. Only their parents.

~~~~~~~~

Sophia's sister, Maria

One recent evening Sophia and I were watching television when one of those Coca-Cola commercials came on showing a group of teen-agers in blue jeans, on bikes, picnic baskets on the handlebars, happy and laughing, on their way to a beach party.

Sophia turned to me, a sad look of envy on her face, and she said, "That's something I never had."

"Neither did I," I said.

The young people in that commercial were fourteen, fifteen, just about the age Sophia was when she took on the world. She was the provider, and on her shoulders fell the total responsibility for all of us, and the responsibility of averting the shame of failure and having to return to Pozzuoli in disgrace.

I sometimes wonder if Sophia today has any fun in her life. To the extent that work can be fun, perhaps she does, but I don't think she has much fun other than that. I really think people must learn how to have fun in their lives, but Sophia's life has been dedicated to work, work, work, and there simply has been no time for her to learn to enjoy life. I have lived a totally different life. Early on, I dedicated myself to having fun and I do. I learned to smile at life, to take things as they are, to make no effort to influence events. But Sophia and I were born with different drives: she was born a grown-up, and I was born a perpetual child, so that she has had no childhood and I have had no adulthood. I am still a child. I always will be.

Sophia has always been grown-up and serious. Of course, now she cannot just go out the door and have a carefree day of enjoyment. She must think of the people who will bother her, whom she will meet, where she can go to be left alone (virtually nowhere). She does not really have complete trust in most people because everyone tries to use her in one way or another. She is diffident and suspicious; being suspicious and melancholic, two typically Neapolitan traits, is bound to produce unhappiness, and that is why Neapolitans sing so much—to try to lift their spirits.

Of course, what is fun for me may not be fun for her. It's just that I can't understand her kind of fun, but that does not mean she's hurting for enjoyment. But I think she was happier when she lived in Italy. She was a totally different person. She smiled more and was much less restrained. But despite the loss of Italy, she seems to have settled into a comfortable way of life in Paris. When she is not working, she reads a lot, gives a great deal of time to her two boys, involves herself in the cooking, is very careful and orderly about her belongings, watches television, and once in a great while goes to movies in the afternoon to stay abreast of the new films. I have never seen her knit, or do anything frivolous like working a crossword puzzle. However, on movie sets she is a whiz at Scrabble and has consistently beaten those two sophisticated, highly literate Englishmen, Peter O'Toole and Richard Burton. When she lived in Rome she used to have poker evenings which she enjoyed, but not in Paris. She attends a few fashion shows, primarily because her profession necessitates being stylish.

I honestly think that Sophia would like to have more enjoyment out of life, but that she doesn't quite know how to. As I said, it is something that must be learned, and is highly individualistic. But Sophia is so intuitive I'm sure she will find the key to unlock that unused portion of her persona. She is stratum upon stratum of fertile soil, and the deeper you dig into her, the more fertile she is. I honestly believe that deep within her there are parts of Sophia that even she has not yet discovered.

~~~~~~~~

Basilio Franchina

When Sophia was young, and movie success was just starting to touch her, she was very suspicious of the people around her. In a way, she was frightened of them. She doubted everyone's motives—why is this one offering me this, why does that one do thus and so—a very defensive attitude. At eighteen, she was like a young animal, a splendid specimen that was admired for her sensuality. But everything that happened, good or bad, she asked Why? Why is this happening to me? Why am I suddenly sought after? What has caused this earthquake around me? Why suddenly do I have all these journalists and photographers around me?

As she got older, Sophia began to analyze her fears. She has a sharp and perceptive mind, and she began to get perspective on who she was and her place in the movie jungle. Since the birth of her children, I have noted a decided broadening of her tolerance, of her knowledge and understanding of people.

~~~~~~~~

I showed my nine-year-old son some stills from my last film and he said, "How sad you look, Mamma." Then he looked at me closely, and he asked, "Are you happy?"

I said, "Do you mean in this film?"

"No," he said, "I just wonder if you're happy."

He already cares about other people's happiness. He is such a vulnerable, sensitive child, I just know he is going to suffer because of it. I wish he could be different. Be less vulnerable. But then again, some

suffering is an important ingredient of childhood.
Curious to say, an unhappy childhood is, in a sense,
a treasure you carry with you all your life. Adults who
were privileged children can't understand that. They
can't understand that my miserable childhood gave
me one big advantage: none of my troubles or problems as an adult could throw me. I had lived through
terrible years that had robbed me of my childhood
but nothing could happen to me as an adult that I
had not faced and overcome as a child. And as a
performer, I believe the hardships of my childhood
have contributed to my talent. "To cultivate a little
sadness," my notebook tells me, "is the mundane duty
of every artist."

Little Edoardo is the extrovert, taking everything
happily in stride, but Carlo, Jr., keeps inside himself,
like his father. After the fire, after we had been
stranded on the roof in the cold for several hours,
firemen finally found us and led us back to our apartment. The fire on the floors below had abated but
wisps of smoke still hung in the air. Dawn was just
breaking over the Paris rooftops. I led the children to
their bedroom but Carlo insisted on first going into
the study where the piano is. Several months before,
without anyone's suggesting it, he had asked if he
could take piano lessons. Now he sat down at the
piano in the smoke-scented room and began to play.
He played a little Bach sonata that is his favorite. He
played confidently and serenely. Then he closed the
keyboard and went to bed.

Twenty-Four

Carlo Ponti

I think a great deal about the future. I want my little sons to live where there is freedom and justice, and solving this problem is my biggest concern. My dream always was that someday there would be a United States of Europe, because that is the only hope for overcoming the worsening crisis of humanity, but there seems to be little likelihood of that now. Freedom and justice in Europe are more constricted than ever. So I have turned my thoughts toward dividing our life between Europe and the United States. At the moment, Italian names abound in the American cinema there—Scorsese, Coppola, de Niro, Pacino, Puzo, Travolta, Minnelli. We should feel right at home.

At this stage of my life, everything is a miracle. Life itself is a miracle. I marvel that a man who is my age, an age when most people face retirement and sit out the end of their days, that I feel like I am starting life anew. I feel young. I have a young, beautiful wife and two little sons, and my spirit is projected toward the future. But that is my nature. I have never been concerned with the past. The pictures I've made, the houses I've lived in, the life I lived are all unrecalled memory, and it's the new house, the new pictures, the life tomorrow that interests me. I always escape to what is possible. Inside me is a very young man.

There comes a time in life when it appears that all possible goals have been achieved, universal fame has been achieved, a number of prestigious awards have been amassed, married happily, two enchanting sons—there would seem to be no further challenge. Where, then, is the motivation to continue acting? Has not striving lost its cutting edge, and complacency subdued wonderment? Not with me. I am as insecure about my acting as I ever was. I do not feel that as an actress I have achieved all that I think I can achieve. So I am still driven by my insecurity into the mist that shrouds potential. After all these years, I am still involved in the process of self-discovery, still subject to an inner force that makes me seek even deeper satisfactions than those I've experienced. The dream beyond the dream.

But that does not mean that my ambition, as such, hasn't slacked; it has. When I gave up two years of my professional career to have my sons, I realized, for the first time in my life, that I could live happily without working. Before that, work was a total way of life. Now, I still adore my profession and love to act, but I will not perform just for the sake of working; only if the project is something that truly excites me.

But no matter whether such parts come along or don't, I would never announce my retirement. I don't believe in that. How can an actor honestly retire? How does he know when the greatest part of his life might come along? I don't know how many times Sinatra has announced his retirement, but why? After a year's indolence in Palm Springs, he's invariably overcome by an irresistible urge to perform again, so back he goes to the old stand, acting and singing things his way. No, I think an actor who doesn't "feel" his profession any more should simply stop acting. That's what I will do if I ever get to feel that way. I was sad to read that Garbo, who is in her seventies, said that she now regrets having cut off her career when she did. That kind of regret, unfortunately, is irreversible.

I myself have few regrets. If I had my choice, I would relive the past twenty-eight years of my life exactly as they were. That doesn't mean that I haven't made mistakes, but I'm even glad of that because that's the way I learned about people and the quality of life. I have learned much from those mistakes, and I have tried never to repeat them. I don't think I've made any really big mistakes but plenty of small ones. They are mostly mistakes in behavior, in judging people, and as I've pointed out, my inability to say no has sometimes made my life miserable. People whom you allow to take advantage of you do not value you as a person, because they know that in your shoes they would say no and mean it. So I have been corrupted by selfish people's persistence, and that has been the biggest mistake of my life. But my philosophy is that it's better to explore life and make mistakes than to play it safe and not to explore at all.

Another regret is two movie roles which I was dying to do but couldn't: the wife in *Who's Afraid of Virginia Woolf?*, and *Anna Karenina*. I first saw *Virginia Woolf* on the stage with a German actress in the part, and I was so moved by the powerful role that before the curtain went down I was urging Carlo to buy the movie rights. Alas, they had already been sold, and I do think that Elizabeth Taylor was splendid in the part, but not being able to play that role is a haunting regret.

Of course, *Anna Karenina* was very well done by Garbo, but nevertheless I wanted to perform it again. I identify with Anna and I think my interpretation would have a quality of its own. But Carlo thinks this is the wrong time to attempt a romantic movie, especially one as costly as this would be, and, regretfully, I am inclined to agree with him.

But there are other projects in view, which shine like distant lighthouses. I am particularly intrigued by the possibilities in a novel about an Italian immigrant woman who comes to New York and raises a large family. At the rate I'm going, I will probably still be before the cameras when I'm eighty. In *Lady L*, I played a woman of eighty—amusing, well-groomed, bright-eyed, a little shaky, but filled with good humor and warm memories, with her children and her nephews all around her.

I hope that's how I'll actually be at eighty (although it won't take me four hours to get made up, as it did in *Lady L*). I see myself surrounded by my two sons, daughters-in-law and grandchildren, my sister and her husband and children, but best of all, my husband, stealing the show from me because he will have turned one hundred just a few months before.

Twenty-Five

Sophia's sister, Maria

As he lay dying, my father took my hand and carried it to his lips and kissed it. Then he said, "I love you." It was the only time he ever said anything affectionate to me. "*Amore*," as he lay dying.

～～～～～

Sophia's mother

I am not a hypocrite. I hated him while he was alive because he was a bastard, and how does his dying affect that? Does it erase anything? Does it change the man he was? No. I hated him alive and I wish I hated his memory just as much. But I am an honest person and I am furious with myself for the conflict I felt at his death. Hatred for what he had done, but also feelings of pity and even of love for those wonderful remembered moments that had marked our illegitimate relationship.

～～～～～

I was on a sound stage in Rome making *A Special Day* when my sister unexpectedly came to tell me that our father was in serious condition in the hospital.

I immediately left with her. My father was in a room with three other patients. He looked gaunt and wasted, and at first I feared that we had come too late.

"We are here, Papa," Maria said, "Sophia and me."

On hearing our voices, he opened his eyes and managed a slight smile. *"Sono felice,"* he said, which means, I am happy. He closed his eyes. He was heavily drugged for his pain, and after a short while I left. I would have stayed longer, but the other patients in the room had visitors who had recognized me and I felt awkward. I just wanted to be an ordinary person visiting her sick father, not a movie star being set upon by everyone in the room and a few nurses and interns to boot. It was certainly not the time and place for it. But before I left, I managed to have a talk with the woman whom my father had lived with for the past ten years, a very nice German woman named Carol, who had been quietly sitting in the corner. She was taking my father's condition very hard. She had been completely devoted to him and he was the only life she had.

That evening, my thoughts would not leave my father. In a way, strange to say, he was the most important man in my life. I had spent my life seeking surrogates for him—in Carlo, the husband who fathers me, in de Sica, who fathered me as a director, and so forth. Despite all the grandiose gifts I had received in my life, that little blue auto my father gave me with my name on it retained a special place in my memory.

My sister, who has a much more forgiving heart than I, had seen him often, and it was she who told me about his illness and about how, when he felt well enough to leave his flat, he would go to movie houses that were showing my films and sit for endless hours watching me. I wondered what went through his mind as he sat alone in the dark observing me on the screen. Whether he ever recalled the early days of our existence when he had not only turned his back on us but in a curious way tried to punish us. That he refused to give Maria his name in that Pozzuoli courtroom; that he made me pay my first million lire for it, and then, a year later, tried to repudiate the agreement—in order to get another payment out of me, I presume. That he even made it difficult for me to collect the three thousand lire a month ($4.60) which, for a few months of my life, he was obligated to pay for my support. And did he recall condemning us to the police in an attempt to run us out of Rome, back to Pozzuoli? Did he have any memory of, or guilt about, all the times my mother asked for his help when we were starving?

I did not expect him to understand the pain of a young girl branded as illegitimate, nor even the raw shame of his wife screaming at me in front of all those *Quo Vadis* people, "You're not a Scicolone! I am! I'm the only Scicolone here!" But surely he must have recalled with some contrition the libel suit. Surely some guilt that he sued his own daughter for libeling his reputation when he himself had branded her reputation with the stigma of illegitimacy. That lawsuit had roused anger in me, and for a time I hated my father for what he had done. But as I got older and learned more about people, I came to realize that hate is an acid that eats away—not the person hated but the one who hates.

I had also faced reality about my father: he was what he was, and festering criminations about him was pointless. As my viewpoint about him changed, so did my emotions. I no longer had any hate or scorn for him—only pity. I felt sad for him because, as I said at the start, he could have had a rewarding and fruitful life, and instead he spurned it, spurned the people who wanted to love him, who cared about him, and he seemed always to be living against himself. A self-defeatist. Destructive. Needlessly creating problems that nurtured his bitterness and hostility. I thank God I inherited none of that from him. I don't want to destroy myself or anyone else. My nature is to give and be involved, without a thought to receiving anything for myself. This wellspring of generous giving probably contributes much to my acting, for what is true acting except the ability of the actor to give his emotions and feelings to his audience?

So I pitied my father who couldn't give affection

and love to his women and the children whom he brought into his life. Perhaps toward the end he had a glimmer of this. Not long before he went to the hospital, at his request my sister arranged for me to visit him in his apartment in Rome. I had not seen him for many years, and I had never been to a place he lived in. I found him much older than his years. I believe he was suffering from cancer. He was very pleased to see me and took me all around the flat showing me his possessions and mementos.

We did not have much to talk about, but it mattered a great deal to him that I see everything in his home. When it was time to leave, and we stood in the doorway saying good-bye, he took one of my hands in his and said, "Lella, I am very proud of you."

That was the only affectionate thing he ever said to me.

A short time after my first visit to the hospital, Maria again came to fetch me. "Come quickly," she said, "Papa is dying. Quickly!"

My father had been moved to a private room. Several of his relatives stood in a cluster at the far side of the room. And to my amazement, my mother was present. She has a terrible fear of death. She never goes to hospitals or funerals. She had not seen my father for years, but the fatal fascination he had for her had held true even to his death. She had borne him two daughters and he had been the only man she had ever lived with. However she may condemn him, he was the one and only love of her life. And now she had defied her obsessive death-fear to be present at his demise.

Also present was the Carol woman. But my father's first wife, Nella Rivolta, the mother of his two sons, was not there. Nor did she come to his funeral.

My father had an oxygen mask on his face, and an attendant stood beside the bed, monitoring the breathing apparatus. Seated on one side of the bed was a handsome young man, thirty years or so of age, who was holding one of my father's hands in both of his.

The young man looked familiar, like someone I had known well a long time ago. Carol led me to the bed and introduced us. Giuseppe was his name, the younger of my father's two sons. He shyly acknowledged the introduction. I felt strange, meeting my brother for the first time at my father's deathbed.

I sat down on the opposite side of the bed and took my father's other hand. I looked across at Giuseppe, joined as we were by my father's hands. There was a soft, gentle quality to his face. I had an illusion that we were old friends. There was a shyness about him with which I identified.

I turned my attention to my father's anguished breathing. Giuseppe had shifted around to look at the monitor beside the bed. It was going erratically. My father's hand felt cold and inert in mine. Life was running out of him.

My mother never took her eyes off my father. Carol sat in the corner, her face covered with her hands. My sister stood beside my mother, watching the breathing machine.

And then the attendant turned off the oxygen and my father was dead. I had never seen anyone die before. The attendant took the mask off my father's face, and placing both his hands on my father's chest, he gave a mighty shove, pushing the last of the oxygen from my father's body.

Carol started to weep. Giuseppe released my father's hand and walked over to the window. I looked at my father's face, now free of the oxygen mask, and I felt compelled to touch his cheek with my fingertips.

"*Ciao, Papa*," I said, and welcome into my heart forever.

My mother had started to cry, not covering her face, letting the tears run freely. My sister, too, was weeping, but she had turned her back to the bed and was weeping against the wall.

I went over to the window where Giuseppe was standing, looking up at the sky. He was striving to hold back his tears. And so was I. Unlike me, as a child Giuseppe had lived with my father, so I guess he felt his loss more keenly. He turned and looked at me; it was a look of distress, of need. I reached out to him and he collapsed against me, releasing his tears. As did I. I put my arms around him and comforted him and felt very much his sister.

United in our sorrow, embraced, shedding common tears, I felt a surge of love for this new brother of mine who wept in my arms. How ironic that at his death, my father, who had given me so little in life, had left me a priceless legacy—a brother. I felt an eerie exultation, as if this young man had risen from the corpse of my father, his flesh and blood, to bring to me the kind of kinship that I had never had with my father.

So there in his death room, I both grieved for my father's demise and experienced the throb of encountering new life. It was a moment of great meaning for me, which will endure for the rest of my life.

FILMOGRAPHY

From *Quo Vadis* to *The Dream of Zorro* she is Sofia Scicolone.
From *The Piano Tuner Has Arrived* to *The Favorite* she is
Sofia Lazzaro.

YEAR	FILM TITLE	PRODUCER	DIRECTOR	CO-STARS
1950	Quo Vadis	Sam Zimbalist	Mervyn Le Roy	Robert Taylor, Deborah Kerr (Sophia an extra)
1950	Hearts upon the Sea	Cine-Albatros	Giorgio Bianchi	Doris Dowling (Sophia an extra)
1950	The Vote	A.R.A.	Mario Bonnard	Giorgio de Lullo (Sophia a bit part)
1950	Bluebeard's Six Wives	Golden Prod.	Carlo Ludovico	Toto (Sophia a small part)
1950	Io Sono il Capata	Jolly Film	Giorgio Simonelli	Silvana Pampanini (Sophia a bit part)
1951	Milana the Millionairess	Mambretti	Vittorio Metz	Toni Scotti
1951	Anna	Ponti-de Laurentiis	Alberto Lattuada	Silvana Mangano (Sophia a bit part)
1951	The Magician in Spite of Himself	Amati-Mambretti	Vittorio Metz	Toni Scotti
1951	The Dream of Zorro	Niccolo Theodoli	Mario Soldati	Vittorio Gassman
1951	The Piano Tuner Has Arrived	Itala/Titanus	Duilio Coletti	Alberto Sordi
1951	It's Him, Yes! Yes!	Amati/Sabatello	Vittorio Metz	Walter Chiari
1952	The Favorite	M.A.S. Prod.	Cesare Barlacchi	Gino Sinimberghi

(Sofia Scicolone-Lazzaro becomes Sophia Loren)

YEAR	FILM TITLE	PRODUCER	DIRECTOR	CO-STARS
1952	Africa Under the Seas	Titanus-Phoenix	Giovanni Roccardi	Steve Barclay
1952	The White Slave Trade	Ponti-de Laurentiis	Luigi Comencini	Vittorio Gassman, Silvana Pampanini

YEAR	FILM TITLE	PRODUCER	DIRECTOR	CO-STARS
1953	Aida	Oscar Film	Clemente Fracassi	The voice of Giulio Neri, the voice of Renata Tebaldi
1953	Good People's Sunday	Giovanni Adessi	Anton Majano	Maria Fiore, Carlo Romano
1953	The Country of Bells	Luigi de Laurentiis	Jean Boyer	Carlo Dapporto, Alda Mangini
1953	A Day in Court	Ponti-de Laurentiis	Steno	Silvana Pampanini, Alberto Sordi Walter Chiari
1953	Pilgrim of Love	Tullio Aleardi	Andrea Forzano	Alda Mangini, Charles Rutherford
1953	Neapolitan Carousel	Lux	Ettore Giannini	Vera Nandi, Leonide Massine
1953	We'll Meet in the Gallery	Athene-Enic	Mauro Bolognini	Alberto Sordi
1953	Anatomy of Love	Lux	Alessandro Blasetti	Vittorio de Sica, Marcello Mastroianni
1953	Two Nights with Cleopatra	Excelsa-Rosa	Mario Mattoli	Alberto Sordi
1953	Attila the Hun	Ponti-de Laurentiis	Pietro Francisci	Anthony Quinn
1954	The Gold of Naples	Ponti-de Laurentiis	Vittorio de Sica	Giacomo Furia
1954	Woman of the River	Basilio Franchina	Mario Soldati	Rik Battaglia
1954	Poverty and Nobility	Excelsa	Mario Mattoli	Toto, Enzo Turco
1954	Too Bad She's Bad	Documento	Alessandro Blasetti	Vittorio de Sica Marcello Mastroianni
1955	The Sign of Venus	Titanus	Dino Risi	Vittorio de Sica, Alberto Sordi,
1955	The Miller's Wife	Ponti-de Laurentiis	Mario Camerini	Vittorio de Sica, Marcello Mastroianni
1955	Scandal in Sorrento	Titanus	Dino Risi	Vittorio de Sica,
1955	Lucky to Be a Woman	Documento	Alessandro Blasetti	Charles Boyer, Marcello Mastroianni
1957	The Pride and the Passion	Stanley Kramer	Stanley Kramer	Gary Grant, Frank Sinatra
1957	Boy on a Dolphin	Samuel G. Engel	Jean Negulesco	Alan Ladd, Clifton Webb
1957	Legend of the Lost	Henry Hathaway	Henry Hathaway	John Wayne, Rossano Brazzi
1958	Desire Under the Elms	Don Hartman	Delbert Mann	Anthony Perkins, Burl Ives
1958	Houseboat	Jack Rose	Melville Shavelson	Cary Grant, Martha Hyer

YEAR	FILM TITLE	PRODUCER	DIRECTOR	CO-STARS
1958	The Key	Carl Foreman	Carol Reed	William Holden, Trevor Howard
1959	The Black Orchid	Carlo Ponti	Martin Ritt	Anthony Quinn
1959	That Kind of Woman	Carlo Ponti	Sidney Lumet	Tab Hunter, George Sanders
1960	Heller in Pink Tights	Ponti-Girosi	George Cukor	Anthony Quinn, Steve Forrest
1960	It Started in Naples	Jack Rose	Melville Shavelson	Clark Gable, Vittorio de Sica
1960	A Breath of Scandal	Carlo Ponti-Girosi-Paramount	Michael Curtiz	John Gavin Maurice Chevalier
1960	The Millionairess	Pierre Rouve	Anthony Asquith	Peter Sellers, Alastair Sim, Vittorio de Sica
1961	Two Women	Carlo Ponti	Vittorio de Sica	Raf Vallone, Jean-Paul Belmondo
1961	El Cid	Samuel Bronston	Anthony Mann	Charlton Heston
1961	Boccaccio '70	Antonio Cervu-Carlo Ponti	Vittorio de Sica	Luigi Giuliani
1961	Madame Sans-Gene	Maleno Malenotti	Christian-Jacque	Robert Hossein
1962	Five Miles to Midnight	Anatole Litvak	Anatole Litvak	Jean-Pierre Aumont, Anthony Perkins
1962	The Condemned of Altona	Carlo Ponti	Vittorio de Sica	Fredric March, Maximilian Schell, Robert Wagner
1963	Yesterday, Today and Tomorrow	Carlo Ponti	Vittorio de Sica	Marcello Mastroianni
1964	The Fall of the Roman Empire	Samuel Bronston	Anthony Mann	Alec Guinness, James Mason, Omar Sharif
1964	Marriage, Italian Style	Carlo Ponti	Vittorio de Sica	Marcello Mastroianni
1965	Judith	Kurt Unger	Daniel Mann	Peter Finch
1965	Operation Crossbow	Carlo Ponti	Michael Anderson	Trevor Howard, George Peppard, Lilli Palmer
1965	Lady L	Carlo Ponti	Peter Ustinov	Paul Newman, David Niven, the voice of Peter Ustinov
1966	Arabesque	Stanley Donen	Stanley Donen	Gregory Peck
1966	A Countess from Hong Kong	Jerome Epstein	Charles Chaplin	Marlon Brando
1967	Happily Ever After	Carlo Ponti	Francesco Rosi	Omar Sharif
1967	Ghosts, Italian Style	Carlo Ponti	Renato Castellani	Vittorio Gassmana

YEAR	FILM TITLE	PRODUCER	DIRECTOR	CO-STARS
1969	Sunflower	Carlo Ponti	Vittorio de Sica	Marcello Mastroianni
1970	The Priest's Wife	Carlo Ponti	Dino Risi	Marcello Mastroianni
1971	Lady Liberty	Carlo Ponti	Mario Monicelli	William Devane
1971	White Sister	Carlo Ponti	Alberto Lattuada	Adriano Celentano, Fernando Rey
1972	Man of La Mancha	Alberto Grimaldi	Arthur Hiller	Peter O'Toole, James Coco
1973	The Voyage	Carlo Ponti	Vittorio de Sica	Richard Burton
1974	Verdict	Carlo Ponti	André Cayatte	Jean Gabin
1974	Brief Encounter	Carlo Ponti- Sir Lew Grade	Alan Bridges	Richard Burton
1974	Gun Moll	Carlo Ponti	Giorgio Capitani	Marcello Mastroianni
1975	A Special Day	Carlo Ponti	Ettore Scola	Marcello Mastroianni
1976	Cassandra Crossing	Carlo Ponti	George Pan Cosmatos	Richard Harris, Ava Gardner, Burt Lancaster
	Angela	Zev Braun- Benjamin Manaster	Boris Sagal	John Vernon, John Huston, Steve Railsback
1978	Brass Target	Arthur Lewis	John Hough	John Cassavetes, George Kennedy, Robert Vaughn, Max Von Sydow
1979	Fire Power	Michael Winner	Michael Winner	James Coburn, O. J. Simpson
1979	A Blood Feud (working title)		Lina Wertmuller	Marcello Mastroianni, Giancarlo Giannini

APPENDIX

CLOTHES, MAKEUP, CARE OF THE BODY, HAIR, EXERCISE, AND THE ART OF COOKING

The actor and the musician have much in common. The musician improves his performance by using a fine instrument, but the finest instrument cannot improve his talent. The actor's instrument is himself —his voice, his body, his looks, the cut of his jib. Without talent, this instrument is worthless, or else the most beautiful women and the most handsome men would be our greatest performers. But a talented actor certainly enhances his performance when he has made the most of his physical possibilities.

From the beginning of my career, I had a natural instinct for what suited me best in makeup, hairstyle, clothes, and body care. I imitated no one. I did not slavishly follow the dictates of fashion. I wanted only to look like myself, uniquely me, which I realized could not be achieved by grotesque or faddish distortion, but only by enhancing what nature gave me, which is an ensemble of irregularities—pronounced nose, large mouth, weak chin, and protruding cheekbones. At first I tried using a lot of heavy makeup. I changed my eyebrows, and varied the color of my hair from one week to the next, from blond to red-tinted to coal-black. All of this indicated that I was not sure of myself, that I didn't know how I wanted to look or indeed what my natural looks really were.

Many women use heavy makeup as a mask to hide behind. Especially young women. I have learned, however, that too much makeup makes a woman look older and can destroy all expression in her face.

After studying how I looked on the screen, and in still photographs, I began to realize that I looked contrived, and that I would be much better off, and my acting more effective, if I kept my face as natural-looking as possible. So I stopped experimenting with hair colors and began to use as little makeup as possible. I use even less makeup on the screen than I do in real life, because the more natural I look on the screen, the better I reach an audience. But even my offscreen makeup is kept to a minimum. I emphasize my eyes, which I consider my best feature, by penciling the upper lid and then meeting it with a hair-fine line drawn along the lower lid. I wish I did not have to wear lipstick but I am forced to because my lips are so dark that if a photograph is taken of me without lipstick it looks as if I painted my lips very dark. Also, I have found a way to use lipstick that de-emphasizes the size of my mouth. The only cream I use is baby oil—nothing else.

I'm convinced that outward beauty is directly connected with inward beauty. Eyes are not beautiful simply because they are big and wide set, but also because they express something that radiates from the inner woman. My eyes are a precise mirror of my soul. If you know me well, you can tell from the look in my eyes whether I'm happy or unhappy, worried or tranquil, bored or interested. Carlo can read my eyes like a stock market ticker. He rarely has to ask me how I am or how I feel—he knows.

I staunchly believe that anything that can help a woman psychologically to overcome the trauma of aging is well worth the effort. Of course chronological age has very little to do with one's mental, physical, or spiritual age. Age is how you feel about yourself. I particularly like what a Frenchman once said to me on the subject: "From thirty-five to forty-five women are old. Then the devil takes over certain women at forty-five and they become beautiful, mature, warm

—in a word, splendid. The acidities are gone, and in their place reigns calm. Such women are worth going out to find because the men who find them never grow old."

When I say women should stay natural, I don't mean they shouldn't use makeup or do whatever they can to present themselves in the best possible light. But makeup and all other beauty preparations should not go *against* the natural grain of one's features but *with* it. For instance, a small mouth should be made to look pretty but it shouldn't be smeared with lipstick just to make it look larger. Small can be beautiful. So, too, a pale, fair complexion shouldn't be disturbed with browns or reds. Violent makeup is never attractive. I would even go so far as to say a woman should *love* her physical imperfections, and not try to erase them but rather to transform them, to make them appear as pleasant and personal characteristics.

I never go to beauty parlors. I hate their gossipy climate and the amount of time they waste. Whatever they can do for me, I can do better. Of course some women are lazy, and some have time they want to kill, but most hairdressers and beauticians do you up in a style they are familiar with rather than in a manner designed especially for you. I admit that as a professional actress I have been in a position to learn things about beauty care that would not be available to the average woman, but I honestly think that if someone really wants to fend for herself, and if she studies her possibilities, and experiments, as I did, she will have much better results than she will at the local beauty parlor. If you have ever watched one of those makeup artists at work in a department store's beauty section, giving demonstrations on the faces of customers, you must have observed that he is making up everyone's face exactly alike. He would have you think that that is the latest style, but believe me, style must be adapted to the woman and not vice versa.

The same can be said of clothes. I don't think you should adopt a fashion because Yves Saint-Laurent or Dior tells you to. If it really suits you, fine, but preserve your critical eye and reject it if you have any doubts. It's all right to dress in the wave of fashion, but don't make waves. You can often adapt a fashion trend to suit your particular needs; the important thing is to feel good and to look good in the dress you are wearing. If I don't feel right in the dress I put on, I have a miserable evening. I don't enjoy myself. I don't feel attractive. So, once you find your own style, what really suits you best, make it the foundation of everything you wear. Dress for yourself.

Another word of warning: Don't rush out and buy a dress because it looks terrific in a fashion magazine. The model wearing that dress is five foot ten, breastless, and hasn't eaten anything but curds and soy beans for months. Your clothes bespeak the kind of person you are. They represent your personality. On meeting you, a person, consciously or subconsciously, forms an opinion of you that reflects what you are wearing. It isn't a matter of whether your clothes are expensive or not; their pattern, color, and the way they are worn—that's what counts. Depending on the person, a modest print frock can be much more chic than a robe from a great *couturier*. Naturally, when money is no problem you have a wider choice of models and materials, but anyone can be smart about her own needs: it's just a question of taste, which is acquired in much the same way a foreign language is learned. Good taste in dressing reflects sound insight into oneself, plus the ability to take from fashion only what suits one best. Styles go in and out of fashion, fads appear and disappear, gowns are short, then long, and then short again. There is nothing solid on which one can rely. The only really concrete things on which you can depend, although they may seem abstract, are your relationship with your surroundings, your estimation of yourself, and the feeling you have of what kind of person you want to be.

When the new fashions come in, I make very cautious use of them. I like to have today's look—I certainly wouldn't go out in a severe schoolgirl-like frock when the fashion features bright, billowy dresses—but over the years the basic style of my dresses has changed very little. I am as true to my clothes as I am to myself.

Of course, the shape of your body has much to do with the shape of your clothes, but I do not have a set regimen of exercise. The only activity I really enjoy is swimming. And I love to walk for long distances. But calisthenics and related workouts bore me, although I do go through periods when I force myself to do a few exercises in the morning. But I am active physically, and I control how much I eat, which I think is as good a program for the care and maintenance of a svelte body as any.

That spring, summer, and fall of 1968, when I was in Geneva, pregnant, a voluntary prisoner of an eighteenth-floor apartment in the Hotel Intercontinental, the ground fog invariably blotted out the city and I seemed to be suspended in the sky, in a universe where nobody lived but me—alone with my great hope, which helped me over the boredom of my isolation. The doctors had ordered me to avoid fatigue of any kind, so I focused my whole life upon the only thing that I really cared about: having my baby.

What am I going to do to make the long months go by? I thought. How can I fill up the interminable hours, get the terrible anxiety of waiting out of my mind? With the help of my faithful secretary I began to mess about with getting meals in the kitchen. At first it was for fun but it soon became a daily routine. And then began a period of fantastic gastronomic experiences. I racked through all my childhood memories, the memories of dishes eaten on trips, the instructions given to me by cooks all over the world, and little by little my notes began to fill up the exercise book I kept by my bed.

I thoroughly agree with those people who consider cooking an art; I'd even go so far as to say a fine art. What actually is cooking? Assembling good basic ingredients, the meats, vegetables, herbs, fats, spices, butter, cream, and the rest, and creating out of them an exquisite sauce, a synthesis of flavors, a little miracle—not unlike the synthesis of the various elements of life that emerge as a painting or a symphony. Of course, I exaggerate a bit to emphasize the creative side of cooking. As for myself, I find cooking the most exciting, and at the same time the most relaxing activity that I know, which is true of almost everything you adore doing.

My childhood poverty taught me the importance of finding, and inventing, new ways to cook and flavor the same cheap, essentially monotonous basic food. In that respect, my grandmother left me a precious heritage. Thanks to her I know at least a dozen ways to cook eggplants, one of the cheapest and most plentiful foods in Italy, and I can perform miracles with a bony or third-rate, stringy piece of meat.

I don't think a good recipe necessarily makes a good dish if the cook does not know precisely the value of each of its ingredients, the intensity of the fire, the exact melting points, and many, many other cooking nuances which can only be acquired by long, *personal* experience with the cookpots.

I also use a little psychology when preparing a dinner for guests. Before I plan a menu I think about the habits, tastes, and even the curiosity of my guests. Until recent times, a dinner party meant an occasion to lavish guests with fancy table decorations and an overabundance of dishes that were inflexibly served according to whatever *mode* prevailed. I have read about some of those fabulous dinners where endless courses of elaborately prepared food were served— to the eventual stupefaction of the guests, I would suppose.

That's not the way I arrange a dinner. I try to find out what my guests can or cannot eat, their likes and dislikes. If I discover they like simple, rather informal meals, they will not be served a formal, elegant, sauced-up dinner. I always try for a menu which will please my guests and make them happy to be at my table. I also try to include one of my specialty dishes, which they will find a pleasant surprise. Perhaps something which is difficult to find at that time of the year, or a dish from another part of the world, or a country dish that they don't know about. If I were entertaining guests in Rome, for instance, I might serve *penne all'arrabbiata,* which is macaroni cut on the slant in a fiery chili-laden tomato sauce, a great Roman specialty, or perhaps *carciofi alla giudea,* deep-fried little artichokes as crisp as french fries, or a flavored ricotta. When Carlo and I used to go to a forest farm near the Po River, I would often serve the game in season cooked in a way that would surprise my guests, or I might serve a dish of eel fresh from the river. Eel used to be something I had no taste for, but when I was filming *Woman of the River,* which was shot at the Po, the president of the district gave a dinner for the members of the cast in a remote part of the countryside. When he announced that all the dishes would feature eel, my heart sank, for I had always considered the eel a repugnant and oily sea snake. We were served seven different eel dishes that night, each one more delicious than the one before, and if I had not been told I would never have guessed I was eating eel. That experience taught me a lesson: not to judge a dish by its ingredients but by what the alchemist in the kitchen creates with those ingredients.

One other thing I always try to do when planning a dinner is to include something of my own on the menu because I flatter myself that I am a good cook. I have repeatedly tried out all the recipes we have in our kitchen, and I have discovered how to vary them a little, adding and subtracting ingredients to suit my personal taste, giving them my own touch. I have a cook who usually prepares these recipes, but if I really want to do something special for my guests, I prepare at least one dish myself. When I can say to my invitees, "This is a dish I made especially for you," I create a very good atmosphere at the table.

One of the most pleasurable cooking experiences was showing President Tito of Yugoslavia how to make spaghetti sauces. He had invited us to his Adriatic island, Brioni, where he has a bungalow directly on the beach. (A red carpet runs right from the front door across the sand and into the water.) One day, he and

I took over the kitchen and I cooked a variety of pasta sauces, a Neapolitan eggplant parmigiana, and other Italian delicacies. Tito put on an apron and cooked right along with me. Cooking is such common joy. We had great fun eating what we had cooked, to the accompaniment of a delicious white wine. I asked where it came from and Tito delightedly pointed to a small vineyard that we could see from the dining-room window. He told me that every year he personally conducted the harvest of the grapes. In late summer he invites a number of his ministers and friends and puts them all to work, gathering the grapes, pressing and barreling them. He said it was a gay and joyful harvest that invariably resulted in the delicious wine we were drinking.

Tito is one of the most extraordinary men I have met in my life. I could not believe his age, because when you are with him his zest and sharpness and strength belong to a man half his eighty years. "The most difficult mission in life," he said one evening, when we were on his yacht headed toward the film festival in Belgrade, "is to find someone you can completely trust." I certainly agree. How often I have been disillusioned. And yet, as I previously said, what other way is there to find out if a person is trustworthy than to trust him?

By the end of the nine months, my cooking notebook was filled. When Basilio came to visit me, he looked through my notebook and urged me to have it published as a cookbook—which I eventually did, with his help and the help of his friend Vincenzo Buonassisi. Entitled *In the Kitchen with Love*, it is a kind of gastronomic autobiography and it remains a lovely memento of my lying-in at the Intercontinental.